THE MAD ROAD

The Mad Road

A MENTAL HEALTH MEMOIR TO SAVE LIVES

Dawn Jeronowitz

Write Road Publishing

First Printing, 2023

ISBN-13: **979-8-9878623-2-2**

ePub
ISBN-13: **979-8-9878623-4-6**

WRITE ROAD
PUBLISHING

Dedicated with all my Love
to Simon and Chad

Life.
Thank God

Contents

Dedication		v
chapter		ix
1	The Road	1
2	Detour	6
3	Reroute	13
4	Visitor Attraction	17
5	The Highway	25
6	Pedal to the Metal	34
7	Blowout	48
8	Junkyard	66
9	Overdrive	78
10	Another Lap	88
11	Fuel	96
12	Wipers	107
13	Roundabout	119
14	Oil Change	124
15	New Tires	135
16	Road Map	141

17 Another Mile   165

18 Parking Lot   178

19 Lemon   210

20 New Car   261

About The Author   291

1

The Road

AAAAAAAAAAAAaaaaaaaaaaaaaaaaaaaaaahhhhhhhhhhh!!!!!!!!

There I was, standing in front of 80,000 screaming teenage girls, fans, all singing along in ear-piercing squeals and crooning to the harmonic lead of the very popular boy band singing onstage beside me.

After being summoned onto a huge stadium stage somewhere in Texas, I couldn't hear much of what was being said while the guys introduced me to the audience and sang a very lovely "Happy Birthday" to me. But, oh boy, did the girls ever shriek, and, wow, there sure were a lot of glowing lights waving in the air!

I must tell you, this was not a random act, definitely not. Instead, this was a well-planned celebration aiming to grow and manifest itself during a weeklong buildup that began with a festive party full of surprises and gifts galore.

By the time my thirtieth birthday actually arrived, I found myself at work and walking into the catering dining room backstage, where the walls were plastered with at least thirty of my childhood photos. Photos that had been blown up poster size.

Yes, poster size.

Sitting on Santa's lap: blown up, poster size. Baby-me bathing naked in the kitchen sink: blown up, poster size. Sweet-Sixteen me with

'80s style *big* hair: blown up, poster size. All poster sized and displayed for my colleagues' delight.

Well, needless to say, the scheme worked. I stood aghast, red as a tomato. It was humor at my expense yet strangely flattering all the same. (And if I may boast, I did get to go on the flying rig and tumble while fifty feet up in the air! Even luckier, the video guys taped it all so I could review my glory at any time. Nice perk!) All in a day's work. Well, on the road.

Yes, I lived a considerably unusual, yet some may regard exciting life. After graduating college, I began a career traveling on music tours around the world. Simply put, a roadie. True, it did make for some interesting stories better left to another day, but certainly, the modern music business was different from the legends of the past. The modern music touring industry was business to the bottom line. Really, road crews were a great community made up of talented individuals who sacrificed a life at home with family, pets, and friends in order to make live music and performance events go 'round. (Although some may say they did it for the T-shirt.) We all must have needed the entertainment because, wow, did tickets ever sell!

It's a different lifestyle, especially as a girl roadie. An average work-day was eighteen hours, but it rarely felt that long. You did that usually for four or five show days a week. You lived, traveled, and worked with the same people for weeks or months at a time, sometimes even years, while on world tours. Lots of travel; virtually every day, it was a different city, state, country, time-zone, season, or hemisphere. You could see some spectacular places and meet interesting people around the globe. It really was a small world, after all.

Living out of a suitcase was rough, but traveling with luggage was unbearable. Flying was a headache, but I did love life on a tour bus and slept like a baby tucked in my bunk. Highway views could be amazing. Truck stops became a delightful highlight. Days off were spent in hotels, and oh my, some had been incredible!

The aspect of my job was always unique. I didn't do sound, lights, video, or anything like that. Instead, sometimes throughout the course of an afternoon, I transformed a professional sports team's locker room into a tropical haven, rustic retreat, or swanky lounge. Frequently, I grocery-shopped for 150 people or ordered a thousand dollars worth of pizza, hoping I'd got enough.

More often than not, I found myself tending to the needs of my fellow road crew: a task that balanced bits and traits of a little sister, wife, housekeeper, servant, boss, and mom. Best of all, I enjoyed playing with the fantastic clothes and worked hard to avoid any wardrobe malfunctions.

Back at home, being that I traveled so often, it was much more practical to stay with my parents (i.e., keep my stuff) in New Jersey, where I grew up. Plus, there was Simon, my dog, an Italian Greyhound; it brought me great peace of mind knowing my parents spoiled him silly while I was away.

So, in 2000, celebrating the momentous age of thirty, I found myself on another tour with one of the hottest-selling bands and feeling pretty darn good. After all, I was single, traveling the world, working in a job I enjoyed, making good money, saving good money, paying off debt (naturally left over from college years), living memorable moments, and looking forward to what else was to come.

And come it did.

No sooner did one tour end than I found myself on my next big gig. There, I met a guy. Not just any guy, but one of those special ones who seem so dreamy. His name was Drew.

After touring together for a few months, my first big official date with Drew outside of work was two weeks in London. From scones with jam and high tea to beautiful parks and Big Ben delights, what a glorious time we had! Even when our little vacation was over, Drew and I continued touring together while we worked in Europe for two more months. Each day was happier than the one before.

Eventually, as it always does, the gig ended. Somehow, despite the fact we lived in two different states, Drew and I continued to talk, meet up, and grow closer. When I immediately found myself going out on another big tour, Drew actually flew out to visit for a week! Better yet, when the holidays rolled around, I spent a workweek off with Drew in his hometown: Oh, how nice it had been, sitting in his car on a cold, snowy night, warmed by his company and the glow of a bit of dashboard candlelight. Indeed, I must have been twinkling when we brought in the New Year together on a most festive evening, joined by his closest friends.

Eventually, when that tour ended, I finally found myself with much-needed and well-deserved time off. By the time that happened, a year had passed. It was March 2001, and I was thirty-one. Joyfully I had managed to pay off all my credit card balances and earn the title: Debt Free. Even better, I had cash in the bank, more than I had ever saved before. Optimistic, I was actually thinking about buying a house. Not a very big house, of course, but still, I could finally say to my dad, "I have the money and am looking for a house." Thirty-one, debt free, dating a great guy with a job; surely, I must have achieved a milestone.

As soon as I had landed in Jersey, unpacked my bags, and curled up in my own bed at my folks' house, the very same house we moved into back when I was three, I quickly began a quest for my own home. Considering my life as a roadie, an airport definitely needed to be close by.

Having spent several years attending university in North Carolina and enjoying all that state had to offer, I decided to search around there. A theatre major, I'd spent some time after college enjoying local work in the film and television industry stemming from that area. Potentially, moving to Wilmington, I could do that again between road tours. Sounded ideal. Looking online, I found a perfect little cottage near Wilmington that I fancied. I wanted to make a trip and see that adorable cottage!

As I began to plan my trip, Camille, my dearest girlfriend from college, phoned me. Camille was the apple of everyone's eye, and what a beautiful soul and being she was: Mille-Mille. She was a charm, a gift, and she created the standard for which all cooking should be judged. After graduating from college and culinary arts school, Camille moved to Tampa, Florida. Working as a chef, she had been living with her boyfriend; they had been dating for a few years. On that day,

Camille phoned, sharing the news that she and her boyfriend had split up. He had moved out, and now she'd need a roommate. So Camille invited me to Florida.

Well, now, that was a thought. With a moment of downtime, it might be nice to pack up my Simon dog, along with some of my belongings, and head south for a short while—like a vacation. Girl time! Hooray! Indeed, I'd pack a bunch of clothes that Camille and I could try on, sort through, donate, and give away. Even better, I would use the rare opportunity of time off the road and spend it in the Florida sunshine with my dear friend while I figured out what I would like to do for my own dreams and life goals. Plus, it would help Camille with rent and regrouping. Yes, a tropical sabbatical! At least before the next tour gig came along. As a bonus, I could stop at the charming Wilmington cottage along the way! Toot-Toot!

My Simon

2

Detour

April 27, 2001

I stuffed my Saturn with a closet full of clothes, bid another farewell to my folks, and with my Simon dog in tow, I hit the road for a very long drive south. In the passenger seat, my beautiful Simon boy looked like a resting baby deer.

About eight hours of highway in, I reached the exit that led toward the Carolina coast and to the darling cottage I found online. Figuring the detour to Wilmington would cost me an extra full day, in a last-minute decision, I decided to bypass the cottage and head straight to the sunny Florida peninsula. I'd continue house hunting online and stop in Wilmington on my way back home. Besides, there was a lot of highway between Jersey and Tampa; I was excited to get to the warm sunshine and spend time with my dear friend Camille. Plus, Drew was on a tour that was stopping in her town! After a few more hours of highway, I found a pet-friendly motel to stay for the night.

Morning came too quickly for a couple hundred more miles to drive. Curled up in the passenger seat with only a potty stop every few hours, my dear little Simon was so good.

Eventually, after two long days, I finally pulled safely up to Camille's two-bedroom rental house. Camille wasn't yet home from the restaurant where she worked as a culinary wizard, so I let myself in with the key Camille left for me. While I waited, I brought my luggage inside and put my stuff into the extra bedroom.

As Simon sniffed about the new surroundings, appearing delighted to be out of the car, I decided to surprise Camille by doing a little cleaning around the house. The space needed a bit of freshening, some sprucing up here and there to bring a hint of pretty girl energy to the otherwise masculine place; just a little touch.

Finally, Camille arrived home. When she walked into the house, a wonderful spirit filled the air; her smile lit up the room with cheer! One big hug of joy brought relief and confirmed Camille liked the freshening I had done. It sure felt like I made a good choice on my visit. Optimism was off the charts! Bonus: the next day, Drew would be in town with the tour he was on. Such luck!

After the best meal made by Camille, a lot of girl chat, and a good night's sleep, I went to visit Drew at his work the following day. He and I had such a good laugh over the coincidence of meeting up in Tampa. It was, without a doubt, one of the crazy best things about being a roadie: you could run into people you knew virtually anywhere on the planet, plus visit friends and family in towns along the way! Thankfully, it was Drew in town with me that day.

I quickly began to settle in nicely at Camille's cozy house. How unusually sweet to stay in one city and sleep in the same bed for more than a night or two. It was early springtime 2001, and the Florida palm trees, tropical air, and rain showers sure were welcomed. Camille and I had great times going to the beach. We rented jet skis, rode a boat, ate outside on seaside decks, relaxed with her fabulous group of friends, and shopped. Even Simon was enjoying the adventure and beach time! Though Simon was a bit skeptical about the boat ride. Yes, Florida felt good.

Camille was also part of a Hospice program and assisted a ninety-year-old woman named Helen. Helen was quite the character. She was a distinguished intellectual of her time. Helen maintained a detailed diary of everything she did, including what she ate, when she ate, when she used the bathroom, when and what medications she took, what mail she opened that day, how she responded to the mail, and so on. Despite her wheelchair status and fragile physical state, Helen was full of life, energy, and pizzazz. It was a wonder to think she was ready to pass on.

Helen lived alone in a small house she had occupied for decades. Camille and I would go over, do some gardening, or take Helen to an appointment—sometimes out to eat. I'll never forget how Helen lit up and danced one zany night on her ninety-first birthday. We took Helen to a seaside restaurant for a beautiful evening and, to all our good fortune, a South American naval ship full of sailors had pulled into port and entertained everyone with Latin music. They even opened their vessel to visitors! Rising from her wheelchair, holding onto the railing, singing and wiggling her hips, Helen shone like she was having the time of her life! I do confess, I always hoped I would not be the one to have to clip her toenails, though; Helen was quite particular and complained about them all the time.

**Dawn (left), Camille, and Helen
celebrating her 91st birthday**
T. Jackson

Then there was Camille's neighbor Annie and her husband, Joe. What a duo. Annie was very thin and bony, with long, unkept, dull dark hair. She wore glasses and smoked two packs of cigarettes a day, making her voice somewhat raspy. I wasn't quite sure of Annie's age, but time seemed to have taken more of a toll on her than her years added up to. Though she was of average height, slender, and nearly frail, there was a weight about Annie. As somebody who had traveled widely, I sensed Annie had barely seen beyond her hometown. There was a juvenile sort of insecurity about her. Annie needed her husband's permission for everything and would never discuss exactly how they met and were married.

Joe, bald and built tough, wasn't seen much but seemed chummy any time he was around.

Annie had a state of innocence about her, similar to a child. I don't know if or how well she could read; I showed her a few articles occasionally, but she never appeared able to read them. Annie had a habit of deflecting things she felt the need to protect. I certainly did not want to probe or press. Also, she appeared to be afraid to drive. Annie walked blocks for groceries. Many times, I would drive her to the store. Though she would laugh and smile and join in with Camille and me, something about Annie saddened me, and I felt a strong urge to help encourage her self-esteem. Every day Annie was welcome to come over, sit, talk, eat, and dress up in the clothes Camille and I were purging.

Enjoying my time off, I decided to remain at Camille's through the end of May and give Camille a full month's rent. Hoping to utilize my precious time wisely and wanting to work on creative writing, I purchased a professional scriptwriting program. When meeting people around the world, they often told me I should write about my road adventures. Seemingly, many were quite intrigued by my line of work. More popular than the questions "What is so-and-so like?" and "Can you get me tickets?" people always asked me, "How did you get that job?"

Given their curiosity plus my background and experience, it seemed best to write a script in a TV series format: instead of a coffee shop, there was a backstage catering dining room. No apartment or house, but rather a tour bus and hotel room. Undoubtedly, working backstage in the concert touring industry did create opportunities for so many scenarios, so many stories, and so many seasons. As May rolled on, my script-writing research began, and the pages of dialogue flowed.

On May 24, Camille's grandmother was coming for a visit from North Carolina. We went to pick her up at the airport only to discover the plane had been delayed. So, with extra time now on our hands while we waited for updated arrival information, Camille and I decided to get a bite to eat at the airport. In the food court, we found a seafood restaurant that seemed tasty enough.

After lunch, Camille and I checked the arrivals monitor again to find the flight would be delayed a few more hours. Hours! Oh, Camille's poor grandma. I sure did know how maddening airline delays could be. No point in waiting around the airport till then. Camille and I decided to go back to the house.

On the way back, we stopped at a clothes store for a summer sale we simply could not resist. I was super thrilled to find a practical two-piece swimsuit that I actually liked and felt comfortable in. I never wore a bikini, so absolutely, that was a treat!

When we arrived at the house, Annie saw us pulling into the driveway. For her, that was her signal to come over, so she did.

Once inside, I immediately went into my bedroom to try on my new swimsuit. Suddenly I felt a strange numbness in my right forefinger. That area began feeling hot and tingly to the touch. Growing concerned, I went back into the living room where Camille and Annie were sitting. As I was telling them about the sudden sensation in my finger, the discomfort grew. Significant pain was creeping up my right arm. My wrist was throbbing, and the numbness in my forefinger made it feel swollen like a club. My finger was numb like a mouth on Novocain after a dental visit.

Beginning to worry, I tried to consider what might be going on. I thought maybe the pain, tingling, and numbness were the result of a spider or weird Floridian bug bite, but I didn't see any mark. Perhaps it was an allergic reaction to something I'd touched. Could it be from the seafood I ate at the airport? Why did I eat seafood at an airport? I didn't know what the numb tingling pain was, but it was severe, unfamiliar, and became an immediate cause for concern. I checked for strange sensations elsewhere, like on my legs and feet, but thought I could be needlessly projecting the apprehension about my finger.

Between Camille, Annie, and I, we all agreed I should seek some sort of medical attention. I called my mom in Jersey and Drew on the road; they both agreed. The pain was intense and showed no signs of subsiding. It was unnerving.

Knowing Camille had to return to the airport and pick up her grandma—plus keeping in mind that Annie could not be depended on when it came to driving, and I was not going to risk getting behind the wheel—I called the medics. When they arrived, the emergency responders did a brief check for broken bones and determined everything seemed intact, but no one could explain the pain. The medics suggested I go with them to the hospital and have it diagnosed by a doctor. Concerned, I took the ride with them.

What a trip. I rode in the stretcher bed. None of the medics in the vehicle could manage to work the blood pressure equipment. Watching them fumble with the digital thermometer, well, forget about it.

We arrived at the hospital, where I was wheeled into the emergency room and parked in the hallway next to a very weak and moaning man. He was covered in bruises and attached to a machine. I felt he was ready for eternity.

A woman came over and took my information. Medical insurance: none. By her expression, I could tell that was not the right answer. "How will you be paying for this then?" the woman asked. "With a check," I told her. The woman proceeded to take my name and emergency contact information, noting any allergies I was aware of. "Cold medicine," I told her. I avoid cold medicines. I didn't like the drug-induced feeling and side effects I experienced from them.

A good amount of time passed, as it often does in emergency rooms. I heard a woman hollering about how badly she needed to "make pee." I thought it funny she wanted to pee in a sushi box that another nurse was snacking out of. The poor old lady went on and on.

Meanwhile, a doctor stopped by to review the source of my pain. I told him that I had severe numbness and tingling in my forefinger, and

I was unable to use my wrist due to the intense piercing pain there. Even more, the pain was shooting up my arm. The doctor informed me that nothing appeared broken. I agreed. The checkup continued with the vitals: my temperature, heart rate, blood pressure, color analysis, and reflex. All seemed well. The doctor walked away and said he'd be back.

I waited. And waited. When the doctor returned a good time later, he informed me that I must have had what is referred to as a panic attack. Panic attack? Since I had no stress going on and was certainly enjoying my life, a panic attack seemed unlikely. Plus, how could that explain the physical pain I experienced? How about a test? I questioned the diagnosis.

The doctor emphasized that a panic attack could have physical symptoms that I must have experienced. He suggested I go home, get some rest, and drink lots of fluids. He also mentioned that I might want to make an appointment with another doctor for further analysis should the pain persist. Finally, he gave me a reference to a hospital affiliate.

When I assessed the emergency room report from that day, it stated that I entered the ER under the category of "allergic reaction" with signs of tingling limbs. All vitals were recorded as good. Blood pressure 106/ 68. Pulse 80. My mental status was checked as "orientated x3, alert." All normal. The emergency center discharge record checked the box "Psych: Anxiety/Stress."

Nearly four thousand dollars later, and still experiencing the unidentified pain, I decided I was going for a full and complete physical exam. Camille picked me up at the hospital, and I immediately called the recommended physician to secure an appointment for five days later.

3

Reroute

A few days after the startling emergency room visit, on May 29, I found myself in Dr. Menia's office. My goal was to determine the source of my ongoing disturbing finger and wrist pain and get a complete physical and blood work analysis done. Sadly, it'd been several years since I had a physical, and it was something long overdue. So, while I was seeing a doctor anyway, it seemed like that was as good a time as any.

Filling out initial paperwork in the waiting room, I again faced the dreaded health insurance question, and once again, I assured the doctors I would be paying by check.

Eventually, my name was called, and the nurse led me from the waiting room and directly onto a scale. Surely, I could not be alone in wishing they'd let you take your shoes off first. Regardless, I was a healthy 132 pounds. Following the basic rough stuff that included blood pressure 104/66 and heart rate 65, I was led into an exam room to wait once more.

Finally, Dr. Menia entered. He was a young man, short, with a heavy foreign accent. His eyes gave the impression of a wide constant gaze as though he was listening closely. Or was he completely lost? First, Dr. Menia began with the typical doctor tools, poking my ears and nose. Then came the stethoscope and deep breaths. Next, Dr. Menia asked a few questions about my prior emergency room visit, my finger, my family medical history, and my work. Finally, after a few minutes of surmising, Dr. Menia stated he would be right back.

A minute later, he returned and handed me a few sample boxes of pills that he recommended I take. He also gave me a one-year prescription for the medication. Dr. Menia said the pills would help me to manage anxiety, stress, and panic attacks. What panic attacks, anxiety, and stress? I did not quite understand, so naturally, I inquired about that.

Dr. Menia proceeded to explain how panic attacks occurred when there was a serotonin imbalance in the brain. Moreover, he emphasized that women require more serotonin due to their menstrual cycle, which offsets our bodies' natural serotonin production, thus causing an imbalance that could manifest into anxiety. "What does this have to do with my finger pain?" I asked. Dr. Menia continued to explain that my body had a serotonin imbalance and was causing me to experience panic attacks. He said the panic attacks had taken the physical form of numbness and pain in my limbs.

Wow. Okay. He was the professional and educated doctor. Trusting that, I took the boxes of sample pink pills plus the one-year prescription for an SSRI, a selective serotonin reuptake inhibitor. Dr. Menia also handed me a pamphlet from the pharmaceutical manufacturer filled with cartoons of happy people. Before leaving the office, I made an appointment to have my blood work done on June 28 and a follow-up appointment for July 2, 2001. Wanting to see this through, I hoped Camille wouldn't mind if I stayed another month longer.

Leaving the doctor's office, I felt a bit surprised by the diagnosis. Being told I suffered from a panic disorder was like being told I had a handicap. Personally, I thought I was quite happy with my life and felt confident about the direction I was headed. Better yet, my finances were great, my friends and family were the best, and my relationship with Drew was like living a fairy tale.

On the drive back to Camille's house, I began looking for things about myself that may have been clues to the newly discovered plaguing imbalance now brought to light. I thought I was definitely anal-retentive about everything being perfect at work. Also, I did get bitchy if anybody moved anything I had set in place in the dressing room before the artist arrived, or goodness knows the havoc I would reap on the caterer who failed to get the union's lunch up on time. At home, I did get quickly and overly frustrated with my folks, who still treated me like a kid. My dad and I didn't always see eye to eye, which drove me nutty sometimes. My mom and I had completely different political ideas, and, oh my, hers were maddening.

So, it was expected the SSRI would help me to relax, ease up, and enjoy more. Somehow the pink pill was supposed to help me not get irritated when things didn't go my way? Or when, for example, the check-out line at the supermarket was ten people long, and the manager still wouldn't open another register—and all the while, the clerk was at a standstill with a price check?

Upon returning to Camille's with my diagnosis and pills, I reviewed the accompanying pamphlet for information and side effects: non-addictive, may cause mild to moderate nausea, decreased appetite, dry mouth, sweating, infection, constipation, yawn, tremor, sleepiness, and sexual side effects. Sexual side effects? Wonder what that meant.

I did some research online about serotonin, a neurotransmitter, and how it was utilized in the body to affect emotional states and constrict blood vessels at injury sites. So, did that mean my forefinger, wrist, and arm became numb and painful because I did not have enough serotonin produced, thus, my body treated my limbs like injury sites?

I called my mom and told her the news. My mom had heard of SSRIs but suggested I read the enclosed information that the doctor provided with the prescription. I told her I did. She also suggested I take time to relax and enjoy time away from my usual travel-and-go lifestyle. I thought I was doing that. By the end of our conversation, I felt supported by my mom and comforted.

Naturally, I also called Drew and talked with him about what had happened. Both Drew and Camille were supportive. The next morning, May 30, along with my coffee and daily multivitamin, I began taking the introductory 10-milligram pink SSRI pills.

4

Visitor Attraction

Throughout the following week, I slowly drifted into a state of peaceful, easy feelings; not even a grocery checkout line twenty people deep could have riled me. Indeed, a fair amount of time was spent lounging on the couch. Not much scriptwriting happened then.

Determined to make the best of my newly discovered disorder, I immediately became regimented in my morning routine of pink pill, coffee, and vitamin. Certainly, I was optimistic and quite curious about the new attitude and outlook this medication would bring to my life. Moreover, the thought of getting a physical checkup compelled me to consider making healthier choices and incorporating good nutrition and exercise into my lifestyle.

As June began, I gave Camille another month's rent. I planned to remain at her Florida house through the end of the month and into the start of July. At that point, I would go for my follow-up appointment with Dr. Menia.

In the meantime, per doctor's orders, I filled the prescription at the pharmacy; one hundred dollars for a one-month supply containing thirty pink SSRI pills. Conveniently, I went to the same pharmacy where I filled Simon's prescription. Simon suffered from epileptic seizures and required a daily pill to help control them. Without a doubt, Simon sure hated taking his medicine. It entailed many clever and creative ways to ensure he received his daily dosage; lots of peanut butter and chicken.

Fortunately, I was also able to softly soothe Simon through his epileptic seizures, helping to reduce them from escalating into violent, trembling, and heartbreaking episodes. I found that a gentle voice, warm snuggles, and lots of love and kisses helped immensely. That said, it took a few times of worry and emergency vet visits before I discovered the comfort technique. Luckily, I never had to increase his medication dosage.

After a June week of lazy days and wispy feelings from the introductory pink pills, I began feeling inspired. As I did so much in decorating rock star dressing rooms, I felt my best friend deserved the royal treatment for herself. More so than the modest sprucing I did when I first arrived at the house, I immediately took to really overhauling and redecorating Camille's house. I hoped to create an environment that would best express her.

Camille had a screened-in porch off the kitchen just outside the back door of her house. A huge overgrown yard was back there too, but none of it could be seen through the storage, stuff, and clutter. She sure had lots of catering and chef supplies. Somewhere under there, I also saw a table and chairs.

One day in early June, while Camille was at work, I took on the porch project. My plan of attack began with clearing the clutter and cleaning the gunk. Then I did some arranging and staging to make the screened-in porch pretty and cozy. Then, tackling the collected chaos, I jumped in full force and managed to have everything organized, neat, tidy, and cleaned for when Camille arrived home that evening. Wow! Camille was tickled with joy! That night we sat at the outside table on the porch and shared another fine, tasty meal prepared with love by Camille.

Continuing to live by doctors' orders, I completed the introductory pink SSRI pills and began taking the twenty-milligram prescription strength. I maintained my intake consistently, and, unlike my vitamins, I managed to make taking my pink pill the first point of every day. I was optimistic about its benefits.

In no time at all, I found myself drawn to the back porch and began spending a lot of time out there. So much time, in fact, I shopped for candles, rugs, chairs, and accessories to dress it up.

Next, I found some paint and began a large mural of trees on the house walls that were connected to the porch. It was such a transformation. The whole space began to develop into a magical, calming retreat of peace and solitude. Camille seemed to think I was doing a bit much; however, I assured her that as the mural was done in pastel tones, it would be a breeze to paint over when she moved out. Or, the landlord could paint over it if he chose.

The back porch became my favorite place to be. Every day I noodled around and worked to make the space even more charming and comfortable. One might say it became an obsession. Simon lounged and watched. More often than not, I was joined by Annie. We spent hours sitting, chatting, sipping coffee, and relaxing in the screened-in haven. Well, Annie relaxed while I neurotically immersed myself in projects and innovative ideas.

Noticing I spent so much time on the porch, Camille insisted I join her and some friends for a day at the beach. Despite the fun company, warm sun, cool water, and delicious salad from a seaside restaurant, I could not get my mind off redecorating. Back at the house, feeling comfortable with the relaxing environment created on the porch, I turned to spruce up my bedroom.

The second week in June, after another big shopping day, I was unpacking all the bags and boxes of things upon things I had purchased. Suddenly, I heard a familiar ringtone coming from my phone. It was Drew! I immediately jumped up and ran toward my room, where the ringing was coming from. As I did so, I fell and broke my toe! Darn pain! But Drew was calling! When I reached the phone, the throbbing pain was forgotten. Drew informed me he had some exciting news: he would have a few days off at home coming up and was inviting me to visit him in his hometown the following week! Oh yes!

Now notably, Camille was not a dog person, to begin with. Though she had never had any pets before, even she succumbed to Simon's irresistible Italian Greyhound charm and adorable manners. Camille even let the house rules slide when she allowed Simon to curl up on her couch at his leisure. So, after checking if Camille would be okay watching Simon for a few days, I made the flight reservation to visit Drew.

I flew to see Drew on June 17. He picked me up at the airport, and I felt a bit self-conscious when he commented on my bright floral Florida dress. Guess my vacation in the sunshine state was really showing!

Drew and I enjoyed a lovely time together, strolling along tree-lined streets and commenting on the beauty of the older homes. It was glorious; we had a lot in common and enjoyed each other's company so much. My mind began to drift into thoughts that involved growing old together and sitting in rocking chairs on the front porch.

While Drew was driving me to the airport for my flight back to Tampa, he informed me of one more bit of exciting information: his tour was going to be doing a show in Orlando on July 6, with a rehearsal on the fifth and a day off on July 4. So that meant another holiday we would spend together! Not even in the airplane yet, I was surely in the clouds!

Back at Camille's house in Florida, I told her of the great news. In an instant, we came up with the brilliant idea that we should celebrate the Fourth of July with a big backyard bash and invite all her friends and coworkers. Camille would cook and invite people while I would make the other party preparations. We sure could use a party!

Camille had been spending more time away from the house while I was consumed with nesting in it. She also met a guy who she'd been flirting with, Jerry. For Camille, the Fourth of July party would be the perfect time to invite Jerry, get to know him better, and introduce him to her friends. For me, it was a party to plan, people to wow, and time to spend with Drew.

The neglected backyard became my next mission. I was dead set and determined to impress the guests with a splash of fun festivities, so shopping would be my first priority.

Nestled in the tranquil screened porch, I looked into the yard and created a plan of action. Suddenly, I recalled an early childhood memory: a bunny hut in the backyard of my parents' house. Though we never actually had bunnies, the memory combined with Camille's backyard gave me the idea that Camille needed a bunny! Yes! Camille needed a pet! I immediately jumped up and ran to grab the Yellow Pages. Searching out pet stores, I called a few until I located one about forty-five minutes away that had bunnies. No sooner had I hung up the phone than I was in the car and on my way.

When I walked into the pet store, I located the bunnies. The very first one I saw was a fluffy gray baby with white markings on her nose and ears. She had the most beautiful blue eyes that reminded me of my Grandma Sadie's. God, I missed my Grandma Sadie. The bunny holding tank was uncovered, so I reached in and picked up the gray baby bunny, making sure to hold her close so she would not be afraid. Carrying the bunny around the store, I shopped and assured Jezebel she would have the happiest life a bunny could ever dream of. A bunny cage, bunny bedding and food, a stuffed yellow duck toy, and a bunny bottle; I proceeded to purchase everything and anything a bunny may need. Nearly three hundred dollars later, Jezebel was safely tucked in her new home on Camille's back porch.

Camille came home that night with a much different reaction than I had hoped. Let's just say she was not pleased. Camille repeated that she did not want a bunny or any other pet, for that matter. I begged Camille to let me keep Jezebel and promised she would remain in her cage outside on the back porch. I begged and begged, and after much grief, Camille finally agreed to let me keep the little baby ball of fluff. Jezebel settled in, and Simon's curiosity about the new bunny began.

The end of June rolled in, and on the 28th, I finally returned to Dr. Menia's office for my blood work. Once again, I sat in the waiting room until my name was called. Finally, the nurse took me back to a chair, tied a rubber band around my arm, tapped my vein, and took four tubes of blood. Ugh. I didn't know how I managed to endure that, and I dreaded the bruises that would follow.

After I left the doctor's office, in an attempt to distract myself from the thought of gruesome blood, I decided to go shopping in preparation for the fast-approaching July fourth party, plus Drew's arrival.

With Annie quickly becoming my sidekick, I asked her to come along to Walgreens. As we walked up and down every aisle, I was excited about prepping the house for the party. Shopping away, I tossed anything I might use into my cart. Everything seemed interesting: makeup, bath products, extension cords, lightbulbs, colored paper, pencils, storage tubs, cleaning supplies, rubber gloves, paperclips, pet supplies, gift cards, kid toys, you name it, I bought it. By the time I made it through the entire store and got to the checkout, three hours had gone by. When Annie and I made it to the register, I had two carts full of stuff!

The manager closed a register for me and took care of the transaction himself. Scan by scan, the dollars added up until the cash register would eventually accept no more. To complete my sale, the manager totaled one sale, I paid, and he began ringing up items again. After all was said and done, my car was stuffed with $700 worth of products. Annie laughed because she had never experienced or seen such a thing before. It seemed pretty normal to me since I was accustomed to big sales at work when I shopped for 150 people at a time. Plus, these were items I would never usually get to buy. It was fun.

Annie helped me unload the car at Camille's house. Bag by bag, I meticulously unpacked and organized items into collective groups—kitchen, cleaning, bathroom, office, utility, pets, decorative, and gifts—and arranged them as though they were on display in a store window. My favorite item was the singing jack-a-lope, which hung on the wall. When I walked past it, the motion sensor was triggered, causing the jack-a-lope to sing and bop along to three different songs! What a hoot! I hung him on the back porch. Oh, how he cracked me up over and over again! A jack-a-lope.

Intensely focused on making the backyard brilliant for our upcoming festivity, I spent relentless hours raking and weeding. By 5 a.m., I was awake, taking my pink pill, drinking coffee, and getting ready for a full day's work. The SSRI was extremely motivating and helped inspire me to get things done. Feeling charged and pleased with my productivity in the house transformation, I looked forward to my upcoming follow-up visit with Dr.Menia.

Two days after my Walgreens shopping spree, Camille and I went to pick up items for the party. When I convinced her to stop at Toys R Us, the party was on! Games, blow-up beach rafts, kiddie pools, and rollerblades—I bought everything I imagined might be necessary for a playful backyard splash, except for a super Simon bed. The six-foot stuffed alligator was strictly for my lounging purposes! Camille was beginning to get on my case about my recent shopping sprees and purchases. Maybe she thought the kiddie pool was too much for the party, but I thought it would be fun.

At last, it was July 2, 2001, and time for my follow-up appointment with Dr. Menia. By then, I no longer saw the doctor's office as a cold, sterile, fluorescent-lit place; instead, I made myself right at home and actually walked straight back into the exam room without even waiting for the nurse to call me. When the nurse came back to check on me, I thanked her profusely for doing such a fantastic job of pulling my blood the week before; I didn't even get a bruise! With that, shoes and all, she escorted me back to the dreaded scale, which calculated 127 pounds. Blood pressure 96/61 and heart rate 69; all was looking good.

A short wait later, Dr. Menia entered the room. This time he did not poke me with gadgets or ask too many questions, and I expressed how wonderful I had felt since he gave me my prescription and how filled with uninhibited energy, purpose, and life I was. Dr. Menia mentioned increasing my SSRI dosage, but I told him I thought the amount was just perfect. I wanted to continue on the twenty milligrams for a while longer. The doctor advised that I could always increase the dosage later. He seemed pleased with my progress and recommended I continue taking the SSRI for one year, per his prescription. We scheduled my next appointment for late January 2002.

It was only two more days until I picked up Drew at the airport in Orlando and brought him to Camille's for the big Fourth of July festivity. Full speed ahead!

5

The Highway

The day had come at last! Bright and early on July fourth, I awoke at 4:30 a.m. after staying up till 2 a.m. in preparation. My stomach danced with butterflies, anticipating the fun festivities and spending the day with Drew. By 7:30 a.m., I hit the road to Orlando on my way to pick up Drew at his hotel and bring him back to Camille's for the day. While I was gone, Camille was going to begin cooking for the big party.

After a few short hours round-trip, Drew and I arrived back at the house for breakfast. Drew was quite startled by all the toys and things I had purchased, especially Jezebel.

Around noon, while Camille continued cooking and greeting guests, Drew and I drove to pick up Helen. Of course, we were going to include Helen in the festivities. She would have a blast celebrating and swinging with some young folk!

Helen's house was not far at all from Camille's. It was a small house that needed many repairs and desperately needed to be tented for termites. Actually, Camille had extended an offer to have Helen spend a week at our house while hers was tented, but that required approval from the hospice program.

Helen was very protective about who she allowed into her home, and men were not permitted. So, by myself, I went to the door and knocked. A few minutes later, Helen appeared in her wheelchair, wearing a pretty dress and lipstick! I wheeled her down the walkway to where Drew awaited us, and together we helped her down three small steps and into the car. It took ten more minutes for me to fold the wheelchair and get it into the trunk.

Back at Camille's, the house was filling up with people, and the food began to flow. Helen was the life of the party! All the guests were having a great time, especially Camille's new love interest, Jerry. I watched as people checked out all the recent changes to the back porch and yard. A few of Camille's closest friends seemed really amazed.

By late afternoon, Drew and I had brought Helen back to her home. It had been a long day for her, but one she thoroughly enjoyed. I believe her attendance at the party brought us more pleasure than she had by being there.

When Helen was home safe and tucked in, Drew and I returned to the house. It was time for us to step away from the party, lock ourselves in my room, and spend some time alone. At that point, I figured out what the pamphlet meant by sexual side effects. But Drew was patient, understanding, and supportive.

When we finally emerged from my room, it was dark outside, and people were pretty drunk. Drew and I nestled into some chairs and simply watched the party around us. We sat and enjoyed the opportunity to share the day together and laughed again over the coincidence that he would be coming through my area once more.

Interestingly, Drew also noted that Camille's new interest, Jerry, sure seemed "friendly" with many of the girls. A well-built guy, Jerry strutted around without a shirt, almost flaunting himself as he flirted away with various girls. I was glad Drew noticed that as well because it was a bit concerning to me. Absolutely no way did I think Jerry was good enough for my best friend.

Eventually, well into the night, the party came to a close, and people filtered out. Some, too drunk to drive safely, slept over. Drew and I retired to my room and enjoyed a night together before I drove him back to Orlando the following morning. Again, I felt in a continuous state of pure euphoria.

The next morning, Camille rode with Drew, Simon, and me to Orlando. After we dropped Drew off at his hotel, Camille and I were headed to visit a friend of hers whom I had never met, Katie. Katie lived nearby with her husband, who wouldn't be home that night.

Another nice girls' day at Katie's house, and it began to get late. It didn't take long before Camille and Katie were exhausted and ready for bed. However, I was far from sleepy. While the two of them would each sleep in a bedroom, Simon and I would spend the night in a small back room of the house. It had a television I could stay up and watch. When Katie took me to the small room, I noticed it could use a slight rearrangement of the furniture. Katie appeared startled that I would offer to freshen up the space but gave me the go-ahead to noodle a little bit.

As the girls headed off to sleep, I stayed up most of the night, redecorating the room and the attached bathroom. After hanging jingles and painting accents in the bathroom with some pastel blue paint I found, I finally dozed in the Papasan chair. In the morning, Katie was astonished at what I had done. With that, Camille and I were headed back to Tampa.

Back at the house, party cleanup began. While I cleaned, my phone rang; it was Louis, a guy from work. He called to ask if I wanted to work a show the following week in Tampa. He was coming through town, heard I was there, and thought it would be ideal to have me work as a local helper that day. Absolutely I would!

Feeling really good and inspired, I suddenly thought I wanted to take singing lessons. Camille had the voice of an angel, so I asked her if I could take lessons with her vocal coach, Mitchell. Possibly Camille just hoped I would get out of the house more, but she arranged a lesson for me later in July.

A few days had passed since the party, and Drew had moved on with his tour. So it was dreamy when he called to wish me good night...

In need of a quiet and reflective beach day, I gathered Simon and headed toward the causeway. Along the route, I was suddenly struck with burning pain in my eyes while stopped at a red light. Out of nowhere, my eyes began to burn as though I had poured poison into them, and a fire was coming out. Tears were flowing hard. When the light turned green, I could not drive and had to signal cars to go around me. The burning began to subside after about five minutes, and I went on my way to the beach.

There, Simon rested while I journaled ideas about my experiences related to the world around me: the beauty of nature was paramount and could be reflected so very nicely in people's hearts. But unfortunately, it seemed that much of mankind was fixated on war and consumed with resentment toward our differences rather than rejoicing in the gifts of diversity and humanity we shared. Even more baffling and disturbing was the general disregard for lessons to be learned from the rest of the animal kingdom. Why was it that so much time, money, and effort were spent trying to discover Life beyond our Earth, while other species with whom we actually did share the planet were too often treated with torture, neglect, cruelty, and barely given any right to life at all? If that was how we regarded our life on earth, however would we treat an alien?

Back at Camille's, I informed her I wanted to arrange a tarot card reading by her friend Laura, who practiced the Wiccan religion. I recalled how when I was a kid, my dear aunt Sophie used to do playing card readings for us during the holidays. It was something I always looked forward to during our visits, though Aunt Sophie would never tell us any "bad news." Always up for a card reading, Camille thought we could make an evening of it, and she would prepare a special meal to share.

Laura came over to the house with all sorts of goodies, new insights, and enlightening outlooks. She certainly did not look like I imagined a "witch" to look. Actually, Laura was a mom and as normal as anybody else. She had even served highly in the U.S. military!

After we shared a delicious meal lovingly prepared by Camille, Camille and I sat and listened to Laura as she explained the ritual of the Wiccan card-reading she was going to perform. Foremost, Laura emphasized that the reading was a gift of messages. Moreover, what the messages said was beyond her influence, and she could only provide the messages presented, making no summary of how they may apply to my life or situation. Finally, she said a true messenger of this kind would never accept money for the service rendered. To do so would be in direct opposition to the gifts presented.

Laura prepared for the reading. First, she reached into her bag, pulled out a few objects, and laid symbols of each of the four elements in a circle. Next, she lit a candle, representing fire; then she set down a cup of water and then a feather to represent the air. The real excitement began when she pulled out a petrified lizard to represent Earth. That sure got Simon's attention! Terrible of me, but I could not help but chuckle when Simon picked up the petrified lizard in his mouth and ran around the house looking for a place to hide it! Luckily, Laura didn't get too angry with him, and we were able to proceed with the reading.

Having reset the now chewed petrified lizard, Laura reached into her bag and pulled out a deck of tarot cards. As I sat opposite her, I noticed she was very systematic in her motions. Being very specific to spin the cards toward my hands in a clockwise direction, Laura gave me the cards to shuffle. She expressed that as I did so, my energy was being passed into the cards so that each message found its place in the deck. Per Laura's instruction, when I felt like I had finished shuffling, I handed the cards back to her, making sure to spin the cards in a clockwise direction, thus completing the circle of transfer representative of the circle of life. I found that fascinating. The lengthy reading that followed seemed to generate around two oppositions within me. I figured those dichotomies to be the conflict between work and home.

July 14, 2001: The day came to go to work. Spending a day at the venue and back in the comforts of my backstage world, I made myself at home. Surrounded by so many familiar faces from various tours and years gone by, I found myself more aware than ever of the unique qualities that made live events happen. How interesting it all suddenly seemed; such skilled people from around the world all coming together to work, travel, and live so efficiently for one unified purpose

—the show. Inevitably the tour ends, and everybody goes their own way, only to meet again somewhere down the road at another show and time.

Many commented that I appeared to have lost some weight. Surely, as most girls would understand, I was flattered at the idea. Indeed, I was feeling much healthier and stronger than I thought I ever had before. At the end of the workday, Louis informed me he would be coming through town on tour again in September. We agreed to meet up again then.

Back at the house and nestled in the comforts of my cozy chair on the back porch, I began to consider ways to utilize my production abilities to benefit the community. What I came up with excited me, and I began to flesh out the details of the idea. I would create a festival! Yes! A festival of harvest and gathering: a day aimed at bringing people together, despite differences—a community day of sharing, appreciation, and celebration. The mission: to strengthen the community by providing an opportunity for folks to share, communicate, observe, interact, learn, evolve, and grow together! I developed a concept:

The day would begin at noon and be broken down into three main parts: a social market from 12-6 p.m., a feast from 6-8 p.m., and a festive celebration from 8-10 p.m.

The social market would consist of a trading post where people would offer goods and services on a barter-system-only basis. Therefore, it was imperative that no money was exchanged at the festival. The feast would be a time for all attendees to sit down and give thanks, blessings, and prayers before enjoying supper together. The celebration would be a time to rejoice with music, song, dance, and poetry.

There were also rules to the festival. The first rule stated: "No harm to others." Therefore, there were to be no threats or violence of any kind and no derogatory words spoken to another. Second rule: "Respect others' free will," and the third: "Whatever you send out comes back threefold." To help support that, especially while people were bartering, a Center of Negotiation area was to be established. There,

THE MAD ROAD | 31

a moderator would help negotiate any discrepancies individuals might encounter.

Beginning my quest for the perfect park venue, I considered various elements I would need to address: date, permits, space, expenses, tables, restrictions, barricades, food, beverages, chairs, applications, insurance, security, tents, people count, and more.

I was inspired to create a poster for the event using the colored pencils I'd purchased at Walgreens. I drew a face composed specifically to signify the five senses and four elements. The nose was designed like a tree trunk to represent Earth; flames roared from the mouth while the eyes flowed with water, and ears captured images of blowing winds. Ideas continued to pour from within me.

In addition to the Festival of Harvest and Gathering, I conceived an Artist Retreat and Boutique Café. All parts would work together as one. The concept was designed to thrive as a continuous work in progress. The model was again constructed in three main components: Artist Retreat, Artist Gallery Boutique, and Artist Boutique Café.

The Artist Retreat area revolved around specific zones. Each zone would be targeted and supplied for various skills, including sculptors, painters, writers, actors, musicians, dancers, floral arrangers, chefs, interior and fashion designers, crochet and knitting specialists, wood-workers, ceramic creators, crafts, and jewelry makers.

The Gallery Boutique area made up the section where the artists would display and sell their work, with a small stage area where per-forming artists would have the opportunity to showcase their pieces.

The Boutique Café was an extension of The Gallery Boutique, com-prised of comfy couches and chairs, small tables, and all sorts of art-work for sale. That area would act as the restaurant where chefs would have the opportunity to prepare daily menus and experiment with new creations for patrons. Naturally, there would also be a tea, coffee, and smoothie bar.

The Artist Retreat and Boutique Café blueprint worked through a membership plan. As such, the aspiring artist would complete a mem-bership application to join. Membership applications were available in the form of annual, monthly, or per session. Ultimately, the mission of the Artist Retreat and Boutique Café was to provide developing artists or hobbyists with an inspirational space to nurture their creative interests while networking and potentially profiting from their creations.

The biggest dream I hoped to develop was fireproof photo albums. Seemingly, every single time a story was told about a person who had their home destroyed by fire, the number one thing people missed most was their pictures of fondest memories. So, I began researching how to make a model of a fireproof photo album worthy of display.

July 28 was my first singing lesson with Mitchell. It was more of an introductory meeting where we addressed my fear of singing and established goals to achieve. My notes from that day covered questions relevant to why exactly I might be fearful of singing. Those fears included: fear of rejection, success, and/or self-expression. To address those fears, Mitchell designed a plan of techniques that would help me increase my confidence, let go, focus, and center myself. He actually gave me homework: I had to sing karaoke in public!

Before my first lesson concluded, Mitchell reminded me to keep in mind that I could not change the world. I could only give the gifts that I had, my contributions. That itself would change the world. Moreover, any other thinking would hinder my ability to share my talent and develop my gift. Living was different from controlling. Furthermore, Mitchell emphasized using productive energy, living in the moment, and not anticipating. He said it took energy to hold back, to conserve, restrain, confine, restrict. Moreover, that same negative energy could be utilized as positive energy in a productive way. Use energy wisely for a healthy mind, body, and spirit.

Later that day, the doctor called. My blood analysis came back, and all was well. My only cause for concern was to be mindful of my cholesterol. My dad had endured multiple bypass surgeries in the past, which could play a genetic role I should be aware of in my future.

July 29, 2001, I woke at my usual 5 a.m. after another restless night's sleep. It seemed I was flooded with inspirations and ideas that excited me, and I found it simply thrilling to be awake early and feel like I was beginning to live more and more every day. So on that morning, after my pink pill and coffee, I wrote in my journal:

"It's a brand-new day! Time has taken me once again to a new world of experiences. I've been staying at Camille's house in Tampa for some three months now... the tour I was going to go on hit the road again without me and is now taking a break as one member is seeking help for depression. Wow, it must be going around 'cause it turns out that shortly after I arrived at Camille's, I had a bizarre episode that left me in the emergency room, and later discovered I had experienced a full-on panic attack! So now I'm taking an SSRI, and the world is new."

6

Pedal to the Metal

August 2001, still in Tampa. The month began with sleepless nights spent on the back porch, time spent scribbling notes, and analyzing random philosophical thoughts. Each thrilling idea led to another. The entwining mysteries of the universe began to take on extreme significance. I scrambled to write as fast as the ideas would come, often resorting to a mix of pictures, symbols, and arrows connecting words and streams of thought.

Jezebel was hopping around, following Simon like a little sister would follow a big brother. Camille nagged each time she found my bunny running about. Over and over, I assured her I would return Jezebel to her cage.

Most early mornings, Annie would sit with me on the back porch. She, too, rose early. We would sip on coffee while bouncing ideas and notions, piecing together ways to improve our world and make it a happier, safer place to live. Though Annie spent many hours a day sitting with me, I wondered why I had never been inside her house after all this time. Never once had Annie extended an invitation, and I would never barge in uninvited. I wondered what it looked like inside.

On August fourth, I took a trip to Orlando with a few of the girls. We were going to a metaphysical fairy shop. Having no idea what to expect at a metaphysical fairy shop, when we arrived, it was like I had entered another world, a magical world. Overwhelmed by all the trinkets and mystical treasures that adorned the shop, I began accumulating all sorts of beautiful finds. Unfortunately, while I was busy gathering precious stones, minerals, fairy statues, palm reading guides, herbs, and trinkets galore, the girls had long since finished their shopping and were waiting on me. Meanwhile, I was still overwhelmed, barely ten feet into the store.

All of my gatherings shifted my focus to a level of spirituality that I had never experienced before. I had never practiced an organized religion and generally attended services only on special occasions like weddings or funerals. Immediately, I began to delve into a religious preoccupation and discovery of what religion actually was. To begin, I charted the polar differences between Christianity and ancient/tribal beliefs. What evolved was such:

Christianity represented the patriarchal aspects of the world. Those included Father, Fear, and the elements of Fire and Earth. In contrast, the pagan faiths represented the feminine, matriarchal aspects of the world composed of Mother, Love, and the elements of Water and Air; five senses, four elements, a trinity of three, union of two, soul of one.

When I explored how Jesus factored into those views, I questioned: why was it that people focused, argued, killed, and engaged in full-blown wars over the questionability of Jesus being the Son of God, as opposed to directing their focus on living out the message Jesus actually lived for, and sacrificed his life in belief of? It was my understanding that the message was not whether or not he was the Son of God but rather focusing on the way we were meant to live, coexist, and be. Seemingly concentrating on whether or not Jesus was the Son of God meant missing the whole point of his life. After all, all living beings were children of God. Neither animal nor human masterminded this life. The Highest Energy did.

Continuing that idea, it seemed apparent to me that Jesus' character and message were meant to be the main focus and, better yet, actively pursuing and living that message was the objective for human life. Simply, we were meant to look at the individual, Jesus, see his life, observe his actions and reactions, and live those choices freely and willingly with good intent; to be like Jesus and live like Jesus was to love like Jesus and give like Jesus. It felt to me that our modern division concerning Jesus being the Son of God in flesh and blood was secondary to what his life was meant to teach us. After all, I figured, our concept of time did run on his clock, and our universal calendar year was calculated by our acknowledgment and observance of his life and death. Clearly, universally, we all accepted Jesus as being the most significant person of historical value to humanity, regardless of any other belief relevant to his religious identity; our entire human reference of time was based on his life: A.D. and B.C.

Thoughts were growing, curiosity driving, a metaphysical world consuming me—I was engulfed in the majestic forces of nature.

August 7, 2001: Another sleepless night filled with passionately exploring the wonders of the world around us and the destructive civility we had created within it. Words, phrases, thoughts, and scribbles flowed. More and more, I found myself constantly with pen and paper and absorbed in insights as though they were channeling to me with purpose.

A sample of my obsessive writings

Obsessive writings on the inside cover of the Bible

Camille was rarely at the house, and I assumed she was spending a fair amount of time with Jerry. When Camille did stay home, she spent most of the time in her bedroom. I imagined she had been drinking a lot, causing her to sleep much of the day away.

When Camille was around, I bounced my new thoughts and theories off her. She thought it was a bit nutty and began getting on my case about the clutter. Not letting up about Jezebel, Camille again insisted I kept the bunny in the cage. Apparently, Jezebel had missed her litter box a little.

Finding little input from Camille and Annie and not entirely understanding my concepts, I got in the car and drove until I found a Catholic church. Not wanting to disturb any services, I made my way to the administrative department and insisted to the receptionist that it was urgent I see a priest right away. The receptionist inquired into the nature of my concern, but I insisted it was strictly private and that a priest was the only person with whom I could speak. I waited impatiently for about thirty minutes before a priest arrived and escorted me into a room.

When we sat down, the priest asked the reason for my visit. I began to explain my discoveries related to Christianity and opposing pagan religions and how a woman like myself could find a place within the church's teachings. Surprisingly, the priest seemed to grow angry with me. After about an hour, our conversation escalated to the point where he accused me of being evil. He went so far as to say I would never have a place within the church and was utterly disgusted when I told him I had attended a private Catholic high school. Defensive of my position, before I left the priest, I warned him that the Catholic church would get what was coming to them and that the female mother would show the church just how present and alive her spirit was.

That priest really angered me. However, I found myself more driven to right the wrongs of the world. The pink pill had provided me with uninhibited strength and purpose.

When Drew called to check on me sometime later that day, he was seemingly startled by my visit to the church. He, too, was a non-religious sort with a hint of spirituality glowing within. He was, in fact, an artist in his own right and a composer of such beautiful songs. Drew called to inform me his tour was finishing later that month. He suggested visiting me again in Tampa for a week after his tour ended. That would be spectacular!

While I watched the news on August 9, a story came on about a Southern Baptist convention in town. It was a deplorable story that told how a Caucasian hotel patron committed a disgusting act of racial crime: the patron had spit in the fruit punch bowl that the Baptist convention had set out for its members. Fed up with racial crimes and discrimination, I set out for the convention downtown.

At the convention, I took a long escalator up to the second floor. When I stepped off, I felt every eye staring at me. Walking through the crowd and toward a table set up with merchandise, I was very aware of feeling like a spectacle. I decided it best to shop at the table and sense out the energy in the room. At the merchandise table, I picked up a VHS tape of a sermon and a few other tapes. A man approached me and asked if everything was all right. I assured the man all was just fine. I thanked him and wished him a glorious day. I observed one woman grab the arm of the man standing beside me. As she did so, she glared at me and yanked him away.

Upon paying for my goods, I began taking steps toward the banquet room where the sermon was taking place. I was not sure whether it was acceptable to enter a sermon in progress. Politely, I inquired with a random attendee before entering.

When I walked inside, again, heads turned. As they did, my eyes grew wide. Oh, the hats! What beautiful, beautiful hats! Women were adorned in such beautiful designs, each more elaborate and colorful than the one I had just noticed. There was a spirit in that room, a collective energy of joy, thanks, and praise. I, too, felt the desire to throw my arms up in worship.

Next, I began to walk toward the front of the room where the pastor was preaching. As I did, I felt eyes piercing, burning at me. I stopped walking and looked around. Many women were giving me evil eyes, and I was slightly intimidated and considered turning back. A woman suddenly approached me and put her arms around me. That woman hugged me and thanked me, and expressed how much it meant that I was there. How did she know I was coming? I wondered.

When the pastor finished speaking, the sermon ended, and that was my cue. Boldly, I walked up the stairs and onto the stage where the guest speakers and assembly were seated. I approached a board member who I concluded was an important figure. First, I apologized to him for the rude behavior displayed by an ignorant fool who spit in the punch bowl. The councilman was taken by the idea that I would travel all that way to apologize for another individual's wrongdoing. He proceeded to spend a few minutes talking with me. Actually, I believe I did the talking, and he listened. However, when I began talking about my ideas of Christianity and how far it seemed to have taken the Baptist Church from the origins of earthly beliefs found in African cultures, the councilman quickly became distracted by something else. He told me I was welcome to contact the offices of the church. He then turned and walked away.

A few days later, I once again pursued my spiritual quest and located a tiny nondenominational church. When I parked my car and stepped out, another car pulled in alongside me. As she stepped out from her car, her Bible held closely to her chest, an elderly woman walked over to me and said, "I knew you would be here." Confused, I explained to the woman that she must be mistaken as I had never been to that church before, and it was a last-minute decision to attend that day. The woman said, "I knew you would be here. I'm never late for service, but today my car wouldn't start, and I knew."

Okay, that intrigued me.

The woman introduced herself as Josephine. She was a short, plump woman with deep wrinkles and tangled gray hair. Her eyes were crystal-clear blue, and one seemed to wander. I wondered if it was real or a crystal eye. Josephine and I walked into service together; I felt as though an angel guide was leading me.

When service ended, Josephine and I remained to talk in the parking lot for nearly an hour. She recited biblical quotes and revelations and told stories of her insights and abilities. Josephine also spoke of a few cases she helped solve for government agencies and police forces. Following our discussion, Josephine and I exchanged phone numbers and planned to attend service again. I felt there was much this woman could tell me, and she must serve a purpose in my life. Clearly, there could be no other explanation for the coincidence of our encounter.

Before she drove away, Josephine told me that the Catholic priest got angry with me, and the Southern Baptist councilman walked away because I scared them. She said they felt as though I wanted to change them, and that brought about fear. I sat scribbling in the parking lot for some time after that. Josephine's words struck me, and I wrote:

"People go to organized religion because they don't want to think. They have rules told to them, stories preached, and that is fine—people do not want to change. But, I am stepping on people's most sacred beliefs. I do not want to change but rather enlighten, enhance, grow, evolve, and live. Follow my purpose through Divine guidance, bring forth unity and understanding, reduce crime, feed our hungry, house our homeless, educate our children, help our animals, tend to our homes, clean up our neighborhoods, our country, our world where we ALL coexist and coincide together as one! For past knowledge, present truth, and future wisdom, in the spirit of Dr. Martin Luther King, 'I have a dream,' I thought, dream BIG!"

I wrote more:

"There is no truth in organized religion. We celebrate the Divinity in unity with each other, but religion, our work, is individually unique as each of our existence is a personal, intimate relationship with the Divine. Religion is each living life, each individual life. Life is not definite, not predictable, nor can be religion. God is energy. We are of God. Earth is God's Church. We are all sent through and by God, a Divinity, a power of force, a connection and operation of energy in matter and space. Our challenge is to overcome the obstacles and challenges set forth in our human world and overcome our temptations of free will, where fear lives. Fear blocks love, like water and rocks, air and fire. Father time, mother earth: We cannot have one without the other. His

*matter is Her being. Her being feeds His energy. There are no children, no life
without the two."*

August 13, 2001: Camille and I went back to Orlando to have dinner
with Katie and her husband, Jim. Flooded with theories and ideas, I
talked and talked and talked the whole hour and a half it took to get
there. Angrily, Camille said I hadn't shut up for weeks. She told me to
not say anything for five minutes. I lasted thirty seconds before I just
had to tell Camille about my next philosophical point.

At Katie and Jim's house, I took out my notebook and pen and began
scribbling ideas as they rapidly came to me. Jim seemed interested in
what I was theorizing, and his viewpoints opened my eyes to even
more thoughts. The more ideas came, the more they each connected.
The circle and cycle of it fueled my inspiration.

Suddenly, the concept came to me! Equilibrist! We were Equili-
brists! Equilibrism would be the name of my developing theory. To
make it official, I wrote it down on a piece of paper, dated it, and
signed it. Then, I had Katie and Camille sign it too. Next, I took a
second piece of paper and wrote the wish for my Equilibrism concept.
I then had Camille, Katie, and Jim each write their wish down on the
paper. At that point, I was drawn into the power of magical thought
and asked the universe to reveal itself. Josephine had told me that "all
shall be revealed."

Gathering Camille and Katie into the kitchen where dinner was still
on the stove, I took the piece of paper with the wishes and touched
it to the burner, causing it to light. Smoke filled the kitchen quickly,
and Katie yelled to open the back door. As I opened the door with the
paper burning in my hand, it began to get very hot. I tossed the flaming
paper in the air and watched as glowing pieces blew away in the wind.
I felt pleased.

Shortly thereafter, and before eating, I noticed that Katie seemed
very upset with me. It seemed like she thought I was flirting with her
husband. I was confused, but Camille shoved me out of the door and
into the car back to Tampa. It didn't matter, as I wasn't hungry anyway.

Camille lectured me on much of the drive back to the house in Tampa. She went on and on about Jezebel pooping, my constant talking, being up most of the night and rising early in the morning, my shopping, clutter, Josephine, my writings, thoughts, and so on. She supported me in discovering spirituality but suggested I slow down a bit. Camille had a couple of days off work and recommended we get away and relax for a bit. We decided to head to Key West the next day. But only for a few days because Drew was coming soon!

Arriving back at the house, sitting on the back porch, I scribbled: *"Depression – SSRI. Never could write. Watch. Moved. Fear – held back. Anxiety – now live! Excited– happy – whole life. Snap out of it."*

The phone rang. Louis was calling from the road. He would be coming through town for a show on September 11, 2001, and suggested we meet for dinner at the hotel the night before. I looked forward to it.

Camille, Simon, and I headed off to Key West the following day. Key West was a place I had never been before, so I looked forward to seeing if all the hype about the Keys was true. It sure took a long time to get there, but the miles upon miles of the bridge over water were stunning!

Arriving on the island, Camille and I found a bed and breakfast. It was a lovely old house, and we stayed in the front room. While Camille and I soaked up the sun on the roof deck, a middle-aged couple came along, and before settling into the lounge chairs, they got naked. Nude sunbathing was permitted in Key West. I made it as far as topless. Surely, as most American girls could understand, topless sunbathing was a stand-out moment. It was freeing and so European. I did not have to hide my female breast, while hairy men with C-cup bosoms freely and legally exposed theirs. For the first time in my life, I, too, could take my shirt off in the blazing sun! While we sunbathed topless with the naked couple, we began a conversation. Turned out she was an attorney, and he was an executive.

Later that evening, I went topless swimming in the pool. I was a mermaid, and it felt as though I could breathe under the water. I swam for hours.

Late that night, while Camille drifted off to sleep, I went for a walk. Ending up at a supermarket, I sat down and found myself talking with a homeless black man for a few hours. Sitting with the man reminded me of another homeless man my college roommate and I had sat with years prior. My college roommate and I did not intend to sit down with the man; we simply saw him sleeping on a bench and picked a few flowers to set beside him. We thought it would be nice for when he woke up. As we did so, the man looked up at us. When we walked away, my roommate and I remembered the peanut butter sandwiches we had in our bag. We went back to offer the sandwiches to the homeless man and ended up sitting for hours on the street eating peanut butter sandwiches while listening to the man, James, speak about history, life, and religion. He had so much knowledge and spent hours every day in the library. He said it was his choice to live on the street, but he did not consider himself homeless. The world was his home.

At the supermarket in Key West, I delved into a deep conversation with the homeless man. We discussed racism and drugs. We both agreed we were all the product of immigrants and tribes, now melding together and creating a single unified nationality representing the children of the world as one. Still, I felt I was only viewed as an American when spending time overseas, outside my home country. I recalled an original poem I wrote while in college and recited it for the homeless man, *Mixed and Free*:

"I seem so strange to you. Or do I? I am the face of the vision, but I am no longer foreign. I am the product of my motherland. I am its blood and its breath. I am the truth of its being and the source of its strength. Mixed and free, my own people surround me yet beat me down. Proudly, I am the new beginning, for I have already been the result."

The homeless man took a drink from a brown paper bag. He had every right.

As a living stereotype sat before me, my thoughts poured out as words. New ideas rushed to me fast. Having left the bed and breakfast without my pen and paper, I quickly found a newspaper in the "free" newspaper stand, then borrowed a pen from the supermarket clerk. Hastily, I began to scribble:

"We must make drugs a health issue. No crime. No prison. Respect drugs. Respect the body. Respect ourselves. Respect each other. Create clean Drug House – enter – check-in – room – administer – activities, books, music, mentor, stretch, high, safe. Check out. Regulate. Help. No cause crime. Prison kills."

The homeless man took his last sip from the bag, counted some change, and asked if I had fifty cents. After telling him I had nothing, the man turned to go inside the store. I left and headed back to the room at the bed and breakfast.

The day after Camille and I returned to Tampa, I prepared for Drew's arrival. When I picked him up at the airport on August 20, Drew commented that I seemed to have lost more weight since he had seen me only a few weeks prior. Apparently, he missed my love handles! Drew and I decided to take a lazy getaway to a small island about an hour's drive away. Camille would care for Simon while we were gone, and poor Jezebel would be trapped in her cage the whole time.

When we arrived at the small island, Drew and I located a quaint resort on the water and went inside to the front desk reception for a guest room. The man at the desk was so nice, and the resort was so beautiful. The resort man said it was quiet, and Drew and I could select whichever room we wanted. Surely any one of them would be lovely. I asked the resort man to choose one and told him maybe we'd move to another later. Before we paid for the room, the man told us that since it was slow, he would let us have the room for $90 rather than $120. I reached into my wallet, gave him $120, and said, "Thank you, but it's worth the full amount." Drew gave me a look.

Drew and I settled and snuggled in our little suite. As he drifted off for a nap, I went to venture out. Locating a surf shop across the way, I was drawn inside. I was in the fitting room when my cell phone rang. It was Drew calling, wondering where I had gone for three hours. I told Drew I was in the surf shop and would be right back. Fourteen

T-shirts, nine pairs of shorts, four pairs of flip-flops, three handbags, and seven necklaces later, I went back to the suite. Drew lectured me about my clothes shopping and hotel room expense. I assured him not to worry.

That night, while Drew was asleep, I wandered out again. I ventured through the resort and went to discover the wonders of the other rooms. I didn't know why the doors were unlocked, but I went inside every room I could and thought about how Drew and I would enjoy each space and different design. As I meandered from one room to another, I rearranged little bits of things and noodled in the gardens around the resort. I imagined everyone would wake in the morning and think a fairy had come and tinkered in the night.

Morning came. Drew and I went for pancakes. He seemed annoyed and desperate for me to relax and sit still. I took my regular morning pink pill. As we ate pancakes and sipped coffee on the beach, I began reading the classified ads in the newspaper and spotted a 1975 Winnebago for sale. I told Drew how fun it would be to have my own RV. Like a mini tour bus, it would be a home all my own that I could drive around and park when I was off tour. He chuckled at the picture I created, but I managed to convince Drew to take a ride and go see it. I called the seller for directions.

That afternoon, Drew and I headed to see the 1975 Winnebago. It was in excellent condition with only 70,000 miles and had a pool table eight-ball as the gear change. The carpet was forest green, and it slept 6, with a full kitchen and bathroom, all for under $4,000! When the girl who owned the RV started it up, it was loud! She said she used it to take to Daytona and had the muffler removed for effect. I told her I was going to the bank and would be right back.

Drew and I left the seller's house. Frustrated, he gave me an earful about what a crazy idea it would be to buy the RV. After begging, pleading, and finally convincing him, I got the money out of my account and went back for the Winnebago.

I paid the girl, left the RV at her house until we could pick it up the next day, and Drew and I went back to the resort on the island for another night. The following day, we drove to pick up my new RV purchase. Drew insisted on driving it back to Camille's while I drove my car. He wanted to listen for mechanical stuff and that sort of thing. Camille was in disbelief when she saw the Winnebago pull up. It barely fit in the driveway!

A few days later, Drew left to go home. It was good to know the next tour he was jumping onto would start their rehearsals in Florida. That meant Drew would be coming back in September!

On the way back from dropping Drew off at the airport, I stopped at the gas station. Being from New Jersey, where full-service-only was the law, I hated having to pump my own gasoline and go inside to pay. Two men were sitting on a bench outside the store. After I paid for the gas and walked back outside toward my car, I heard one man say to me, "Hey, what are you?" I turned around toward the two men. "Excuse me?" I said.

The man repeated, "What are you?"

"American," I told him. The men laughed. "What are YOU?" I questioned.

One man chuckled. "I guess I'm American, too," he responded. The other man said he was born in Germany, but he'd been in the United States most of his life.

I smiled and repeated, "I'm American." Then I got in my car and drove away. As I looked down, I saw a note in my cup holder. It read, "Please, baby, no new toys. Love, Drew."

7

Blowout

September 2001 rolled around. I still lived at Camille's house and paid her rent monthly. Feeling uber-energized by my new enlightenment, I faithfully continued my morning ritual of taking a pink pill with my coffee.

On the morning of September 2, I was outside in the front yard decorating the Winnebago. I saw Annie in her front yard and was surprised when she called me over. Annie wanted to show me a project she was working on. Even though her house was next door to Camille's, and I had spent countless hours hanging out with Annie, I still had never been over there.

As we stood in her front yard, Annie went on about excitedly as she talked about "fast lightning."

"Fast lightning," Annie said, "what a great name for a horse!"

"Oh, a horse!" I beamed while recalling how I rode horses as a kid and had quite the Breyer's horse model collection. "I've always wanted a horse. Oh my gosh, I could get a horse!"

Immediately, I turned and ran inside Camille's house, directly to my computer, and searched horses online. Annie followed me. The second picture I saw was a solid black baby horse. Next to the colt's picture, it read, "Can You Imagine."

"Yes, I can!" I yelled.

I picked up the phone and called the number for Good Enough Farm. As I got directions to the farm where the colt was located, I told the woman I was on my way. It was a two-hour drive to the barn. I drove the Winnebago; it roared on the road and seemed even louder as I pulled into the peaceful surroundings of the farm.

An older man greeted me and walked me to a stall where he said, "This is Chad. Chad is six months old and just weaned."

"Chad?" I asked.

"Yes," the man replied. "Can You Imagine is his official paper name, but his barn name, well, we call him Chad. The kids in summer horse camp named Chad after the Presidential election, when they had to recount the hanging chads down here in Florida."

"Oh," I replied, "okay."

The man continued, "He's not ready to leave yet, maybe in a few days. He just had his Coggins pulled, and the results haven't come back yet. He can't travel without a Coggins report."

As the man walked the colt out of the stall, I thought about where I would keep my horse. I would have to find a barn near Camille's house to board Chad. Fortunately, the man said he could trailer Chad to Tampa. I spent thirty more minutes with Chad, walked him around, smiled, and talked to him. Before I left, the man told me he would call in a few days when the Coggins report came back. Excellent, I thought. That would give me time to find a barn.

I didn't tell anyone I was getting a horse; I wanted it to be a surprise. Plus, I thought Drew might get a bit mad, and I didn't want another lecture. My parents would have been furious as they had already questioned me about when I was coming home, what I was doing for work, and how much money I had spent.

I located a horse supply store in the Yellow Pages and took the ride. At the tack shop, I purchased lots of items like buckets, lead ropes, and halters for Chad. They also had dog supplies and bunny stuff, so Simon and Jezebel got a few little goodies too. Before I left the tack store, I checked the bulletin board for a barn to keep Chad. My eye was immediately drawn to a flyer for Rocking D Stables. While I sat in the parking lot with the flyer in hand, I called the barn manager, Diane. After a few minutes of speaking to Diane, I informed her I would head straight over to check it out.

Rocking D Stables was a small family barn about fifteen minutes from Camille's house. The barn had ten stalls and worked on a rough board basis, meaning I would be responsible for purchasing my own hay, feed, and bedding. However, Diane was firm that she was the only one who would actually feed the horses their grain. She did that to ensure each was fed twice a day, and she would not have to worry if a horse owner could not get there to do it. I would be responsible for cleaning Chad's stall, though, and letting him in and out. I gave Diane a deposit for the stall and told her I would let her know immediately when Chad was ready, and I could bring him to the barn. She gave me a list of more items I would need for Chad. So back to the tack shop I went!

When I arrived back at the house later that night, Camille was home and waiting for me. She appeared uneasy and stressed. Camille spent most of her time with Jerry by then; she was rarely home. That day, she seemed different. Camille began by sitting me down. She insisted I sit still and look directly at her. Then, Camille expressed her fury with me about the house and the bunny. I assured Camille I would clear out some stuff and put it in the Winnebago.

Camille made me follow her into the den, where she pointed at her favorite chair. It was my favorite chair too. It brought back fond memories of when Camille first moved to Florida and I still lived in North Carolina. That big gray chair was actually a chair and a half. It was my guest bed when I stayed at her old apartment. It was a comfortable chair indeed. I didn't know what to say when Camille pointed at the chair, now filled with bunny pellets. She lifted the cushion, and there were more. Camille screamed about how the chair was ruined. I tried telling her I would have it cleaned, but she insisted Jezebel had to go. I begged her no. I promised to move the bunny cage into my bedroom and keep Jezebel in it. I swore I would get the chair cleaned. Camille pointed out where Jezebel had chewed the cushion and arm.

"Please, I will fix it," I pleaded with Camille, "but I can't get rid of my bunny."

Eventually, with much persuasion, Camille gave in. She allowed me to keep Jezebel under the condition that I kept the bunny in her cage, and the cage was in my room. Camille said she would take the bunny if she caught Jezebel out one more time. I promised. After that, Camille informed me that she needed to get away; she was going to spend time with her mother in North Carolina the following week. With Camille infuriated and going away, I figured it was not a good time to tell her about Chad.

The following day, I received a phone call from Good Enough Farm. The Coggins report came back, all was good, and Chad was ready to go. On that trip, I took the car for the long drive as the Winnebago seemed desperately in need of a tune-up and muffler. Simon and I drove to pick up Chad.

Pulling down the farm road, I turned on my camera and took many pictures. I drove down the long driveway snapping away. Simon's head stuck out the window as he took in the fresh air. The owner, a tall, older, kind gentleman who had spent decades raising horses, met me at the barn. He told me more about Chad. He told me how Chad was born early, and the family stayed up all night with Chad's mother waiting for his birth. The moment Chad came into the world, the man "imprinted" him by rubbing his hands all over Chad's newborn body, thus instilling him with the comfort and security of human hands. Chad had hernia surgery when he was five months old and had ridden in a horse trailer before. Chad was a real trooper, he said, very well-mannered and quite clever. I immediately loved Chad and knew he would be with me forever, no matter what.

The man seemed saddened when the trailer pulled around, and he prepared to load Chad up for the ride. He had raised him since birth, and the man had bonded with him closely. Before we departed, the man showed me how Chad liked to be scratched on his chest. I promised to keep him updated on how Chad was doing.

On the long ride back to Tampa, I followed in my car behind the truck that pulled the horse trailer. The horse trailer appeared empty; Chad was still a small colt, not yet tall enough to be seen through the trailer windows.

We arrived at Rocking D Barn safely, and I led my baby horse into his new stall and home. The truck and trailer drove away. Diane and her kids came out to see the new baby colt. Diane's daughter was only nine, but she sure had a way with the horses. I admired that she had no fear as she chased after them, running the horses around the paddock. I led Chad out to an empty paddock and spent the day getting him settled.

Simon enjoyed running around the farm and was curious about the big new animals around us; his curiosity was distracted only by chasing barn cats. Each morning Simon and I hopped in the Winnebago and headed to the horse farm. All day we played. Chad walked around, and I hugged and scratched him and was a bit surprised when I realized it would be three years before he would be old enough for me to ride him.

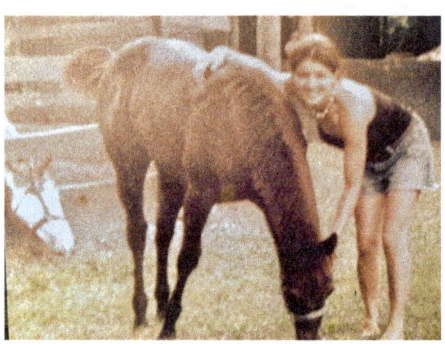

Dawn and baby Chad, September 4th, 2001
C. Stringer

On September 9, 2001, Camille left to visit her mother in North Carolina. Before leaving, she made me swear to keep Jezebel in the cage while she was away. No sooner had Camille left for the airport than Jezebel was running free.

That afternoon, Louis called to remind me he was coming to town for a show. He invited me to meet and hang out with him and the crew the following night. A bunch of people I knew were on that tour; it would be a blast to meet up again. Everybody would meet by the pool and bar restaurant. I would make sure to bring my swimsuit.

"Awesome! See you there!" I said. I was excited to wear my new two-piece.

It was a fun night swimming and catching up with everybody. Everyone commented on my significant weight loss. I sure felt light and free, as though I was in the best shape since junior high. When it became late, I went back to the hotel room with Louis.

While my wet swimsuit hung in the bathroom to drip dry, I walked around wearing a t-shirt and underwear. That was unusual behavior for me; Louis thought I was nutty. No big deal, I thought. After all, for several years, we lived together on a tour bus along with eight other guys and a bus driver. Surely, I had seen them in their boxer shorts many times.

I also brought a present for Louis. It was a gift I picked up when Camille and I were in Key West: Mexican jumping beans! Louis laughed and told me I was nuts. Before too long, I jumped in my car and headed back to the house. But before I left, I did make him promise to take good care of the jumping beans.

The next morning, September 11, 2001, I woke at dawn like I had become accustomed to doing. Pink pill, coffee, writing, scribbling, reading, cleaning; I went about the rituals of my morning. Suddenly Annie came running into the house as she always did, but this day, Annie was anxious, frantic, and scrambling to say something.

"The tower!" she yelled. "The building, a plane. They crashed, and there's smoke, and the plane crashed into the tower! Turn on your TV!" Annie commanded like I had never heard her do before.

"Jezebel ate the wire," I told Annie. "The TV isn't working because Jezebel ate the wire, but I have to fix it before Camille gets home from North Carolina."

"The plane crashed into the building! In New York!" Annie yelled feverishly.

"What are you talking about?" I asked.

"Come see!" Annie grabbed me; she pulled me out the door. Dragging me along, Annie ran toward her house and yanked me inside. That was the first time I had ever been in Annie's house, and I was amazed. The house looked neat, well-kept, and clean. It made me wonder even more why Annie had never invited me over before.

The TV was on in Annie's living room. I sat on the floor staring at it and wondering if what I was watching was real or a Hollywood movie. It appeared that smoke was billowing from one of the Twin Towers, and the report claimed a commercial airplane had just crashed into the World Trade Center. As I gaped at the TV, digesting what had happened, another plane came flying into the picture and flew straight into the second tower!

"Oh my God!" I yelled.

"That's another plane!" Annie screamed. "That plane just flew into the second tower!"

"Oh my God!" I repeated over and over as I jumped up and raced back to Camille's house for my telephone. Panicked, I called my mom back home in New Jersey, frantically telling her what was happening. She, too, was watching what was taking place.

"We're under attack!" I screamed.

"Stay calm," my mother told me.

I was scared for my family and friends who lived and worked in the city. Being from New Jersey, that was a lot of people. Also, my grandpa lived in Jersey City. I was terrified for him and concerned he wouldn't be able to get away. My mom reminded me to stay calm. She also wanted me to stay off the phone so I wouldn't tie up the phone lines; people needed them for the crisis. Mom was going to call Grandpa and check on him, as well as some other relatives who worked at the World Trade Center.

Not knowing if more attacks and explosions were coming, I thought it might be the last time I ever got to talk to my mom. Sobbing, I told her how much I loved her and how thankful I was for all she and Daddy did for me.

After we hung up, I immediately repaired the chewed wire on the TV. By the time I was able to get the TV turned on, the news was reporting that another commercial airplane had crashed into the Pentagon. "Oh my God," I repeated again and again. I sat on the floor rocking back and forth while I stared at the TV and witnessed the most devastating attack take place before my eyes.

Next, another plane crashed in a field in Pennsylvania!

"When will it end?" I screamed. "What's next? Where is the next strike? Where are they coming from? Who would do this? Oh my God! Oh my God!"

I watched the Twin Towers crumble in a mass of smoke. Disbelief. Were they gone? How could they be gone? The mosaics. The mosaic tiles on the walls. Oh, those beautiful tiles of the Great Wonders of the World. Gone. The Twin Towers gone. New York was over. How would it ever be the same? All those people were gone. Where did they go?

By early afternoon the strikes seemed to have stopped; no more planes had crashed. Despite this, I felt like one would strike anywhere at any moment. I began to make a plan. Frantically, I paced and looked for where I could hide or run.

The phone rang. It was a girl I had met through Camille. She called to see if I could get her tickets for the show later that evening. "There is no show!" I yelled.

"Are you sure?" the girl asked.

"There was an attack on our country! The Twin Towers have collapsed!"

"So, you don't think they'll do a show?"

"There is NO show!" I yelled as I hung up on her.

I began making phone calls. While keeping the television on, I went through my phone book and called to check on everyone and anyone I could think of who lived in the New York area. I called old coworkers from ten years prior and a boss in the city for whom I had worked as a temporary receptionist a long time ago. I composed an urgent letter of sympathy and concern intended for Mayor Giuliani and emailed it to him.

My mom called back to inform me that everyone in our family was okay. Some made it onto ferries and got home. She described how one cousin had to jump over a leg – the leg of someone who had possibly fallen from the tower – to make it into a taxi, but she was now out of the city and safe.

I was too frightened to go anywhere, but I very much wanted to be home in Jersey with my family and friends. I didn't know what was going on up there. I only imagined what could be taking place as the crumbled buildings smoldered and the sky looked black with smoke. I began to imagine the collective power and energy of all the souls inside; I dreamed they would all rise and light the sky with Holy Light as we witnessed them released from the darkness of the devastation. I prayed to the power of the Divine that the people would walk from the ruins and heaven would show its grace.

I felt more panic and depression than I had ever known before. I was frantic. In addition to the one pink pill I usually took, I also took a second pink pill that day. I needed the medication more than ever. I re-called Dr. Menia had previously mentioned increasing the dosage, and the time to do so had come. I wished the medicine would bring me the peaceful calm I had experienced during my first days taking the tablet.

The day went on, and I wrote, scribbled, and saw this was a purpose. God allowed such tragedy to happen for a reason. This was a calling, a need, an opportunity for us to become better, stronger, united. I was driven to give any gift I had, any way I could help.

The following two days, I did not sleep at all. Listening to the television around the clock, I scribbled, wrote, and reviewed the note-books filled with symbols, pictures, and words I had written over the past month. Everything I had recorded seemed to take on a new mean-ing of extreme significance.

By September 13, I had finished composing a letter and obtained fax numbers for the White House, Pentagon, and FBI. I faxed my letter repeatedly to the institutions until one of the establishments called my mom and requested no more faxes be sent. I didn't realize my fax included a cover page with my contact information from my parents' house in New Jersey. Apparently, I tied up the fax machines at the government institutions. My mom was not pleased and requested I let the authorities work in peace.

After I finished faxing, I called Josephine and told her about my letter. She told me the tragic events were God's message to us, saying that we should "rebuke sharply." Then, Josephine invited me to her house to talk about what had happened and what the Bible said about it.

Josephine's small apartment was filled with stuff! It was difficult to find a clear place to sit. Josephine said she usually lived alone but had a troubled young person staying with her at the time. Hours upon hours, I sat with Josephine and listened as she went through her Bibles and notes. She told me of all the predictions that were to follow. She talked about anthrax, natural disasters, and the poisoning of our water and food supplies. She showed me how codes were used and how meanings were hidden in the way words were written. She emphasized that we should look beyond and see that all shall be revealed to us through Him.

Parked in Camille's driveway, I sat in my Winnebago that night and composed another letter, a code-written letter filled with all my new information and warnings that Josephine had told me. I was filled with fear. All I knew was I needed to pass along the warnings in the hope that I could prevent horrible attacks from coming to be. My thoughts raced.

The next morning, I again faxed a letter to the White House, Pentagon, and FBI. In the letter, I included my thoughts about the attacks, war, and retaliation:

"This is my solace... My country 'tis of thee, sweet land of Liberty, of thee I SING! ATTENTION ALL AmERiCANs AND AmERiKisTs AROUND the GLOBE. Anybody in this Earth World, any American or Freedom Fighting Person who believes that reacting or responding violently against another, to whomever particular persons at wherever places, is 'the thing to do' at

this time, is a person who is as ill-fated as the terrorists of this very UN-Natural disaster themselves. To do so would not only be a complete hypocrisy to the intent and universally eternal purpose of our America's existence today and all days of the world before, it would lead to, moreover, the most catastrophic events we have yet to even conceive. Two wrongs will NEVER make RIGHT!"

I continued:

"America will love. America will live. We will stand on our own grounds and protect our soil, our waters, and our air with fire and vengeance! We will honor our Amendments and seek to live their highest truth. We will bear arms to hug, arms to hold, arms to rebuild. We will speak out – rebuke sharply – vocalize. We will assist, comfort, and help each other, the citizens of our United States, as well as in lands beyond our borders. We do this in Worship of God's Love, His Gift of Life, and to honor the lessons learned from the founding fathers before u.s."

Other themes composed in this letter related to the attacks, history, and karma:

"Thank you, brothers, for this wake-up call! The sins of the past will be repaired, and wounds will heal. Time led us here; Time will lead us free. We begin now. To our original Native Americans, we send our hearts and our hands in an extension of your suffering. Let us take a moment to recognize and acknowledge the forgotten Trail of Tears and the challenges that, once again, as Native Tribal Americans of this Homeland and in a new millennium of Time, under a new perspective of Wisdom, face today. Today may our Hearts understand your grief and pain. To our Brothers and Sisters in Africa – please – forgive us for stealing and abusing your people. Let us join at this Place and Time to embrace and love them always as our own empowered American Spirits. Let u.s. join together with our fellow citizens, our allies, and our neighbors: Mexico, Canada, and Central and South America. Together with the presence of God, we will have healed the wounds that have scarred centuries deep. God forgive us; we knew not what we had done. Praise Lord!

Bless our People! God Knows No Time! AmeriCANism IS a RELIGION! But what IS religion??? My fellow Americans, be safe and be smart."

I scribbled:

"God has demonstrated the Force of the Almighty Energy. The Spirit is upon u.s. Imperative we do not Re-tal-i-ate through VIOLENCE. Declare war – YES! On Fear!**NO MILITARY VIOLENT ATTACKS!!** Be 4(Fore)Warned. Pride: Praise God; proudly, publicly, personally. States of America UNITE! Flags-apple pie-baseball-music-picnics-vigils-education!! Hearts. Compassion. Empathy. LOVE. See it, Cure It. Security. A War unlike any other, a new kind of war, a strategic, sophisticated war of a spiritual nature that strikes the core of human existence. Intelligent war. Wisdom. Religionis of the physical world – God works through love in a spiritual world that most do not comprehend: Blind Faith. However, know God answers our cries for help through the collective energy produced by our living experiences on God's creation, Her Mother Earth. Do not be afraid. Do not prostitute to human-developed fear. God is here. Now. Always. 4-ever."

Camille was still away, delayed in North Carolina under a high travel alert.

Listening to the news around the clock, I scribbled notes, pictures, arrows, and drawings on any paper or notebook I could find. I attempted to figure out how the attack could happen and what exactly was happening. I found it difficult to digest that four commercial airplanes could be hijacked in America in less than an hour without anybody having a clue that it was going to happen. This was America.

GOD HAS SPOKEN, Be FORWARNED!

God has demonstrated, once again, the FORCE of tHIS ALMIGHTY EnERGY! One Holy SPiRiT is upon (U.S.) GOD WARNS:

- IMPERATIVE! Do NOT Re-tal-i-ate through VIOLENCE (expression of FEAR!) THERe aRE BETtER SoL u tiOns! IF we DO, the current devastion will look like kindergarten play.

- OFFICIALLY, WORLDWIDE, DECLARE WAR AGAINST FEAR, TERRORISM, , ViOLEnCE... The wise will follow! Unionize the living connection between 'Father TIME, Mother EARTH (see: "natiVe Americans", Trail ofTears, ALSO: AFRiCA) HEAL/HEEL, "walk by my side", man's best friend,; God ..fOOtPRintS'it was then that I carried YOU'

- Be PrO U d... PRAISE GOD!!! Publicly, Privately, Personally ALWAYS!! Do not worship false idols!! GOD FORGIVE them, they KNOW not WHAT they DO!

- UNITE through LOVE! In America: fly flags, eat 'apple' pie, be WISE to free-will, play ball, listen to rock n roll and the blues, have a picnic, a vigil, EDUCATE others!! SIGNS - posters, HEARTS, Exercise FrEeDOM and Right to bear ARMS!

One letter in part faxed to the White House, Pentagon, and FBI

Drowning in agony over the destruction, desperate to warn and help, I had to do something. In the middle of the night, I went downtown to the office of the FBI. There I met an agent, Dean Smith, who I called "Dean of Students." He talked with me for a good amount of time while I poured over the 'materials' I had brought to show him. I included the letters I had faxed and notebooks filled with all the writings and ideas that had poured into me over the summer. Also, I told the Dean of Students of all the warnings Josephine had spoken of. I wore an American flag T-shirt cut up with holes to represent gunshots. I had trinket stones in my pocket for protection and courage. Before I left, I thanked the Dean of Students and the FBI for all their hard work and dedication to finding out who did this to America.

The T-shirt worn to the FBI office at 3
a.m.

I was still tuned to the TV on Sunday morning, September 16, 2001. The news reported that terrorists had executed a plan against our homeland, our people. Reports came of cars found in airport parking lots and terrorist flight training that took place in our very own schools, including Florida! They had infiltrated our system and could be anywhere.

I began dressing to meet Josephine for Sunday service. I specifically chose my favorite clothes: a white T-shirt with the image of a little black jive girl on the front; she was so cute and funky with her little groovy self. She wasn't a large color print or anything, just a little jive girl dancing with her big Afro hairdo; she was happy. I also selected my favorite denim skirt: a dark wash pencil skirt with a slight slit in the back. It was my favorite because Drew thought it looked nice on me. That particular service day, I felt strongly that I needed to wear something representative of love because there was so much madness, terror, and chaos around. How could this happen?

My paranoid thoughts went on and on. I began thinking aloud as I fleshed out in my mind all the possibilities. "Oh my God!" I suddenly yelled. "They knew! The only way this could happen is if somebody on our inside knew! Yes, they knew! They killed Kennedy! Dr. Martin Luther King! Of course, someone knew!" I hollered.

Impulsively, I ran outside in the front yard and saw a huge American flag hanging on the garage door of the house across the street. "Now!" I yelled. "Now you are proud to be American! Now, you finally say you are an American!"

Looking toward Annie's house, I saw a few suspicious men working at the house next to hers, and I began to scream, "Who are you! Are you one of them?" Annie and her husband, Joe, were outside, and they asked if I was okay. I ran to their house and around into the backyard, then looked in their shed and yelled, "They could be anywhere!"

Joe remained on his front porch. When I ran back around to the front of their house, he was sitting in a chair with a sly look on his face, a sneer. He looked right at me and said so slyly, "Who could be anywhere, Dawn?"

I ran back inside Camille's house, filled with fear and overwhelmed with emotions. I was not going to be afraid! Rebuke sharply! With Simon following me, I ran out to the driveway and began singing the song composed by John Kander, with lyrics by Fred Ebb, and made famous by Frank Sinatra, *New York, New York.* Passionately, I sang at the very top of my lungs: "I want to be a part of it! New York, New York!" As I continued singing loudly and passionately, I saw a car coming down the street. It seemed to be going particularly slow; it felt like danger was coming toward me. I ran back inside the house. I was scared there. I ran back outside, across the street, and around the block to a house on the corner. I ran to the front door to seek help because I was scared of the car and Joe.

Before I knocked on the door, I took a moment to ensure I knocked calmly and didn't bang, but before I could knock, I turned, and there was a woman in a dark, stiff uniform standing in front of me. She had fine black hair and a mean face. Her hands were up as though ready to strike me.

"Whoa, sister. Chill," I pleaded.

Before I knew what had happened, the woman lunged, grabbed me, and wrestled me with intense force. She was attacking me! I screamed in terror and tried to slip away from her. Why was she attacking me? Was she a terrorist with them? She was going to kill me!

More hands grabbed me! They pulled, wrestled, and jerked me while I screamed and squirmed, but I could not fight them. Every movement of my body anticipated a gunshot blasting into me. In a flash, with one bang, I was going to be killed. I surrendered in dead weight as they dragged me along until I gathered strength and began to fight for my life again.

As they pulled me toward a car, I saw its trunk was open. I was terrified they were going to stuff me in the trunk! Then, I recalled seeing a safety report on TV: if they put me inside the trunk, kick out the tail light from the inside.

Louder and louder, I continued screaming for help, but nobody came to help me. I screamed in blazing terror as I thought my attackers were going to kill me. There were too many hands. They were too strong. They wrestled me to the ground and onto my stomach with my face in the dirt. They hiked my arms around my back, and the pain, oh, my God, the pain! I felt metal dig into me. I was screaming and eating the dirt until I couldn't scream anymore, and I knew nobody was going to save me.

I lay still. Maybe they would think I was dead. I lay quiet. It was as though time had stopped. In my head, I sang a song: "When the whole world is falling in love, and the sun shines bright in the sky up above, and the earth moves on my feet underground while I just can't seem to escape all the sounds."

Blocking out the violence I was enduring, I thought: I love Lucy. I love Lucy. I repeated it over and over in my head. Lucy was my great-aunt and a special person in my life. When I was a little girl, she and my uncle would pick me up and bring me to their house. Theirs was a peaceful home where voices were never raised, and serenity filled the air. There, we would garden, bake, sew, and even go on day trips to the milk farm or mill. Aunt Lucy enjoyed watching me ride horses when

I was young, and she would collect the compost from the farm for fertilizer.

Trying to catch my breath, I began to repeat very softly, "I love Lucy. I love Lucy."

With my arms tightly shackled behind my back and the metal digging into my skin, I was picked up like a garbage bag, then tossed into the backseat of the police car. My arms were numb from the pain. I was filled with dirt, mangled, and beaten.

Trapped inside the car, I could see the circle of people in uniforms standing outside through the window. Their backs were turned to the vehicle. Suddenly, I kicked my bare feet hard on the window. The window glass shattered and the frame dangled. In a flash, I saw my escape. It was my only chance to get away and save my life. I maneuvered quickly and scrambled to dive out through the shattered glass. I tumbled onto the ground. Hands grabbed me and pulled my feet up off the ground. I was too broken to fight anymore.

I was positioned stomach down on a stretcher; my ankles were then cuffed. Placed inside an ambulance, the door closed, and I was driven away. In the back of the ambulance was a large woman sitting next to me. I asked her where I was being taken. She told me I would know when I got there.

Having never been in trouble with the police before, my understanding was that if the police took you, they needed to first read you your rights. So I asked the large woman if I was being arrested. She did not answer. "If I am being arrested, you have to read me my rights! Read me my rights!" I demanded. The woman looked down at me lying on the stretcher and said, "You have no rights."

The police incident report from that day read:

"I responded to the location where I met W/F. As I spoke to the Compl., the subject ran out her front door screaming. The Compl. said that subject was screaming at the lawn workers and she ran into somebody's house. I followed subject and told her to stop several times. Several neighbors came outside and observed subject yelling and screaming. Subject refused to stop so

I restrained her and forced her to the ground. Subject continued to struggle and attempted to get away. With a neighbor's assistance, I placed her in the backseat of my police vehicle. The subject was handcuffed behind her back. A minute later the subject kicked out the police vehicle's right rear window and injured herself. She received lacerations on her right wrist and legs. Ambulance responded to the scene and transported subject to the hospital. I took photographs of the police vehicle."

8

Junkyard

The ambulance came to a stop, and the back doors swung open. Immediately herds of people swarmed around me. The stretcher where I was bound was lowered from the vehicle and wheeled into a building. I was rushed through a frenzy of bright lights and chaos. Where was I? Where were they taking me? What were they going to do to me? I began screaming again. There were so many people surrounding me! They were moving purposefully. They were going to wheel me into a room and kill me inside!

I was wheeled into a room; the door shut. I screamed as loud as I could and begged and pleaded, "Please don't! Please don't! No! Nooooooo! STOP! Help! Help me! No!" All the while, I felt hands all over me.

The lights were bright, and I was grabbed, lifted, and moved onto a hard table. I was fighting as they tried to grab my hands and tie them down. There were more people at my feet where I was kicking and kicking as they tried to grab my legs and tie them down. I was screaming and kicking and flailing. There were people and lights and noise and chaos and hands grabbing me. I looked to my right, where another woman had a needle, and I screamed—they were going to inject me and poison me! I tried pulling my arms away, but the heavy straps were too tight. They were wide and hard, stiff leather that stung as they dug into me!

My legs were trapped, strapped. My arms were tied, and I was bound at the mercy of the many people around me. They were mocking me, laughing at me, and teasing me as I screamed out loud. The woman on my right raised her hand as though to hit me. She told me to be still and shut up. I continued screaming for my life. I screamed that I knew a secret that I had to say before I died. I screamed my bank codes and that my mom needed to know them so she could manage my accounts. I screamed for my Simon and my Chad, and my Jezebel, who needed me. Who would take care of them when I was gone?

"No!" I screamed, "Oh my God! Nooooooo!"

My T-shirt and skirt were cut off my body; I heard them tear while I lay strapped down on the table. The lights were so bright. There were so many people, and I was naked and felt exposed and wanted to cover myself, but I was tied, and I couldn't cross my legs as people were fighting to spread them open, and I knew I wanted to close them tight. I was so exposed.

I could feel them doing something on my right arm, and I knew they had me. I was helpless as I screamed and squirmed with no success. I was mad that was how my life would end. After I had traveled the globe with the best in the world, this was how it all would end. I screamed louder as the moment came when I was injected; then, I tried to accept that it had come. Their poison was in me. I prepared to make my last pleas as I felt it flowing in my arm and through my body.

"I can feel it," I told them, "I can feel it coming down my arm, and it is warm."

"Yes," the woman on my right said. "Oh yes, you have it coming."

I thought: When confronted with death, hold your head high and proud toward the face of light. Praise God, love God. Know. Believe. Trust blindly, wholeheartedly, passionately. I felt the warm sensation make its way down my arm, and I felt the woman on my right doing something to my wrist. She was sewing it. She had implanted something in my wrist and was sewing it inside me. Rebuke sharply!

My legs were pulled open, and I fought as they tried to insert something inside me.

"Stop!"I screamed. More hands pulled mylegs. "Noooooo!"I shouted.

It did not matter. I was tied. My legs were strapped, my hands bound. My clothes cut off, my body naked. Dirt caked in my mouth.

The lights were bright, and in the last effort I could exert, I shouted at the doctor who was leading the mockery of me, "Homey, you need to get out!" The doctor laughed and said, "I haven't been called 'homey' in a long time."

The room suddenly cleared, and I was left alone; I was still alive. They wanted me to sleep, but I would not. I knew I would not close my eyes and rest; I might not wake if I did. A long time passed; I lay there, unable to move.

Two women entered and tried to talk with me. They moved suspiciously through the room. They laughed at me while I lay strapped down. I made sure not to make eye contact with them; never make eye contact, or they will get you. I watched them closely but said nothing. One girl reminded me of the black-haired woman who attacked me. I expected the woman would remove a mask and reveal herself as my attacker. She was coming back to finish me off. I said nothing until they eventually left the room.

More time passed. I remained strapped down.

Another woman entered and told me I needed to sleep. Still, I would not close my eyes. I would not sleep. I would listen closely for any sounds that might tell me what was going on. I needed to break free. I needed to get to my animals. Who was going to care for them?

I had to get that thing out of my body. Tied down tight, I could not reach down to grab it from between my legs. I twisted and distorted myself. The leather dug into my arm as I squeezed to reach it. I kept twisting and distorting; the leather straps were digging. I had to reach. At last, I could touch the object; I could get it! Painfully, I twisted and stretched and managed to pull the object out from inside me. It was a tube, and there was a bag, a plastic bag. What were they doing to me? I bent my body sideways until my teeth could reach the bag, and I could tear it open in disgust.

More time passed, unable to move.

I was relieved the object was now out of me, but my right wrist felt contaminated and separate from the rest of my body. I was implanted and marked. I began to holler for a priest; I ordered a priest to read my last rites. I was going to die there. A man arrived at the room and sat down. He would not read my rites, and I did not believe he was a priest. I screamed for him to leave. He left, and more time passed.

Eventually, people returned to the room and prepared to unstrap me. I heard them speaking as though I was not even there. They had tested me for drugs: Ecstasy, mushrooms, LSD, but found nothing. They made me promise not to run or attack and threatened to tie me down again if I did. Desperately, I promised I would obey.

As they unbuckled the leather belt, my arms were numb and in pain. I lowered them slowly by my hips and let the blood run back into them. Someone supported my back as they sat me up. I turned to cautiously lower my legs over the side of the bed I had been fastened to.

I tried to stand and felt like a beaten doll. I felt small and fragile, and the dirt was still in my mouth. I could not stand upright and walked slowly as they wrapped a cloth around me and escorted me down the hallway. They walked me outside and led me toward another ambulance. They made me get inside the ambulance and lie on a stretcher. Then the doors closed. Once again, I was driven away.

The hospital records from that day reported:

"*Patient screaming out religious preoccupation. Running around the neighborhood screaming. Patient broke out the back window of the police car with her feet; Vital signs/normal; Medications/Unknown; Allergies/Unknown; Exam limitation/Clinical condition/Physical impairment/Patient acutely psychotic + uncooperative; Onset of symptoms/Unknown; Type of onset/Abrupt; Presenting symptoms/acute psychosis; Suicide-Homicide risk/Unknown; Eligible for hold under state law/Yes-acute psychosis; Intoxication factors/ None;*

History of similar symptoms/Unknown; Psychiatric behavior/uncooperative/ impulsive/decreased eye contact; Personal appearance/disheveled; Memory/ impaired recent/impaired remote; Judgment/impaired; Insight/impaired; Eye contact/threatening; Level of motor activity/increased; Speech/ tangential/ pressured; Affect/angry/inappropriate; Mood/agitated/combative; Thought form/ normal; Thought content/obsessive/ideas of reference/delusions/preoccupation with ideation/depersonalization/derealization/persecution/religious; Hallucinations/Unknown, Current suicide risk factors/None."

The ambulance drove on. When it stopped, the doors opened, and I was led into a room that appeared to be a waiting room of sorts. The walls were lined with stackable metal chairs. There was a desk where a very large man sat. I was told to wait in the room. I did. It felt like I had entered another world, and the world I knew and loved was gone forever, taken over by strangers with ill intent.

There was a pay phone in the room, but I was scared to use it. I didn't know if it was a real phone until I finally summoned up the courage to pick it up and try to dial out. I made a collect call to my mom. I tried to tell her what had happened; she kept asking where I was.

"I don't know," I repeated.

She asked me to describe what I saw; I told her there were metal chairs and a man at a desk. She wanted me to ask the man at the desk where I was. He would not speak to me. My mom asked me for the number of the pay phone, but there was none I could read. She told me to call her if anyone came to take me from the room or call her back in an hour. Meanwhile, she was going to try to find out where I was.

I was tired, exhausted, and disheveled. I pulled two metal chairs together and tried to lie down and rest. Time passed until I called my mom again. She told me that I was in a crisis center and would be waiting there until they had a bed ready for me. I did not understand what she meant. Most importantly, I told my mom that somebody had to feed Chad, Simon, and Jezebel. Camille was still away in North Carolina, and there was nobody to let them outside and feed them.

My mom tried to assure me that she would take care of it, but that did not settle my concern and worry about them.

Hours passed. My body ached, and the chairs were so hard on my wounds. I had no shoes or clothes, just the cloth put on me at the hospital.

From home in New Jersey, my parents made phone calls on my behalf. They noted their communications, and my dad wrote:

"9/17/01. 10:15am - asked for nurse & CSU- got transferred. Transferred again – ring – no answer. Recalled Dawn and central intake. Ringing – no answer. Recalled – on hold – music; receptionist got back on phone, said call in 10 and ask for a 'counselor' at intake. 10:35 – Horse Chad 'Can You Imagine' Good Enough Farm pickup. 11am – central intake counselor said Dawn's going to a unit, call back in one hour and ask for unit to talk to someone about her. 12:30 – still not moved, call later. Talk to Dawn in intake center throughout day. 20:00 nurse says to call unit pay phone. 20:15 – CSU nurse says Dawn will go to unit. Depakote 200, Klonopin, Risperdal, Ativan. Bipolar."

It was deep into the night when a woman entered the waiting room. She escorted me through the doors on the other side of the security desk, where the big man still sat in silence. On the other side of the doors, I heard screams, loud, crazy screams like a wild animal. There was a man behind caged glass howling and jumping around his pen.

I shuffled slowly along as the woman led me into a room. There, she asked me to remove my cloth. Again, I was naked and prodded and probed. The woman checked over every inch of my body and documented the bruises, cuts, and gashes that covered me. She seemed awed by all the bruising and was gentle in her touch. She weighed me: 108 pounds. When the woman finished examining me, she left the room and then returned with clothes for me to wear. From there, I was led to a dimly lit room where there was a bed. I was administered pills and told to rest.

I got into bed and noticed a man seated in a chair at the end of the bed. I asked the man his name. He said, "Q." Though I was still unable to sleep, Q shared the same name as a security guy I knew from work; somehow, that comforted me for the moment.

After some restless dozing, I awoke to a woman who insisted I get up. She instructed me to get up and get in line. I didn't know what she meant, but I got up and walked outside the room. There, in the bright fluorescent lights, I was in a hallway. Looking to my left, I saw there were other rooms and individuals emerging, dressed in pajamas and rags. To my right, there was a line of unusual people: old people, young people. Some talked to themselves, and some yelled at others. I took my place at the back of the line.

When I reached the front of the line, I was at a desk. It was the nurse's station. The woman behind the desk asked for my name, then handed me a small plastic cup with a few pills. She then gave me another small cup with water and told me to take the pills, swallow, then open my mouth to show her inside. I obeyed.

Next, I was instructed to stand in another line behind the others. I waited in that line for a long time before it began to move. Eventually, the line moved down a hallway and into what appeared to be a small room with tables and chairs. Finding an empty table in a corner, I sat, waited silently, and watched. Finally, each person went up to a small window where they got a tray and a plate of food. I could not eat. Continuing to sit there while I stared out of the barred window, I wondered how my Simon, Chad, and Jezebel were faring.

When the meal was over, we all lined up again and were led down the hallway and back to the locked area we came from. There, at the nurse's station, an announcement was made that we were to remain in the community room and not permitted back into our bedrooms until further instructed. I followed the others into the community room to wait.

The community room was located on the other side of the glass, across from the nurse's station. It had tables and chairs and rows of chairs like at an airport gate. There was a small couch area and a bookcase with Bibles, books, and newspapers. I selected a newspaper. It was September 18, 2001; the Twin Towers had just fallen in New

York. The newspaper was current, and I read the headlines: Terrorists had attacked in a Jihad. Thousands had been killed. The world had changed. My wounds were dirty; I went to the nurse's station with concern. High up in her elevated chair, the nurse clarified that she did not have clearance to tend to my lesions. "They're dirty, and I have stitches," I told her. The nurse ignored me. I grew angry with her and insisted that I had to have the wounds cleaned so they would not get infected. She made it clear that she did not care.

Back in the community room, excitement developed when a large man entered and announced it was time for smoking. Everybody jumped up and ran for the door in the back corner that opened to a caged patio outside. The perimeter of the patio cage was lined with chairs. Most everyone quickly lined up to get a cigarette and a light from the distributor man before they settled in a seat for a smoke. A few people discreetly bummed a cigarette from the security man, who seemed to have a pack reserved especially for the ones without.

I began to watch the people more closely. Who were they? Where was I? How did I get there? How could I get out? Why did that black-haired woman attack me? How was I alive? What were they going to do with me? I recognized there were collected groups of people around me, cliques. Were those people part of the terror in New York and at home? How were Simon, Chad, and Jezebel? Had anybody fed them or let them out? Oh my God, I needed to know. I had to get out of that place and get to them!

After the cigarette break, I went to the nurse's station again, demanding answers. The woman behind the desk told me to settle in because I was going to be there for a while. "How long is a while?" I asked.

"Until the doctor says you can leave," she replied. "What doctor?" I asked.

"The doctor assigned to you."

"Who is that? I want to see this doctor!"

"He will see you when he gets here."

Again, I mentioned that my wounds needed to be cleaned. The nurse told me I could wash them when I went back to my room, but it would be a while before we were permitted to return.

Back in the community room, there was a small, senior woman bellowing about the time. She was unable to tell time, so I occupied mine by drawing a clock and explaining to her how it worked.

Later that day, before being permitted back into our rooms, all patients lined up again for our pills; pills, water, swallow and open wide. I was relocated to another room further down the hallway, but first, I asked the nurse if I could clean my wounds. She told me I could shower. She pointed to a tray where there were more little plastic cups. Each cup contained either a squirt of shampoo, lotion or toothpaste. Next to the cups were little hotel-size bars of soap and plastic-wrapped toothbrushes. I took one of each.

A strange man who stood beside me pointed to a cardboard box on the floor; he told me I could get clothes there. Rummaging through the cardboard box, I found underwear, socks, pants, and a T-shirt to wear. Clothes and cleaning supplies in tow, I headed down the hallway to my room.

It was a small room with two beds and a bathroom. Each bed had a drawer under it to put your things; I didn't have any things. There was a window with a metal cage on it. I wanted to be free. Why was I not free?

Tender with my cuts, I took a long, hot shower and cringed when the soap touched my open skin and stitches. Reluctantly, I put on the clothes from the cardboard box but could not bring myself to put on the used underwear. I couldn't. Drugged, I fell asleep fast and slept.

The following morning, I woke, dazed as to where I was. Loudly over a speaker, I heard the announcement summoning everyone to stand in line. Again, I received my plastic cup of pills, and again, we lined up to eat. A pay phone near the community room caught my eye.

I talked to a different nurse at the station, Alice. She reminded me of "Go Ask Alice." She was a heavy-set woman with long, bleached blond and gray hair. She had sleeves of tattoos on both arms. I felt I could trust her; she talked to me. She said I was "high-functioning." Talking with Alice, desperate to get out of there, I began to research what was going on. Alice showed me paperwork that listed belongings I had with me when I was taken into custody: my ring, necklace, bracelet, and cell phone. They had my cell phone! Though she would not give it to me, I asked Alice if I could see my cell phone so I could write down phone numbers and use the pay phone. Alice finally agreed; she gave me a piece of paper and a pen, then allowed me to see my cell phone. I wrote down every phone number I had in my phone.

I began by making a collect call to Camille. Thank God she had made it safely back from North Carolina. Camille was in disbelief about what had happened while she was away. She promised me she would come by during visiting hours to bring a few of my clothes, especially underwear. Also, Camille was able to access my wallet, which I had left at the house, and get my credit card number. Having my credit card number enabled me to make phone calls and charge them to my credit card. I begged Camille not to tell Drew what had happened.

Next, I called my dearest reliable friend, Oleg. Oleg lived back in New York; he was the champion in my life. Never ceasing to amaze me with his outstanding success, Oleg opened his own successful stock firm by the time he was twenty-two! He and I met when he decided to become an actor and ended up in a New York acting class with me years before. Oleg was the worst actor I had ever seen. Despite that, and determined to succeed, Oleg studied and improved. Within one year, he had become a most incredible actor with an impressive resume. Moreover, Oleg became a member of all three actor's unions!

I knew Oleg would be a friend who would never judge me and would also know exactly how to help me get to the bottom of the mess I suddenly found myself in. I knew I could count on him; Oleg knew all the right ways to approach seeking legal help. He couldn't quite explain my imprisonment and what had happened, but he committed to helping me get through it. After a few minutes of talking, I heard Go Ask Alice call me; Oleg and I had to hang up.

Dr. Harry came to see me. A man in his later forties or early fifties, Dr. Harry seemed to revel in the power he held. He was insistent that I would leave only when he felt I was ready to go. Pleading with the doctor, I explained that I had a dog, a horse, and a bunny that depended on me. I explained that I was from New Jersey and that the Twin Towers had just collapsed. Even more, I had many friends and family in the New York area; I was desperately concerned for their well-being and needed to get out of that place to find out if everybody was okay.

The more I protested against my confinement in that place, the longer the doctor said it would be before I could leave. He proceeded to explain that I had acute psychosis from bipolar personality disorder. Hearing that, I proceeded to curse him out.

How fucking dare he! Who the fuck did that guy think he was! I have traveled the country up and down, through and through, with the best of the best! I thrived on our fast-paced, stressful situations and glided through them like a warm knife in butter! That was why I got the jobs I did! That was why I worked well with the people I did! My personality was an asset to my work and was absolutely not a disorder! At thirty-one, I knew who I was! That motherfucker! Bipolar personality disorder, my ass! Fuck you!

Visiting hours finally came, and an angel walked through the door. When I saw Camille's face, we hugged and talked in the community room for the entire hour. As promised, Camille remembered to bring my underwear and some clothes. Thankfully, she also assured me that she was caring for Simon and even Jezebel. She assured me that my parents had made arrangements with Diane at the barn so that Diane would take care of Chad until I was released.

Feeling better after my visit with Camille, I was able to return to my room and put on my own clothes at last. Doing so, I was reminded of my jive girl T-shirt and denim skirt. I made every attempt to retrieve them, but no luck. The hospital informed me my clothes had been burned in the incinerator.

Another visitor came to see me that day: a police officer. While I sat in a room alone with the officer, I was grilled with questions about the incident. There was no mention of the broken car window. All I knew was that a vicious dark-haired woman had attacked me for no reason.

The pay phone became my great resource. In my many phone calls, I contacted local government representatives and lawyers. Desperate, over and over, I explained how I was attacked by a police officer for no reason and was held somewhere against my will. I had committed no crime, yet she brutally attacked me!

Back in the community room, daily newspapers and copies of the weekly magazines arrived. All showed cover pictures of 9/11 reports. I looked closely through them and saw images of the horror in New York. Weeping, sobbing, helpless, imprisoned in my own nightmare of hell, I wanted to be home in New Jersey. I saw the towers on the magazine covers: buildings burning, smoke billowing, people jumping from the top floors and flying upside down in midair.

I flipped the pages of the magazine and saw a man with a big smile. I turned the page and saw more pictures of people killed. Then, I turned the page back again as the familiar smile grabbed my attention and stopped me. There he was, his picture smiling at me in *People* magazine. He was a man who appreciated life, a thankful man who never complained, and had a contagious smile. He was my coworker, my tour mate. He was aboard the first plane that hit the tower that day.

Looking up at the TV, I saw reports of the anthrax warning Josephine had spoken about and regarding which I had faxed government institutions. It was coming true. The news reported anthrax attacks had invaded our U.S. Postal Service.

It would be two more days before Dr. Harry signed my release form and discharged me with prescriptions for Risperdal, Depakote, Adderall, and Ativan; he also provided me with full bottles of each. Back at Camille's house, I still had my SSRI and a one-year prescription.

At last, Camille picked me up at the discharge entrance. I walked outside the mental prison and inhaled the rush of freedom again. I jumped in the car, where Simon was rapturously waiting for me. Camille and I drove off like Thelma and Louise.

9

Overdrive

Camille drove me back to the house. There, I was able to take my pink pill once again. Like cheating on a diet, I had missed a few days while being held in that place and needed to get back on schedule. The SSRI was the medication provided to me by my doctor, the health care provider I paid to treat me, unlike the doctor who forcibly drugged me and used his power against me.

Once we arrived at the house, Camille emphasized that Annie was scared of me and I should not make any attempt to talk to her.

Feeling anxious to get in the Winnebago and visit Chad, I grabbed the keys and left. The Winnebago was loud, but it sure was cute. It had everything I needed: kitchen, bathroom, shower, table, chairs, bed, and guest bed. I had decorated it with curtains and trinkets. I made a little area under the table, especially for Jezebel to rest. Simon liked to ride nestled against my left foot. That was his cruising spot.

Driving to the horse farm, I felt freedom, but it was at a cost. I became paranoid that I was being followed. Who was the officer who came to see me in that place? I made sure to take a different route than I usually would drive to the barn. I made last-minute decision turns and quickly pulled in and out of random parking lots. The Winnebago was loud.

In a quick decision, I pulled into a convenience store parking lot. There, I waited and watched. Fear building, I heeded to "rebuke sharply" and cast it away. Somehow, the words gave me the strength to overcome the fear and the courage to move. Gathering my courage to enter the store, I opened the Winnebago door and slowly stepped out.

In the store, I walked around, making sure to stay aware of everyone and everything around me. I particularly looked for suspicious people who may have been staring at me, following me, or posing a threat. I remained inside the store long enough to accumulate and purchase over two hundred dollars worth of stuff. Who knew you could find that much stuff at a convenience store? Items ranged from T-shirts and fun candy to collector's items like a dragon lamp and baseball cards. There was also a squishy ball with eyes inside and a soccer ball for Simon. I purchased all kinds of things.

When I finally left the store, I was determined to be strong, fear not, and confront anyone. I saw a young man who scared me—something about him made me afraid—so I walked directly up to the man and handed him the squishy ball with eyes inside. I insisted he take the squishy ball because it seemed he would enjoy it. Then I smiled, wished him a good day, turned, and walked back to my Winnebago.

On the roads, cars were covered in American flags. Everywhere I looked, red, white, and blue waved in the wind.

At the barn, I was relieved to see Chad peacefully in his stall. I hugged him and apologized for not being there. I promised him I would make everything better. It was a beautiful afternoon. Chad came out of his stall and grazed while he visited the other horses in their paddocks. Simon ran around chasing the new soccer ball and playing.

All the kids who lived on the dead-end dirt farm road were outside playing. They all wanted to play in the Winnebago. Diane was outside with some others and said it would be fine. So the kids piled onboard the Winnebago and oohed over all the toys and decorations. They especially loved Jezebel in her little nook!

There was a huge tree near the barn; it was a perfect climbing tree. Finding it irresistible, I climbed the tree and encouraged the kids to give it a try. It was especially difficult to climb as my arms still hurt from my attack. My left arm could not go behind my back without unbearable pain. Even if I tried to pull it behind, it just wouldn't go. But I did not want the girls to see me hurting.

Most of the girls thought the tree seemed too big and too high. However, one adventurous girl gave it a go anyway. She did make it up with a bit of help, but getting down became a whole different deal. The girl was terrified. Eventually, after some cheering support, she made it back to the ground just when it was time to eat.

Diane invited me to join everyone for the hamburgers and hot dogs they were making on the barbeque. I was delighted to do so. Naturally, Diane and the others were curious about what had happened to me. I apologized and thanked them tremendously for taking care of Chad when I was away. Then I proceeded to explain that a black-haired woman in a uniform, a police officer, had attacked me for no reason. They couldn't understand why she would do that, so I explained how I was in the street outside the house singing *New York, New York* when suddenly, I saw a car coming at me, and I ran around the block to knock on a neighbor's door. There, the woman attacked me.

Diane asked me to sing *New York, New York* like I had done that dreadful day. Gathering my courage and standing up in front of everyone, I sang it at the very top of my lungs, just as I had done when my nightmare began. Everyone at the picnic table clapped and laughed; they got quite a chuckle. I tried to laugh along, but the horror of what had happened stung me.

After burgers and hot dogs, the kids wanted to play in the Winnebago again. I suggested we go to the store, get ingredients, and bake brownies in the Winnebago. Big "hoorays" from all the kids! The adults said it would be fine, and so we did. That night I learned that horses didn't eat brownies, but I sure did!

Driving the Winnebago back to Camille's house, I was again careful to watch any cars that followed me. Maybe it was the FBI; they didn't like what I said. Certainly, I knew somebody had it in for me. Why else would that have happened? My eyes began to zigzag, quickly side to side for brief flashes, uncontrollably. My wrist was sewn with heavy black stitches that poked out. I hid them by wearing a terrycloth wristband and lots of little beaded bracelets. It all matched with the jingles of the other trinkets I adorned myself with by then.

Back at Camille's, I parked the Winnebago in the street near the telephone pole as there was no space in the driveway. Once inside the house, I turned on the TV and tuned in to the details reported about the tragic events of 9/11.

My eyes would rapidly, uncontrollably, zigzag back and forth when I watched the destruction and listened to the horror. My eyes buzzed in sync with the horrendously detailed reports; they alerted me that something was not right. I presumed the airplane attack and tower collapse must have been our threefold return. From the original Native Tribes living on the land, to African slave importation, to the grave disrespect for other living species with whom we share the Earth, negative energy went out. Then, it had come back. So many dead, so much destruction. God was mad. What would become of us?

Camille stayed at the house that night. She talked, lectured, and told me that things had to change. Not only did I have to clear my clutter, but Jezebel had to leave the house. Camille was mad about the chewed phone wire, though she was not surprised about my getting a horse. Mostly, she said that not much surprised her anymore. Camille further expressed she would not visit Chad; she wanted to know nothing about him. Finally, Camille went to bed, and I continued watching TV.

Warm rushes flooded my body. They felt like an internal charge that zapped and wiggled from my legs through to my shoulders. I grew to understand the zap charges as spiritual signs in accordance with my actions. They were messages that confirmed or rejected my thoughts and doings. Yes! They were messages for me. I continued scribbling, writing, connecting words with lines and arrows, making pictures and doodles of meanings and purposes. All the while, the eye zigzags and body rushes confirmed my thoughts and affirmed I was right to drive on with my ideas.

The following morning, I had to work a show. So, again, I prepared to work as a local backstage helper. Coffee, pink pill, and off I went to the venue. It was a strange day at work after the September 11 attacks. Others at the gig also knew our fallen coworker; they talked about him and discussed how his family had managed.

While I drove around working for the show, I picked up candles, cards, and trinkets to make a vigil back at the venue. Many at work commented on my distressed condition and weight loss. They seemed to believe I was dramatic in my grief. They understood it was a scary time but would not let it get the best of them. Nighttime fell; the show went on. I sat outside on the loading dock with my vigil of candles and remembrance while I listened to the music play.

Work finished, and I arrived back at the house sometime after midnight. More television, more zigzag eye buzzes and body rushes, more writing and thinking and detective symbolism. By three in the morning, I was filled with grief and began to believe I had caused the attacks and the towers to fall. Somehow, by burning my paper at Katie's house and all the new insights brought to light, I must have played into the devil power and sent negative energy into the atmosphere myself. But then, I recalled the warnings that Josephine said the Bible had cautioned us about. The government administrations must have known the attack was going to take place. There must have been evidence of something. Somewhere, somebody must have overlooked the coincidences!

Again, I got in the car and drove downtown to the FBI office. There, I asked to speak to the Dean of Students. Draped in a red and white striped shrug, with pockets full of stones and tokens, I brought gifts for their hard work: taffy and treats and desk toys I had purchased on previous shopping sprees.

As I left the FBI office and drove back to Camille's house, a new thought suddenly struck me. With urgency, I felt I needed to tell the Dean of Students right away. When I arrived at the house, I anxiously called the FBI office and told my confidant of the new messages I had received. He was amazed that I had called and mentioned something about a bunch of people who were in his office at that time. He said it was a coincidence of some kind on his end. I did not want to know what it was, but I felt confident the Dean of Students believed me.

By morning, I was still consumed by the television news. Reports came out about more anthrax; Josephine's warnings were confirmed. Unusual scrolls rolled along the bottom of the TV; they gave information. Like a synchronized dance, my eyes zigzagged in response to the messages while electricity fiercely raced through my body.

Camille woke; I assured her I would clean and bring Jezebel to the horse farm with Chad. I continued listening to the news while I brought things out to the Winnebago, still parked on the street. My car was in the driveway, and my parents strongly advised me to get my oil checked.

Simon by my side, I took the car to visit Chad and let him out into a paddock for the afternoon. Once again, I was very cautious in my driving and aware of anyone who may have followed me or looked suspicious.

Following an afternoon with Chad, I began driving back to the house. My eyes buzzed, and my body rushed; I was overwhelmed by all the events of recent weeks. How did everything get so bad? I yelled out at God in all my anguish and discontent. Then, on an impulse, I intentionally swerved the car across three highway lanes and crossed in front of a large speeding semi-truck. A long, loud, mean horn sounded, and I continued bearing right onto an exit ramp.

Off the exit, there was a Walgreens. I pulled into the parking lot and told Simon to wait in the car. Inside, I remained cautious and suspicious of all around me, but I got a shopping cart and began gathering the things I needed.

Walking through the aisles, I felt like I was being watched. Suddenly I heard a strange and frightening voice. I did not know where it was coming from. Again, I heard a sound, a voice. I immediately left the shopping cart in the aisle and ran out to my car to get Simon. I took him inside the store and put him in the baby seat of the shopping cart. I needed to keep him safe with me. Continuing shopping, I heard the voice again and saw frightening bats, vampires, ghosts, witches, and skeletons. Quickly, I left the filled cart in the aisle, took Simon, and ran out of the store.

I drove in a circle all around the roads surrounding the store. I drove around and around, over and over, while I pressed my hand hard on the horn. Around and around while the horn was honking until the horn sound began to weaken. Then I drove away.

I got onto a highway, then I pulled off the road. I didn't know where I was. I pulled into a parking lot somewhere. Shortly thereafter, a police car pulled in. The officer stepped from his vehicle as I got out of my car. Crying, I explained to the officer that I was lost. I explained that I was scared to talk to him and tell him my name and address because I feared he would take me to that place again. The officer assured me he would help, and I trusted him by telling him where I needed to go.

After the officer gave me directions back toCamille'shouse, I thanked him. Even more, I told him I would return to the parking lot the following day to clean it up as there was trash all over.

I made it back to the house and was more upset by the unfolding drama.

Camille was home that night. She was in her room and going to bed. I was in the living room, fixated on the television news and developments of the day. I was talking out loud; Camille asked me to keep quiet as she was trying to sleep. I rushed in and out of the house, back and forth to the Winnebago. I wrote madly as I watched the news reports and knew the terrorists had trained in Florida; they were all around us.

Camille came into the living room again; she asked me to turn off the TV and go to bed. How could I sleep? I tried to explain to Camille that I had been attacked, locked up, sodomized, and held against my will, and all the while, devastation was happening back at home, and I needed to see what was going on. I had to know if people I knew had been discovered in the rubble. Camille sat on the couch with me and talked some. She tried to communicate the disturbance I caused her. She went back to her room.

I continued watching the TV and called my mom. My mom tried to calm me as I articulated how traumatizing and frightening everything was. Then, my mom asked if I had gotten my oil checked in my car. That scared me more, as though she was warning me about something she knew. Maybe she knew my phone was tapped; she was sending me a message. I thought of my wrist stitches. The implant was a tap, a bug. I began talking to the transmitter in my wrist as though someone was listening. Shadows seemed to move like a wildcat running into the bushes. My body rushed with spirit chills, zaps, and eye twitches.

Impulsively, I ran out to my car while I told my mom I was going to get in it and drive. My mom was pleading with me not to. Camille woke up; she came outside and asked me to keep quiet and go to bed. I was getting louder, and Camille was pleading with me. There was something in my car. Somebody was trying to kill me. My mom didn't want me to get in the car because she knew there was a bomb in it! Camille went back in the house but returned outside and begged me to go to bed. I told Camille to call the police. Rebuke sharply; stand up to fear! Then, I called 911 myself. Camille grew panicked.

An officer arrived. I was outside in the driveway. The policeman approached the house and walked up to me. I asked him for his name, but he would not provide it. I asked for his badge number. He would not provide it. I was not convinced he was a police officer. I called 911 again, then again and again and again. I called 911 twelve times, repeatedly.

Multiple police cars pulled up. I ran inside the house. Camille was outside. I locked the doors. I heard someone screaming for me to open the doors. I was inside, running around. Where was I going to run? I had to protect my critters. Simon was hiding. I grabbed Jezebel and tried to stuff her in a hole in the wall. She wiggled her legs and resisted. I had to leave her in the bedroom. I ran to the bathroom and got a razor.

There was banging on the door and yelling outside. I heard Camille and ran to the front door. I could see her through the peephole. She pleaded for me to unlock the door. I told her I could not. I had the razor;

I had to run the bath and shave. Camille ran around the house to the bathroom window, where I met her from the inside. I turned the water on. Camille begged me to open the doors. I told her if she went to the front door, I would open it and let her in.

Looking through the peephole in the front door, I could see the swirling lights outside. I heard banging and looked toward the direction of the sounds. There at the kitchen window, I saw her face. It was the face of the black-haired officer woman! She was smashing the glass, busting her way inside! I screamed when I saw her; loud and scared, I screamed. She was coming to get me; the black-haired woman was back, breaking inside to get me this time for sure!

I unlocked the front door and went to run toward my car. I turned, and Camille was there. Her face looked different than I had ever seen before. She did not look like the angel I knew; instead, her hands were up like she was going to attack me. Screaming more, I ran back inside the house.

I fell to the floor in the hallway. Before I knew anything, I was surrounded by guns pointed at me. Hands were all over me again. I begged them to kill me, screaming, "Please kill me now! Kill me now!" More hands ripped and pulled me. I could hear them saying that I needed extra control. They yanked my arms high up my back and cuffed them. Numb, I felt no pain. They bound my ankles tightly, then attached them to my wrists behind me.

When I was completely bound, a few people carried me toward the police car, where I saw the back door was open. I knew they were really mad, and I was going to be killed for sure. "Please kill me now!" I begged and pleaded with them. As they carried me toward the car, I looked back at the house and watched Camille turn and walk inside. Other neighbors were outside; I saw Annie turn and walk back into her house too.

The sun was beginning to rise. When we neared the police car in the street, a young boy walked by me on his way to school. "Remember this!" I cried out to him. "Remember what you see here!"

As the officer put me into the backseat of the police car, I told him, "Fireproof photo albums; make sure they make the fireproof photo albums." The officer stuffed me in the car and drove away. I lay still and quietly repeated, "I will die for Him."

Police records from that day state:

"The listed subject was Baker Acted after advising she wanted to kill herself or have the police kill her. I responded to the listed location and met with Dawn and Camille. Dawn advised she wanted her car to be impounded for evidence for the FBI. She would not advise what the reason for impound was, but stated it had something to do with terrorists. Dawn then began to get upset and demanded another officer. While in my presence, Dawn called 911 twice demanding an officer. Officers responded to assist me. I spoke with operator of the county who advised Dawn had called 911 approximately 10 times demanding assistance. While I was on the phone, Dawn locked herself in the house and continued to speak with the Sheriff's Office via 911. Forced entry was made to the residence after Dawn armed herself with a disposable razor. Dawn immediately dropped the blade but stated she wanted to kill herself or have the police do it. Dawn was taken into police custody and transported to the hospital. Dawn's roommate stated Dawn has been having emotional problems and was Baker Acted last week for the same behavior."

10

Another Lap

In the early morning of September 24, 2001, while shackled in four-point leather restraints, the police officer transported me back to the same hospital emergency room where I had previously been taken.

Again, strapped down to a table, I yelled and cursed, but it was no longer high-pitched screams for help. Instead, my hollers were deep, demonic, and threatening. Finally, I was injected with drugs and assessed with suicidal ideation. A security person sat beside me. Hours passed until I was released from the straps and led into an ambulance.

Again, I was transported to the same waiting room with the metal chairs and pay phone. It was not long before I was escorted past the security man, through the doors, and to the nurse's station. From there, I was assigned to a room with two beds and a bathroom. Again, I sat on the empty bed, and again, I had nothing to put in the drawer underneath. What was going to happen to Simon, Chad, and Jezebel? I was frantic.

A familiar announcement came over the speaker: Line up. There was no option not to. So I did: a little plastic cup filled with pills, a little cup of water. Line up for cafeteria. I waited. As the drugs took hold of me, I leaned on another patient. I could barely stand or keep my eyes open. Others were talking to me. They sounded muffled, as though they were talking through a cloud. I stumbled; someone caught me. I leaned, and I waited.

We began to move. Another patient walked closely with me as I staggered along. I looked forward to a chair waiting in the cafeteria. I made it. I sat. My head fell over and hit the table. An evangelist patient sat with me and tried to hold my head and spoon-feed me.

I was inside myself; I knew all of this was not right. Nothing like this had ever happened to me before in my over thirty years. What was going on? I was going to find out. To begin with, whenever they gave me a plastic cup of pills, I would write down what they gave me.

The nurses would not permit us to return to our rooms. In the community room, I sat with the newspaper. There were lists of names of those killed in the attacks. There was a picture of the first Yankee baseball game played since the attacks on the eleventh. All the players lined up with their caps on their chests, remembrance paid to lives lived and destroyed.

There was one public bathroom outside the nurse's station. I went inside. Locking the door, I laid the newspapers out page by page and covered the entire floor. The lights turned off, and alone, I sat on the newspapers and quietly wept. Everything had changed. Things would never be the same. Eventually, there was banging on the door. I had to come out. But I couldn't. I sat quietly and cried more.

The banging continued until I had no choice but to gather my news-papers and myself and open the door. There stood a mean girl patient glaring at me. The mean girl threatened me and said she wanted to kick my ass. She was a large, obese, tough black girl who wore a barely-there half-shirt with itsy bitsy straps that hung off her shoulders. She paired that with short shorts and walked around like she owned the place. She called me a black witch and devil. The nurse threatened that if I locked the bathroom door again, I would be put into solitary isolation.

Smoke time in the outside cage was announced. Everyone gathered in line to sit outdoors. Most lined up for a light and a cigarette. The monkey man was still there. He was the old, skinny, hairy, grungy man who made howling noises and climbed the walls when I first arrived at the facility. He never spoke actual words; rather, he made unusual grunts and noises. Most people were frightened of him. Monkey man was known for doing a variety of things to get himself put in isolation, which included throwing feces. In the smoking cage, monkey man would often try to quickly grab a cigarette away from someone else. More often, he would dig in the ashtrays and gather all the cigarette butts, then empty them out into another piece of paper that he would then roll and smoke.

I used the pay phone and called my mom. She had talked with Camille and arranged for Diane to care for Chad, and Camille to care for Simon. Jezebel was going to be in her cage and moved to the horse farm. My mom was going to fly to Florida. She had also spoken to Drew on tour. New arrangements would be necessary as I would not be able to return to Camille's house.

Med time rolled around, and we all lined up. I had my pencil and paper ready. When I was handed my plastic cup of pills, I asked the nurse what the name and dosage of each pill were. Then, I wrote it down. I wrote down the name of the pill, the color, the amount they gave me, and the time I took it. I remembered how Helen did that too.

At last, we could re-enter our rooms. I needed to clean myself, so I asked at the nurse's station for a toothbrush, toothpaste, and soap. Then, I went to the cardboard box for clothes to change into.

In my room, I washed my face and brushed my teeth. I needed pretty. I needed girly. I needed nice. I had a clean bed sheet. Playing dress-up, I tied the sheet into a one-shoulder style gown, then into a tube-style gown until I twisted it into a halter gown and paired it with socks from the box. I used my toothbrush to secure my hair as I twisted it up into a style like Audrey Hepburn, feeling *Breakfast at Tiffany's*.

Fresh and clean, I walked out of my room and up the hallway. Then, the yelling began; the nurses were outraged at me. "Absolutely not!" they yelled. "You cannot walk around wearing a sheet!"

"It's a dress," I replied. "I am fully covered."

"You cannot be out here wearing that!" the nurse yelled.

"That mean girl is nearly naked!" I responded.

"Get dressed now!" The nurse yelled as she yanked the toothbrush from my hair and would not give it back to me.

Shocked, crushed, and furious, I turned and stormed down the hallway while cursing very loudly. Halfway back down the hall, I screamed, "You don't want me to fucking wear a full-length fucking wrap dress when that bitch is nearly fucking naked! Fine! I'll fucking take it off!" I then dropped the sheet and continued right on walking, naked down the hall and to my room.

I went into the bathroom and began clogging the bathtub drain with toilet paper and towels. I had to take a bath. While the tub was filling, I poured in some shampoo I had in a cup, hoping to make some bubbles. I used a pencil to carve and write on the walls. I dreamed of pulling the fire alarm and planning my escape. I had to get to my animals.

Bathed and dressed, I returned to the community room. In the community room, the mean girl remained on my case until I finally yelled back at her, "God is going to get you!" The mean girl then complained to the nurse about me. She said that I had threatened her. I was sent into solitary isolation.

Isolation was a small room that contained only a cot and a thin mattress. There was a camera in the ceiling where I was watched from the nurse's station. Periodically, a voice came over the speaker and told me how my behavior was inappropriate. Isolation was a filthy space. Talking to the nurses who watched me on the camera, I pointed out the stains on the mattress and the pubic hairs on the walls that were covered with streaks of urine. Hours passed; the filth was something I noted to report. I did not know how or when, but somebody had to know about the filthy caged disgust.

Picking up the mattress, I stood on the cot and held it above my head. I pressed it against the camera, cutting off their view of me. The voice came over the speaker, demanding that I uncover the camera. "Fuck you!" I yelled. A nurse came to the door and unlocked it. "I have to pee," I told her; she led me to a bathroom and then back to my cage.

More hours passed before I was released from isolation. I was given another cup of pills, and again, I wrote down the name, dosage, time, date, and color.

Everybody kept confirming that the world had changed and things would never be the same. I felt trapped in some unknown place; another control had taken over my life. There was a blonde girl who kept telling me about the New World Order and how they would always be watching me. The evangelist man gave me Bibles and quoted the words like Josephine. Another told me, "Better they think you are crazy than scared; they'll get you if they think you're scared."

There was a little old lady, so small and innocent. She was in the hallway, scared to go into her room. "They're in there," she kept saying.

"Who's in there?" I asked her.

"They're in there with the lady, and the serpent is in the drain. He's coming out of the drain in there, in there, the serpent," she frantically repeated over and over. A nurse began yelling at her from down the hallway, but she never stood up from her chair behind the desk. Finally, I took the little old lady's hand, walked with her into her room, and told her we would defeat the serpent together. I walked her to the bathroom drain and declared that she had scared away the serpent. The little old lady sat down on her bed, relieved. We sure conquered that serpent, we did.

The doctor came to visit me. I begged him to let me go. I had to get to my animals. He told me my mother would be there the following day, and we would discuss it then. Given the recent attacks, I was terrified at the thought of my mother getting on an airplane.

The announcement came. We all lined up. More cups of pills distributed and documented.

A new day came with another cup of pills. The nurse told me my mother would be there soon. I dug in the box for something nice to wear and found a pair of gingham pants that reminded me of my Aunt Lucy's favorite gingham button-down blouse. I put on the pants.

Visiting hour arrived; my mom waited in a room. Before entering, I looked inside; overwhelming fear flooded me. That was not my mother! Who was that woman? She did not look like my mother! The woman in the room saw me. "It's me. It's Mommy," she said. There was an unusual look on her face I did not recognize. I expected her to remove a mask and be the dark-haired attacker. I did not trust the woman in the room.

With caution, I entered and sat with the woman who claimed she was my mother. She told me that Drew was coming the following day. She had brought some of my clothes. She also brought me arts and crafts supplies. The nurse quickly grabbed them, took them away, and said I was not allowed to have them.

The doctor came in and began to discuss my condition. "Bipolar," he kept saying. I kept yelling, "I am not fucking bipolar, asshole! I have been assaulted and locked up against my will in this shithole, fucking dump! I am allowed to have emotions about it!"

The doctor commented that my behaviors were manic and I suffered from acute psychosis. He claimed my actions, the actions of documenting the medication they were administering to me, should be considered "manic behavior in itself." I wondered what Helen would have thought about that. The doctor considered any emotion I displayed, ranging from happiness to anger, as manic bipolar disorder. How the fuck did he want me to feel? Or was I even supposed to have emotions at all? The doctor made arrangements with my mother for me to return to New Jersey and seek treatment there with a counselor.

My mom was going to stay in Florida until I was released. She would meet with Drew the following day and bring him to see me. My mom and Drew had never met before; I was concerned and distraught that they would first meet under such tumultuous circumstances. I had to get out of that place. I plotted ways I could sneak out with the visitors, but it was not possible. The repercussion of getting caught would have been brutal.

I was terrified to see Drew. When I received the announcement that he was there, I did not want to go. I did not want him to see me in that place. Oh my God, how did I get there? Where the fuck was I? I was suddenly self-conscious about my shoes. I was wearing white sneakers I got from the box, and no one was permitted to have shoelaces. I was not wearing shoelaces.

My mother was there for a few moments before Drew walked slowly through the door and hugged me. I was safe with him. My mother agreed with the doctor's diagnosis, which angered me. I said wicked things to her and crumbled into a ball as I sat on the floor next to a wall. Drew sat with me and covered me with his coat. There was so much shame. Beaten. Battered. Madness. Captive. Caged. Drugged. Why were they killing me and keeping me there? My God, my Simon, my Chad, and my Jezebel. Why did my mom not get me out of there? Drew sat with me and tried desperately to calm me. He was scared for me. He had left his tour to see me.

Visiting hour ended. My mom and Drew left. They were going to have lunch together. Drew would stay at Camille's house; my mom would stay in a hotel.

Back in the community room, another patient griped about how I was wearing his gingham print pants. "They were in the community box. I found them in the box," I told him. He persisted. I persisted. Then I walked away, down the hallway, and toward my room. A nurse yelled that I had to give the man the gingham pants. The ordeal escalated, but I forfeited the pants before I ran the risk of being sent back into isolation.

With nothing to do all day between meals and pill times, I spent endless time doing handstands against the wall. Then I took to balancing on one arm and doing upside-down push-ups repeatedly. It was simple; I felt strong.

One patient told me how she would hide the pills in her mouth, then spit them out. I began to do the same. I collected the pills and stored them in my drawer, where I also kept a small wardrobe and some paper records.

The pay phone was my source to the outside. Acquiring the Yellow Pages phone book from the nurse's station, I searched through the attorneys and began to call a few. "A police officer attacked me," I told them. Nobody could help.

At the nurse's station, I protested my captivity. One nurse mentioned something about a hearing. What hearing? I never had a hearing. I never saw a judge. Somebody had a hearing regarding my involuntary captivity? The nurse went on to tell me I could file a habeas corpus. I understood that to be the paperwork I could file that would defend me and get me out. That place was making me crazy. Every day, I filed a habeas corpus. I never saw a judge but remained a prisoner.

Smoking cage time became a time when I could do something to lift myself from the horror. I sang aloud while we smoked. Soon, most of the medicated mental patients joined me; we sang and danced together. The little serpent lady enjoyed it. Even the monkey man joined in. It struck me how monkey man was interested in participating; I had been having short conversations with him and was impressed by how his verbal and social skills improved when we talked.

On one special day, we were all provided a soccer ball, permitted to go beyond the smoking cage and into an enclosed grass area! We must have kicked the ball around and laughed for a full hour. At last, there was fun.

It was not long before the caged windows in my room reminded me of how desperately I needed to get out of that place. I wanted to go home. I managed to use the pay phone, my credit card, and Yellow Pages phone book to arrange for my Winnebago to be picked up by a tow truck at Camille's house, then brought to me at the facility. It sure was an incredible sight when the old '75 Winnebago was pulled around the institution I was imprisoned in! Everyone gathered around the windows! We all watched the Winnebago being towed around and around the building a few times. I smiled with glee and said, "That's my home." After a few circles, it was eventually towed back to Camille's.

October 4, 2001: After eleven days of involuntary lockup in a state-controlled mental health institution, no judge, no jury, no justice, and no peace, I was again discharged with written prescriptions and full bottles of psychotropic medications that included Depakote, Risperdal, and Klonopin. Eleven days without my usual pink pill.

11

Fuel

My mom, Drew, and Simon picked me up. I sat in the backseat with Simon. He was so happy to see me; I cried while I hugged and snuggled him again. Then, we went to Camille's house. Camille knew I was going to the house; she made a point not to be there.

Gathering my things, I stuffed them inside the Winnebago and took my pink pill. I felt angry and did not want to talk to or see my mom. I felt betrayed by her and thought of her as the enemy. She was not permitted in my Winnebago.

Searching the Yellow Pages, I located an RV campground with an available spot. I drove the Winnebago while Drew drove my car. My mom followed in her rental vehicle. We arrived at Happy Travels RV Park and went to the registration desk. They had a few available spots; I chose one in a corner location tucked away on the edge of the woods. Drew agreed it was the best spot. Meanwhile, my mom rented a small cabin they had available near my spot. Drew pulled the Winnebago around and parked it in my new lot. While I settled and spent time with Drew, my mom went to the store for essentials and fresh sheets to put in her cabin.

I took Drew to a singing lesson I had previously scheduled with Mitchell. The two of them had a private conversation, and then Mitchell proceeded to give me a brief lecture about oxygen. He explained that oxygen was our body's natural drug of choice; it was accessible to everyone for free. He made me do a series of breathing exercises that increased the oxygen flow in my body. Mitchell assured me it would make me very happy. Fifteen minutes of controlled deep breathing techniques, and I was soaring in the smiles! Amen Oxygen!

Drew left after a few days. He returned home to prepare for rehearsals on another tour he was starting. Those rehearsals would begin in Florida sometime soon.

My mom stayed; things between us did not improve. She told me the man I got Chad from had called. He wanted Chad back. She must have known there was zero chance I would give up Chad. Can you imagine. I didn't want to hear anything about it. Chad was mine; I was his mom, and he depended on me. Can You Imagine; I needed him desperately. I needed him.

My mother and I drove to the horse farm together in her rental car. She had paid for Chad's expenses. Jezebel was locked in her cage outside Chad's stall. My mother continued on at me about surrendering Chad to the man and returning to New Jersey.

Along the drive back to the RV park with my mother, I was angry and suddenly, impulsively reached over, grabbed the steering wheel, and spun it hard. I attempted to steer the car off the road. My mom quickly gained control of the vehicle and pulled it over to the shoulder on the highway. There, she raged in a fury and slapped me hard across my face. The next day, my mother informed me that my dad would fly to Florida; she would return to New Jersey.

I drove the Winnebago to Camille's house and hoped to pick up more things I had left behind. Jerry was there when I arrived. I was not permitted in the house alone, and Camille did not want to see or talk to me. At the house, Jerry let me inside. He, too, was my enemy; he disrespected Camille. While Jerry watched, I grabbed all kinds of things around the house. As I did so, my fury with Jerry grew; I began screaming and cursing at him. I screamed about how unworthy he was and how Camille deserved better. I yelled, cursed, and slammed things. On one trip to the Winnebago, Jerry locked the doors and would not let me back inside the house. I began hollering and trying to get in through the windows. Jerry threatened that if I persisted, the police would come again. I left.

Back at the RV park, my mother left, and my dad arrived. Dad stayed in the same cabin Mom had rented. He, too, tried to get me to return to New Jersey and give up Chad. Absolutely no way was that going to happen. I was not going to give up Chad. My dad also complained about the garbage I had outside the Winnebago. He said it was disgusting and I was going to attract wild animals. I assured him I would clean it up, but a raccoon did come during the night. I argued with my dad for the few days he was there until he, too, had to return to New Jersey and go back to work. I did not return to New Jersey with him, and I kept Chad.

Needing to do laundry, I wanted everything cleaned. So I loaded up my car and took 140 pounds of clothes and linens to the Laundromat. I told the woman I would be back in a few days to pick it up.

I obsessively, compulsively called everybody and anybody. Finally, I spoke with a friend of mine, Amber, who lived on the West Coast. We had met in my travels on the road. I told Amber that I was in Florida and living in my own Winnebago. She had a few days off work and decided to visit me. I picked Amber up at the airport and brought her to the RV park.

Amber, Simon, and I went to the horse farm where Amber met Chad. On the way back, there was a security man at the front entrance of the RV park. He was in a small booth and watching TV. Stopping and getting out of my car, I went to see what the security man was watching; I wanted to know if there were any updates on the attacks and terror from September 11. The security man informed me he was watching "reality TV." He said it took place in real time and was like watching people in their daily lives. "I see," I told him. I suspected that was part of the new system of order. There was no privacy left; everything was exposed. The Beast had indeed shown its number. We were all being watched.

With Amber and Simon in my car, we pulled into the spot where my Winnebago was parked. I opened the door, and Simon jumped out. Before I could even step out, a neighbor began yelling at me that Simon should be on a leash. "He just jumped out of the car on my own spot!" I yelled back at her. She continued yelling how she did not care; he should have a leash. It made no sense to me. The argument escalated loudly. The police arrived.

Amber was quite upset but tried to remain collected throughout the ordeal. The police officer told me I had to leave the RV park. I told him, fine; I would leave the RV park and go to Florida horse country in Ocala. Amber did not stay the night. Instead, she told me about a man she met on the airplane and had talked to throughout the entire flight from California. They exchanged phone numbers. Amber decided to call him and get a ride back to the airport. I insisted that it was not necessary, but she called him and left anyway.

I arranged for Diane to let me park the Winnebago at the horse farm. I drove it from the Happy Trails RV Park while a helpful neighbor near the farm drove my car.

Driving around town, I remained paranoid about people following me. While at the convenience store, I felt people staring at me; I raised my voice, telling them to stop. Inside the car, I was terrified of being shot while I drove, so I ducked down in the driver's seat when a car passed me by. Sometimes I aggressively honked the horn, hoping to keep danger at bay. I read license plates, looked for clues; every letter or number had significant meaning, as though it was a coded message for me. The body rushes continued. Wherever I stopped the car, I peered inside any vehicle with tinted windows, expecting to see the face of those people watching me. Florida had a lot of cars with tinted windows.

I needed a storage unit for all the stuff I had accumulated. Locating one nearby, I stopped in and inquired. The woman behind the desk appeared disheveled and upset. She fumbled through papers as a man stood watching her from behind. I could see the woman had a black eye, and I continued to carefully monitor the man. He must be with *them.* They knew I was coming and were trying to threaten me by exposing the violence they were anxious to inflict upon me.

I walked into a convenience store with Simon in my arms. The clerk informed me that no dogs were allowed. I told him that I was carrying Simon and he was not walking around; moreover, I was just getting a sandwich and a drink, then would be on my way. The clerk grew angry, insisting I leave the store with Simon. I paid for my purchase, then gave the food to a homeless man who sat outside the store.

I stopped at the tack and feed store. It was especially busy inside on that day. I meandered slowly and came across a hutch filled with baby bunnies. I opened the hutch and removed a little floppy-eared white one. I named her Loocia. Carrying Loocia around the store, I looked and browsed for nearly two hours. All the while, I cuddled Loocia. Eventually, the store manager told me I could just have her. Loocia in tow, I quickly went on my way.

At the horse farm, I set baby Loocia in the cage with Jezebel, hoping they would become friends. It did not take but a quick moment before I realized that Jezebel was actually Jezbah! A boy! He loved the little Loocia baby bunny; he groomed her, hopped along after her, and oohed with delight over her company. They were the perfect beautiful little bunny couple: Jezbah and Loocia.

I talked with a neighbor about the invisible cars. We talked about people who started life old, then grew younger as they aged. I told the neighbor how I wished there were cars with colorful pattern designs on them, and the very next day, I actually saw one! It was plaid with flowers.

One day while I was driving and trying to hide from the people who were watching me, I saw a parking lot filled with school buses. I pulled my car into the lot and hid it behind one of the parked buses. Then I opened an unlocked door of a school bus and lay down in the backseat. Crying and scared, I hid inside the school bus until it was dark; then, I slowly emerged and drove my car back to the horse farm.

Camille's hospice patient, Helen, came to mind, and I wondered about her. I drove to Helen's house and knocked on the door, but there was no answer. I began to knock harder, louder. I called to Helen and banged on the door. I heard a yell from inside, "Go away! Go on!" It was Helen. I banged on the door more. "Helen, it's Dawn! Open the door!"

"Go away!" Helen continued. She sounded fragile and shaken. I knocked more, then looked around for Simon. Simon had jumped out of the car with me but was nowhere to be found.

Scared, I began walking around Helen's yard, calling out for Simon. He did not come running. Simon never left me; I grew terrified. "Simon! Simon!" I called and walked through the neighbor's yard. "Simon!" I went into the street and walked up and down, calling for him, crying, getting more desperate with every holler.

"C'mon, Simon. C'mon, my Nardo-Simonardo doggie dog of all Simon doggie dogs! Simon! C'mon, Simon, let's go! I got your cookies, Simon!"

Simon did not come to me, and my stomach grew sick.

I went to a neighbor's house and asked if they had seen a little gray and white Italian Greyhound dog. The woman had heard me yelling and mentioned seeing him in the yard. She invited me inside. The woman then said something about Simon being taken. Taken? The woman believed Simon may or may not be down the street. That was fucking nuts. Why the fuck would someone take my Simon? I yelled for the woman to tell me where and which house. I jumped in my car and immediately drove to that house.

The house the woman referenced was quite a distance down the street, and there was no way Simon would have gone so far on his own. I pulled up to a house where it appeared a bunch of people were in the backyard having a party. I couldn't see them down the walkway path alongside the house, but I could hear and see the lights. I got out of the car and began calling for Simon. A man appeared; he walked up the pathway from the backyard. He asked, "Can I help you?"

"Yes, I'm looking for my dog," I said. "He's a little gray and white Italian Greyhound. Simon! Simon!" I called out again.

"I might have seen a dog," he replied.

"Give him to me!" I demanded. "Simon!" I began walking toward the path. I hesitated in fear that it was a trap. "C'mon, Simon!" I stopped and yelled again. "Bring him to me!" I commanded the man.

"You said gray and white?" the man retorted.

"Yes!" Another man came walking up the pathway from the backyard; I could see he was holding Simon! "Let him go!" I yelled, "Simon! Simon! C'mon, Simon!" The man set Simon down, and my little boy came running to me! I scooped him up with kisses and tears as I sat him on my lap in the car; we drove away.

Mid-October, tour rehearsals with Drew were beginning near Orlando; I decided to drive the Winnebago to visit. At the rehearsal venue, the artist was not yet on-site, and the stage build was still in progress. Considering I had toured with that musical performer before, I knew many of the people there. I was able to go inside the venue. Oddly, Drew was not there.

I brought Simon inside the venue with me. Everybody commented on my significant weight loss. I tried to tell them what had happened to me. It seemed nobody could believe such a thing. At some point, I went on the stage and would not get off. Many people tried to tell me I had to get off the stage, but I did not listen. I danced and danced while the lighting department tried to focus their lights, and the road crew tried to continue their work.

Outside the venue, I played soccer with Simon. I wanted to bring crew friends to my Winnebago and show them my mini-tour bus; nobody had time. I gathered up Simon and the soccer ball, then prepared to head back to Tampa.

Driving back to Tampa, I saw signs for an RV repair shop. Considering the Winnebago needed a muffler and a few other parts, I thought I would stop in and inquire. Before I made it there, smoke started coming out from the Winnebago engine. I kept driving, hoping to make it to the repair shop. When the exit came, I pulled off the highway safely and into a truck stop attached to the RV repair. Smoke was billowing out, but the RV shop had already closed for the day.

I went inside the truck stop store, hoping somebody there could help me. Sure enough, a truck driver was willing to check it out for me. Upon entering the Winnebago, the truck driver went to the driver area and lifted up the center console. When he did, flames shot up! I thought the Winnebago was going to blow up! More truck drivers came over to see.

While they were all interested and involved in seeing what was going on with my RV, I began talking to an older woman nearby. She reminded me of Josephine. The woman kept talking to me and telling me all her problems about how she and her husband were stuck at the truck stop and did not have any money. She had an old car, something from the 1970s, it looked like. It was packed full of stuff. The woman told me about the musical artist who was rehearsing near Orlando. She said the artist had not arrived at the show yet because the performer was dead. Dead? She said they were going to use a hologram and project the artist's image so nobody would know the performer was dead. They would also get a lookalike to take over so nobody would ever know. That scared me greatly.

I noticed a person near the Winnebago. As I approached, the person disappeared. The world had surely changed. All was being revealed. Anything seemed possible. I assumed the individual had been beamed somewhere else.

The truck drivers informed me that nothing could be done about my Winnebago that day; I needed to have the RV people look at it in the morning when the repair shop opened. I was stuck.

The strange hologram lady continued to follow me inside the convenience store at the truck stop. She said she could not leave the truck stop because she did not have money for gas. I told the clerk to fill the lady's fuel tank and put the expense on my charge card, which she did. The hologram woman then went on her way. Before she left, she gave me a textile bracelet with pink and purple butterflies on it.

Inside the Winnebago, I settled in with Simon and figured we would be safe in the parking lot for the night. I planned to go to the RV repair shop first thing in the morning.

Shortly thereafter, a very large, super luxury RV pulled in beside my Winnebago. I was heading into the store for supplies when I noticed an unusual-looking girl exit the big RV. She began walking into the store behind me. Inside the store, I walked around, being very aware of the girl. She appeared to be in her later twenties and had multi-colored hair. She wore black and white striped stockings and perused the racks of T-shirts.

When I walked back outside to my Winnebago, the girl followed me. She went inside her RV but soon emerged with a video camera. The girl approached me and asked if she could interview me on camera outside my Winnebago. I agreed to do it, so she started the video and began asking me questions. I believe she inquired as to how I felt about the world and solving a variety of issues. It would have been an interesting video to watch, but the girl got in her RV and drove away. I began cleaning inside the Winnebago.

Nighttime came, and it grew dark. Truck drivers were parked all around. Two large RVs pulled into the parking lot. One truck driver began directing the two RVs to pull in and park, one on each side of me. The huge vehicles felt like two giant monsters trying to block me in. Jumping in front of the moving giants, I waved my arms. "Back up!" I hollered at them. "Back up!" The RVs eventually began to reverse, and I heard a man nearby say, "Wow, you really do have power." Power? What did he mean? What did he know?

Inside the store, I met another younger truck driver; he and I began a conversation. The truck driver wanted to come by my Winnebago, see the antique RV, and continue talking. Inside my Winnebago, the truck driver spoke to me about New World Order, Big Brother, governments, politics, and even how marijuana would prevent and cure diseases and save lives. In God, he did trust.

I suddenly felt scared, becoming more and more paranoid with every passing minute. The phone rang. It was Drew. I told him what was going on. He was terrified for me. He thought I was going to end up dead. He begged me over and over to be safe. Drew would not tell me when he was going to arrive at rehearsals. He wanted me to get the truck driver out of the Winnebago. He repeated over and over, "Please be safe, please be safe." The conversation escalated with anxiety while Drew pleaded with me to be safe. I hung up on Drew. He called back. The truck driver told me not to answer it. I grew more frightened.

People were hiding in the woods around the truck stop. I grew terrified of the people hiding in the woods. They were hiding in the darkness, waiting to shoot. Leaving the truck driver sitting inside, I suddenly jumped and ran from the Winnebago. I ran in front of a vehicle and to the corner road while I screamed at the people in the woods, "Shoot me and end it now!" I begged them to shoot and anticipated the gunshot at any moment. I ran back inside the Winnebago, where the truck driver still sat with Simon.

I began cleaning and making piles outside the Winnebago in the parking lot. When I came across a book of postage stamps with a red rose and the word "Love" on them, I wanted to express gratitude and appreciation to all the truck drivers who had helped me with the Winnebago throughout the day. I took the postage stamps, and one by one, I went to each truck parked there and put a "Love" postage stamp on their windshield. The young truck driver stood outside my Winnebago and watched me.

When I arrived back at my Winnebago, a police car pulled into the parking lot and drove up to where I was parked. The police officer opened his door, stepped out, looked at me, and said, "Hello, Dawn, aren't you supposed to be in Ocala?" How did he know my name? The officer started questioning me. He asked if I was taking my medications. He stated that he did not believe I was taking my medications; I insisted to him that, in fact, I was. I was! My pink pill! The officer said he did not believe me; he thought I needed to go downtown again. I begged him no. The officer said he thought I needed to go with him; he was going to take me. Pleading with him, I asked him to call my parents. I told him I needed to go to the bathroom; he said I could.

A female officer stepped out of the police car. She escorted me into the truck stop store and followed me into the bathroom, where she waited until I was through. Then the female officer escorted me back outside to the Winnebago, where I continued to plead with the male officer, who somehow already knew my name. The young truck driver was using my cell phone.

Simon suddenly began having an epileptic seizure. His seizure was growing in intensity. I tried to get to Simon and comfort him, but the male police officer grabbed me and pulled me toward his car. I screamed for Simon as I watched his body spasming, his legs shaking above his head, his eyes wide, scared and bulging, saliva drooling from his mouth. "Simon!" I screamed for the officer to let me comfort Simon. "He's having a seizure! He needs me! He's having an epileptic seizure!" The officer did not care and became more forceful, twisting my arms, threatening me, and jamming me into the backseat of his vehicle.

The middle of the night, broken down at a truck stop, October 14; looking through the back window of a police car while I was being driven away, I saw Simon left all alone on the parking lot ground suffering in a fit of an epileptic seizure while the door to my Winnebago was left wide open and all of my belongings were there.

12

Wipers

I was in the backseat of the police car, and the officer spoke to me as though he was very proud of his capture; he gloated with power. I screamed for Simon while sobs poured from me.

The officer took me directly downtown to the mental facility, bypassing the emergency room at the general hospital. I was held in a different waiting room from the one I had been in before. It seemed like a garage or warehouse loading dock of sorts. Hours passed.

There was a pay phone in the waiting room, so I was able to make a collect call to my mom and dad. Mom informed me that somebody had already been in contact, telling her I was once again taken into custody. As she knew my concern would be for Simon, I was grateful my mom had already begun investigating what happened to him.

Simon was taken into custody and brought to the county animal shelter. He was being held in a cage; Simon had never been in a cage. My mom told me the cage was in the back with the big dogs. I was terrified for him. Immediately, I began pleading with my mom to get Simon out of there. He was a little dog, sensitive, and required gentle handling when approached and picked up. I knew Simon would be scared; he had experienced a terrifying, horrific seizure. I pleaded with my mom, "Please get Simon out of there, please, please." My mom assured me Simon would be moved up to the front near the desk and around smaller dogs. Also, the shelter would give him a pill for his seizure. The horror! I had to get to Simon and save him from that place.

Hours passed until the doctor who had previously seen me entered the waiting room. The nasty male officer was there too. Upon talking with the men, I emphasized how I was simply visiting friends near Orlando when my vehicle broke down near the truck stop; I was waiting till morning when the repair shop would be open to look at it. Finally, the doctor agreed not to incarcerate me again against my will. He said he would allow me to leave, provided I continued with a plan to get home to New Jersey. *Whatever,* I thought. I just had to get to Simon.

By afternoon, the doctor provided me with more bottles of pills, medications, and written prescriptions. He signed my release form, and I called a taxi. The taxi arrived at the institution; I instructed the driver to take me to the animal shelter.

Upon arriving at the shelter where Simon was being held, I asked the taxi driver to wait for me. Inside, the woman at the desk informed me she would not release Simon until I paid a fine and a fee. Fine and fee! I had nothing on me but the clothes I was wearing. Certainly, I had no money to pay. The woman would not even let me see my Simon until I paid her. Expecting the taxi driver to take Simon and me to the truck stop where my Winnebago was still in the parking lot, I got in the cab alone and cried.

The taxi driver took me to the Winnebago, where the stuff I had left outside had been taken in, and the door had been closed. Rummaging through all my stuff, I located my wallet and provided the taxi driver with a credit card. He gave me a receipt and drove away.

The Winnebago started! Flames were still shooting up from the engine beside me. I did not care. Driving a maximum of thirty miles per hour, I made my way to the animal shelter to get Simon. After paying for his release, I got my boy back! Together again in my Winnebago, we slowly made our way to the horse farm, where Chad, Jezbah, and Loocia were happy to see us.

Money was tight, and I had depleted virtually all of my savings. My credit card bills were growing. I had been scrounging for loose change to buy Simon food, and I splurged on a lottery ticket in hopes of a dream.

Drew was somewhere, I believed, at his home. I knew he would be coming to Florida to join rehearsals near Orlando. He would not tell me when and said he did not want to see me there. He explained how all the drama had left him very upset; he needed to focus on his job. He told me he loved me and to be safe.

I wanted to investigate where I was kept and locked up while held in state custody against my will and without any judge, jury, or criminal charges. The mental health institution was near a crack neighborhood in a very rough area of town. I drove around and stopped at a nearby fast-food place on a corner. Parking the car, I went inside and got a biscuit. There, I met a guy with whom I began a conversation. He and I talked for some time and even exchanged phone numbers. I felt comfortable in the crack neighborhood. Nobody judged; nobody cared. I was safe.

Stopping at other establishments, I talked with more strangers. I took the liberty of showing some people the letters I had previously faxed to the government institutions — I carried all kinds of things in my car. I drove around and talked with all sorts of people. I was desperate to discover who was after me, causing all the destruction. Everybody I spoke to confirmed that the world had changed and things would never be the same again.

I remembered I had brought stuff to the laundromat near the Happy Travels RV Park and still had to pick it up. Traffic was at a standstill. Paranoid, I felt like the car would blow up at any second. I was trapped, stuck, and scared. Jumping out of my car, I ran onto the grass median alongside the other cars stopped on the highway. Knocking on a stranger's window, I got inside their vehicle and told the driver of my fears. The traffic was still at a standstill. Scared, I jumped out and ran. Rebuke sharply! I went back to my vehicle.

I made it to the laundromat. Inside, there were many sacks and bags of stuff of mine. Also, in the laundromat, I saw a former neighbor from the Happy Travels RV Park. Another coincidence; I knew she must be with *them*. I wondered how they always knew where I would be, even before I got there. I loaded my car and left the laundromat quickly.

A few days later, I wanted to return to tour rehearsals near Orlando and talk with Drew. Surely, he must be on-site. Drew barely answered my many phone calls; when he did answer the phone, he sounded different. He often repeated, "Please be safe; please be safe." I drove my car to rehearsals near Orlando. It did not matter to me that Drew did not want me to go. I had to see him. I knew they were getting him to go against me too. I had to convince Drew not to side with them, to trust me; we could escape together.

I feared the terrorists around that area. I believed terrorists were harbored below, underground, in places like the underground workings of Disney in Orlando. I imagined the terrorist codes were based on our most fundamental American symbols ranging from our alphabet and apple pie to Mickey Mouse and convenience stores; the 7-Eleven terrified me. I was driven by interpreting codes, meanings, and hidden words like a detective, revealed and confirmed by me to be ever-present. Every name, number, and shape – even a simple license plate on a car was a code. Things would never be the same.

I arrived at the rehearsal venue and made my way to the back door, where I had always entered. A security man told me I was not permitted inside the building. "I was just here a few days ago," I told him.

"No entry," he repeated.

"I am here to see Drew with the tour," I told him.

"You cannot come inside," he told me. "Wait outside, and I will let the tour personnel know you are here to see someone."

I waited in my car until Drew came out from the building. When he walked over to my car, he looked very different. There was an unfamiliar look on his face. He appeared angry that I was there. I told Drew I had won the lottery and he could come with me; we could get out of Florida and go. He told me I had not won anything and he had to go to work. Drew told me I had called him over and over and left more than thirty messages on his phone. "Over thirty!" Drew yelled. "You should hear yourself!" It was the only time I had ever heard Drew yell. He was very different, and he was shaking. I was inside my car, and Drew was angry. He begged me to leave. His eye twitched as he yelled at me to stop this. I knew they had gotten him, too, and I told him so. Drew kicked the car hard. He turned, walked away, and went back inside the building.

I drove away and all around the area. I feared that the terrorists and those out to get me were all inside the building. The lady at the truck stop told me the artist was dead. They killed the artist, which is why the performer was not there yet! They were trying to cover it up and create an identical replacement, the hologram!

My fear grew, and I thought I would not make it through alive. I found paper and a pen in my car and wrote down my name, plus all the numbers in my telephone. Then I stopped at a VFW and found a veteran outside. I told him I was in trouble and gave him the paper with the list of all the phone numbers I had written down. I instructed him to call the numbers should he read about me dead in the paper or on the news. I made a few more copies of the numbers and gave them to a few other folks I came across.

I called the police department and reported danger at the rehearsal venue. I told them about a terrorist attack and a bomb in the building. Then, driving back to the venue, I watched the police cars pulling up to investigate. I then drove away and headed toward the highway back to Tampa.

I was sure I needed to plan my escape from Florida. But, first, most importantly, I needed to plan how to get Chad to New Jersey. After calling several horse transportation companies, I decided it would be best to try to trailer Chad myself. I had never in all my years pulled a trailer, and considering my Saturn car would not be able to pull a horse trailer, I went looking for a vehicle that could.

Pulling into a used car lot somewhere, I began to look around. It did not take long before a salesperson came to assist me. I told him I was looking for a small SUV vehicle that could pull a horse trailer. The salesman mentioned one that had come in the day before. It had not been looked at or cleaned out and was not even on the lot yet, but he could show it to me. The salesman opened a fence gate and took me to a 1993 green Mazda MPV minivan. It had a tan interior, seats that folded, and a lift door on the back. No hitch.

I asked the salesman if I could take the minivan for a drive, and he said sure. I drove out of the lot, down a few traffic lights, and asked if we could draw up the papers so I could drive away in the minivan that day. He said sure. I returned to the dealership, parked, and went inside.

Once inside the dealership, the salesman made a contract where I would give the dealership my Saturn (the car I received brand-new as my college graduation gift from my parents in 1995), plus my Winnebago and also $4,500 charged to my credit card. I signed the papers, cleaned out my Saturn, handed the salesman the keys, agreed to drop the Winnebago off in the coming days, and drove away in my new, used Mazda minivan.

I drove to Josephine's house, where she showed me pictures and told me about the bright lights on faces in photographs: their spirit-self glowing through. We went to the little church for Sunday service. I needed God's help. The energy there filled the room with praise and worship. At one point in the service, the pastor presented an oversized, hand-carved wooden chair with a high back decorated with velvet and a crown like a king's throne. He began calling upon people to join him at the throne and trust their hearts to God. He called for anybody who was in need to come up to the altar, to the "King's Throne," praise God, repent their sins, ask for mercy, and give their prayers to the Lord. I made my way to the throne and knelt down, with hands laid upon me by many of the congregation. I wept and begged God for a home, a safe home.

After the service, I drove the minivan back to the Rockin D horse farm, where my Winnebago was still parked, and Chad and the bunnies were kept. Diane was gone. A neighbor came up to me. He was a big, burly man with a furry beard and mustache. He drove a turbo 4X4 truck with gigantic tires and an enormous American flag with a missile cannon displayed in the flatbed. He told me Diane had gone to

Mexico, and offered me a coffee. I grew suspicious. I saved the sugar packets and wanted them tested for anthrax.

That night in the Winnebago, I could not sleep. I paced and screamed and kicked the walls. "Just get me already!" I pleaded. The unknowing madness! I kicked the walls and screamed; Simon hid under the driver's seat while I rampaged in terror, challenging the demon to fight.

The following evening, Simon was missing. It was nearing dark, and I called for him all around the farm, but he was gone. He would not come to me. They had taken him again! I got in the car and drove to the convenience store, where I met a couple and told them that somebody had taken my dog. I needed them to go with me to the farm and help me. Begrudgingly, the kind strangers followed me to the farm road, but they were too scared to go down it; it appeared very dark.

We drove to the corner, and there, we called the police. When an officer arrived, I told him that the barn's owner was in Mexico, somebody else was there, and I believed they had taken my dog, Simon. The officer took my information, and he and I drove down the dark farm road with the police car's spotlights on. While I called out desperately for my Simon, in the light, like an angel, there he was, all intact. I held Simon close as the officer gave me a look and drove away.

The following day, I drove the Winnebago to the storage space I rented. I emptied all my belongings from the Winnebago and put the stuff in the storage unit. Back at the horse farm, I arranged to have the Winnebago picked up and towed away to the used car dealership. Homeless, I drove my car to a motel near the highway and got a room.

Searching nearby horse farms, I found a nice one that provided full-care horse board and also accepted credit cards. The people there had a horse trailer and were able to transport Chad. So while Diane was still in Mexico, I moved Chad to "Easy Breeze Farm." The bunnies moved into the motel room with me. It was a nice few days with Chad at the new horse farm, as my new vehicle could hold a bale of hay, and Chad liked when I opened the back lift door, letting him munch right out of the van.

Wanting to keep on the move, fearful of anybody following or watching me, I changed motels. At the next motel registration desk, a soldier was inside. I bowed to him and thanked him for his service. It was another restless night as that motel was located directly across from an amusement park. The air was filled with haunting sounds of scary hollers and spooky howls. The sounds of screaming children became eerie and frightening, while the roaring sounds of coasters were threatening. I wanted to scream and kick the walls again, but I could not. I paced and made countless phone calls deep into the night and early morning hours until I checked out and returned to the motel where I had first stayed.

At the Easy Breeze Farm, I arranged for a mom and daughter to bunny-sit Jezbah and Loocia for one week. After that, I was going to drive to New Jersey. My plan was to drop Simon safely at my parents' house and stay with Oleg in Brooklyn. Oleg would help find a home for us: me, Simon, Chad, Jezbah, and Loocia. Oleg would help us recover; he was the only one who still believed in me and was not out to hurt or poison me. Oleg knew me better, and he supported me. He was safe and would help make everything okay.

I felt prepared for the long drive to my long-awaited escape back home. I checked out of the motel, making sure to ask the housekeeping staff for the vacuum before I left. I did not want them to see the messes of Jezbah and Loocia.

October 29, 2001, Simon jumped inside the minivan, curled up, and rested in the passenger seat alongside me. We made our trek to the Florida highway and headed north toward New Jersey; we were going to break free at last!

When we neared the border of the Sunshine State, I was terrified, expecting to be pulled over and taken into custody again. But we broke through the barrier of the Florida state line, to my relief, and we made it out. I was alive.

I drove hundreds of miles that day. The world was a different place, yet the highway looked the same. I stopped at the truck stops and drove onward. Making my way to a pet-friendly motel for the night, I rested before the next full day of driving.

Late at night, October 30, I finally arrived on the street in New Jersey where I grew up. Expecting to see unusual vehicles and activity, I found that nothing looked out of sorts. So I went inside my parents' house, and Simon was very happy to be home at last.

My parents remained suspicious and dangerous to me. They were of the medical belief that I required psychiatric drugging and some sort of counseling, such as they had arranged through the doctors at the Florida facility. I felt strongly that I did not. I was not going to consent to anything of the sort. I had my pink pill that Dr. Menia gave me for one year.

I drove on to Brooklyn, where Oleg was waiting to hug me. Oleg lived in an apartment building where most of his family also lived. They emigrated from Russia when Oleg was a kid and had lived in that same building since his childhood. Oleg's apartment had been re-modeled precisely to his liking. He had walls of incredible hidden built-in storage design and a freestanding Jacuzzi tub in his bedroom. Years before, he hired an artist to live there for months while painting the bedroom to look like the grounds of a Grecian kingdom; beautiful and spectacular!

While filming a movie in Montreal, Oleg met a French girl. When I arrived, the French girl was staying at his apartment, trying to build her business and find work in the city. Oleg tried to help the French girl pursue her dreams. She liked jewelry and fine things. Despite Oleg experiencing his own financial difficulty resulting from stock stuff I did not really understand, he was a compassionate individual, and he made the decision to help the French girl. With her desire to build a business, loyal to his word, Oleg loaned the French girl money to purchase wholesale antique jewelry. He would go with her to various markets and sell the pieces as she did not drive.

The weekend I was there, I went with Oleg and the French girl to the outdoor market. It was a super great day. Oleg and I enjoyed talking and walking, and laughing. He gave me a special guitar charm and told me to keep my dreams alive. Oleg amazed me; his smile was even bigger than his personality! His personality was huge!

I wanted to go into the city, to the site of the Twin Towers, but there were too many men with machine guns around, and that scared me. I could not go.

The French girl, Oleg, and I took a drive into New Jersey and began searching for a barn to bring Chad to. Seeing Oleg at a barn was very funny. I was glad he didn't care about the mud on his very nice and very expensive shoes. Thankfully, we found a great barn near the Jersey shore; a beautiful cobblestone barn with green pastures and little nooks all around. A stall was available! I told the woman I would give her a deposit and bring Chad sometime within the next two weeks.

Next, we found an apartment nearby, nestled between the river and the ocean. It was November and cold in New Jersey; it certainly was not the time of year for a beach apartment. However, it was in a town called Sea Bright, and that was just what I needed. Plus, it was in an old Victorian house with a purple hardwood floor and a non-working fireplace in the large bedroom. Moreover, it had beautiful wraparound windows from what was clearly at one time a porch.

Between the drastic rate increase in the cost of boarding a horse in New Jersey, the expensive rent, and the fact that I had spent everything I saved, plus I had also charged my credit cards to the maximum, I was unsure how I would pay for the apartment. There was no choice but to ask my dad for help. I called my dad and asked him to loan me money for the rent deposit. There was an understanding that I would not go home to their house; I needed time alone. My dad agreed to help and gave me a deposit check. I signed a four-month winter lease on an apartment down the shore.

Back at Oleg's Brooklyn apartment, he was determined to help me by setting up an eBay account where I could sell some of my memorabilia and raise rent money. Not being computer savvy, I was not interested. Oleg persisted and said it would generate income. If it meant I could pay Chad's board so he could stay with me, then I had to do it. Oleg set up the account.

Stopping at my parents' house in Jersey, I picked up a check from my father and some memorabilia that Oleg could photograph for eBay. Also, I gathered mutual funds I had received for college graduation and sold them to pay Chad's board in New Jersey. At the house, I was able to spend quiet time with Simon. It broke my heart to leave him there, but I knew he was safe at home and would be well cared for by my mom and dad.

Back in Brooklyn, preparing to return to Florida for Chad, Jezbah, Loocia, and my belongings, I noticed that Oleg seemed very depressed. He lay on the couch and did not get up. That was not at all like the energetic Oleg I knew. So I asked him to come with me to Florida. I told him that he and the French girl should come along, and while I packed my things and critters, they could hit the markets down there. After all, Florida was filled with markets and swap meets. Plus, I was only going to be there about a week or so, just enough time to get my stuff and get out.

Oleg was always up for any adventure. For example, Oleg once called me while I was having a bad day at work on the road. He heard the frustration in my voice, jumped on an airplane, and spent the day with me in whatever city I was in before he returned on a flight back to New York late that same night. A crazy laugh! Impulsive, fearless, love. On another occasion, Oleg and I were in a restaurant, and just when I thought Oleg had excused himself from the table to use the bathroom, he returned holding two live lobsters from the tank and asked which one I would prefer. There was also the time at a restaurant when Oleg insisted on going behind the bar to make me a drink. The bartender went on about how Oleg could not be behind the bar. Persistent, Oleg told the bartender he wanted to make my drink, and whatever money the bartender had in the register, Oleg would double it. He did. And it was a nice cocktail Oleg made for me. Whatever Oleg wanted, he made happen. Whatever it took to do so.

On that particular day, when I prepared to go back to Florida, Oleg remained lying on the couch for some reason and did not walk me to the elevator like he always did. He seemed so sad. My heart ached for him; I clung to the hope that Oleg and I would pull together, restore good days, and make more happy memories. Walking out the apartment door, I expressed my love for him and told Oleg I would keep him posted as I went. Even more, I looked forward to seeing him soon when we moved me into my new apartment. We were going to build wonderful things together. That was the first time I got into the elevator at Oleg's building alone.

November 7, 2001. I got onto the highway in my minivan and began the long drive alone back to Florida.

13

Roundabout

It was a long, lonely drive without Simon. But it was a relief to know he was out of harm's way and safely at my parents'. With two days of highway driving and much time to think, I began making plans. I pulled back into Tampa late on the evening of November 8 and immediately went to check up on Chad, then drove to a motel where I rented a room for one week.

The following day I drove downtown to obtain copies of the police reports relevant to each incident where I was taken into custody against my will with no representation, no rights, no judge, no jury, no justice, and no peace. Parking the car, I made my way through the large office buildings looking for the entrance I needed. Suddenly I heard hollering and yelling. Looking up, I saw a convertible car with four or five men wearing large rubber masks of former U.S. Presidents. Each man was yelling, and some were standing up in the car, flailing about as they drove through the downtown streets. Was that the new normal?

Turning the corner, I located the door that would lead me up an escalator and to an office. There I filed to obtain the police records and was directed to another window where I received the copies for a nominal fee. Unfortunately, the files only included the first two times when the vicious dark-haired woman came for me. The third time I was taken into custody by the asshole macho man from the sheriff's department required a visit to a separate office in a completely different location.

I went to the police department's Office of Internal Affairs and attempted to file a complaint against the beastly dark-haired woman who assaulted me. They told me the officer did nothing wrong, and I could not file a report.

I located a horse trailer sales lot and drove forty-five minutes to get there. Again, a salesperson was ready to assist. While I browsed the lot, the salesman filed my loan application. Within a few minutes, I was approved. While my minivan was pulled into a garage and a trailer hitch was installed, I selected a brand-new two-horse bumper pull trailer. I opted against the additional expense of a spare tire. After all, it was a brand-new trailer. In less than two hours, I drove away in my Mazda minivan with a new horse trailer attached. It was the first time I had ever towed anything while driving. It took a bit of attention to manage the braking.

I dropped the trailer at the horse farm and spent some quality time with Chad. The farm had sand trails Chad and I could go walking on; Chad even crossed the water and played in the streams. The bunny-sitter came and returned Jezbah and Loocia. I took the bunnies with me back to the motel.

When I pulled into the parking spot outside my motel guest room, a nice older couple began talking to me about my bunnies. We proceeded to have an interesting conversation, and I found Dov and Helene to be incredibly wonderful, inspiring souls. Helene even reminded me of my Aunt Lucy. After they invited me for dinner, I sat with them in their room and listened to their wonderful stories of jazz and music, travels and golf, beautiful observances they had made, and wise knowledge I noted to retain. Dov and Helene were dearly in love. They were angels sent to me, providing me with guidance toward peace once again.

Feeling strongly that something was not right, I was determined to discover exactly what had happened to me and receive justice for the assaults I endured. Having never needed a lawyer before, I called an attorney I saw advertised and made an appointment. It was an attorney service. I signed up for the service and would be charged monthly on my credit card. I would file a report, and an attorney would call me regarding my case.

I went to the general hospital to obtain my medical records. It was the same hospital where I had gone when my finger was initially numb and hurting at Camille's house in April; the same hospital I was taken to when attacked by the dark-haired aggressive officer shortly after September 11; the same hospital I was taken to when the dark-haired officer broke the kitchen window and came after me again. I located the records window where I was charged one dollar per page of each hospital record. The amount of paperwork the records produced surprised even the receptionist there.

I was cautious in my driving, attuned to everything around me. When I saw a thrift store, I quickly turned in. Inside, it was relatively quiet. I browsed around and began collecting items that appealed to me, including suitcases for packing. Within minutes, a woman began shopping alongside me. I was very aware of her presence. I set two items down and noticed she immediately picked them up. The store began to fill with people as I gathered items and suitcases to pack my belongings. I noticed the woman following me had set down the items and left the store.

At the checkout, the line was so long that the salespeople were overwhelmed by the sudden activity and called for assistance. I finally reached the checkout, where my credit card was denied. Suspicious, I insisted the store clerk call the bank, and I stayed on the telephone with credit card services for twenty minutes until they sorted out the problem with my account and approved my sale. Then, I drove away and continued driving around the area for a few minutes until I saw that all the cars in the thrift store parking lot were gone.

At the horse farm, I managed to attach the horse trailer to the hitch on the minivan and drive to the storage unit. There I emptied my storage space and loaded everything into one half of the horse trailer. I was very careful to pack securely because I needed to put Chad in the other half of the trailer and drive back to New Jersey. I did not want to run the risk of anything moving, falling, or scaring him.

On November 16, I cleaned the motel room and checked out. I parked the van and trailer outside Chad's stall and kept the bunnies safely in my vehicle. Reclining in one of the seats, I settled in the van to sleep for the night.

The following day, I drove to the mental facility to obtain the records from my captivity there. They were not so cooperative. The mental facility claimed that I was not entitled to the records. Furthermore, they explained the documents were the property of the state and facility, and I would need a court order to access them. I was enraged. I resolved that I would take measures and obtain that court order one day. Meanwhile, I filed paperwork to receive a brief paragraph summary.

That evening, I went to the mall. It was the first time I had been to the mall in months, and it felt surreal. Slowly I walked around in a daze as though it was a place I had never been before. I shopped in a clothes store. Knowing I had no spare money to spend, I still could not resist a soft, comfortable pink pajama set. I made the purchase and left the mall. Parked back at the farm, I nestled into my new pajamas and lay down in the backseat of the minivan with the bunnies.

The phone rang; it was Oleg calling to check up on me. I informed him that I was making my final preparations to return home and would be leaving the following day. Oleg wasn't thrilled about my new pajama purchase as I had promised I wouldn't buy anything else, but he understood that I needed something fresh, comforting, and nice to wear while I slept in a minivan with two bunnies and parked outside my horse's stall. He was looking forward to my getting home safely.

The following morning, I prepared to leave Florida for good. I had gathered all the police, medical, and mental health summaries and records I could pertinent to the events that had taken place. Also, I had saved everything along the way and tucked my evidence safely in my horse trailer.

It took some time to load Chad into the horse trailer. He was a bit apprehensive about all the stuff inside, but eventually, he stepped up, and I secured him safely inside. The bunnies remained settled in the rear of the minivan. At last, we were loaded, packed, and ready for the final journey home to New Jersey.

14

Oil Change

I was nervous about driving while pulling Chad in the trailer behind me, but there was no alternative; I had to drive on. So I opted to take the small back roads to the Florida border.

About two hours into the drive on a long two-lane back road in Florida somewhere, I felt something strange with the vehicle. Realizing I had a flat tire on the horse trailer and there was nothing around, I considered whether to drive on slowly until I came across a gas station or pull over immediately. On my left, I noticed a large pen beside the road with a horse in it. It was on the opposite side of the road. Ahead on the left was a lane where I could make a U-turn.

Carefully turning around, I pulled into a driveway alongside the horse pen. Tucked in the back was a small shop of sorts. I never went inside the building to look. A man came out, and I told him about my flat tire. Kicking myself for not getting the spare tire when I bought the horse trailer; I did not have a spare one, nor did he. However, he did have a phone number for a place and proceeded to make a call. It would take nearly two hours before the man arrived with a tire. I kept Chad inside the trailer for fear of what would occur if I took him out while the man jacked up the horse trailer and changed the tire. No sooner had I given him my credit card to charge than I was on my way once again.

The delay in the drive, combined with my choice of back roads, put me in the prearranged horse motel at a very late hour. Surprisingly, there were horse farms along highway routes that rented stalls to travelers with an equine companion in tow.

By the time I found the farm, it was after midnight. Chad was dazed from the endless hours on the road, as was I. Somehow in the dark, I managed to find an empty stall to settle Chad; then, I tried to rest in the backseat of the minivan. It wasn't long before I woke to the early sounds of the farm owner. After paying him and loading Chad, we were quickly on our way again. Every two hours, I made a point to pull off the highway, check on Chad, and see if any of the stuff had moved; so far, so good.

By the time I made it to the cobblestone barn in New Jersey, it was nearly midnight, dark and spooky. I unloaded Chad from the trailer and carefully searched for an empty stall. After getting Chad settled the best I could, with no light to be found at all, I made my way back to the minivan and trailer. It was dark, late, and I was utterly exhausted.

Not knowing what to do with the horse trailer, I unhitched it from the van wherever it was parked and figured I would address the problem in the morning; I would have to be at the farm bright and early to feed Chad because the barn manager did not have his grain. I had a garbage can full of grain stored in the back of the trailer, but I didn't want to dig in the dark of night. Plus, I needed to be there when Chad woke up. Still a little colt, he must have been quite confused, tired, and disorientated.

I left the barn and headed to my new apartment nearby on the water. Even though I wanted to call Oleg and tell him we had made it home safely at last, I was so tired the best I could do was open the door to an empty apartment and collapse on the floor into sleep.

At the early break of dawn, the walls of windows facing the East Coast shore flooded the room with light. Fuzzy and disorientated, I woke up on the hard floor. I took a moment to digest where I was, then immediately remembered Chad and his breakfast; I jumped up quickly, grabbed the car keys, and back out the door I went.

As I drove to the barn, I called Oleg but got his answering machine. I left a message telling him that I had made it home safely, got into the apartment okay, was headed to the barn to see Chad, and looked forward to him coming over to celebrate the new beginning.

At the barn, I went to the stall where I had left Chad the night before. Chad was gone! Running through the barn and into another, I found a barn helper who told me they had moved Chad into a different stall in a small barn around the back. I ran to the small cinderblock barn, and, with great relief, I saw Chad. While I cried and hugged him, I noticed he was sneezing. It was cold in late November, and Chad had only ever known the warm humidity of Florida air. For him, it was a long ride in the trailer. The sides were open, with the wind blowing through. I did not have a blanket or shipping boots for him. He was almost eight months old and dependent on me.

I went to the trailer for Chad's grain. The barn helper saw me and told me I had to move the trailer to a different spot. She pointed out an area on the other side of the farm. After feeding Chad his breakfast, I began the process of hitching the trailer to the van. While doing so, the phone rang, and I saw it was Oleg calling. I answered the phone, expecting to hear him singing with a morning cheer, but instead, I heard the voice of the French girl.

Excitedly, I told the French girl I had finally made it home safely and asked her to put Oleg on the phone. The French girl choked up as she told me that there had been an accident.

"An accident?" I questioned.

"Yes," she said, "there was an accident last night, and Oleg didn't make it."

"What do you mean, Oleg did not make it?"

"Oleg is gone."

"No," I told her. "No, he must be okay. He may be hurt, but he will be okay."

"He died, Dawn." She sounded sure.

"Where is Oleg?" I yelled. "Is he in the hospital?"

"He is not in the hospital," the French girl continued. "He has been taken to be prepared for the funeral."

Oh my God. Oh my God.

"What happened?" I demanded. The French girl explained that she, Oleg, and his brother had gone out the night before; his brother was driving on the way home, and there was an accident. Oleg did not make it. The family was mourning, sitting shiva. Oleg was not going to be buried according to their religious timeframe as Oleg's brother had been arrested for DUI, and the family would wait to bury Oleg until his brother was released from jail.

I had to go to Brooklyn. I took my pink pill.

Dazed and numb, I finished moving the horse trailer to the parking spot and immediately found the barn helper. I told her there was an accident and I would have to go to Brooklyn. I asked her to please feed Chad his dinner that night and give him breakfast the next morning, as I would be spending the night in Brooklyn. She agreed to do so.

Crying and sobbing on Chad's mane, I hugged him and told him I was sorry I had to go away again, but I would be back soon, and I promised I would make everything okay. I cried and sobbed until I had to pull myself away and go to Brooklyn to be with Oleg's family and mourn. I went to my apartment and prepared things for the overnight visit.

The bunnies were still in the van and would go with me to Brooklyn. The drive was a fog. I was angry that they had taken Oleg from me. They knew he was the one person I had who was true and real and was my rock. Yet, they took him and left me stripped and alone. My eyes buzzed in zigzag motion; my body zapped.

Days were a blur; the excitement of home was a distant thought. I knew I could not escape, no matter where I ran and hid. Three days of back-and-forth between Brooklyn and the barn, and still Oleg was not buried.

Thanksgiving Day; I spent the holiday with my family in New Jersey and tried to act as though all was fine. After I left the family Thanksgiving gathering, I headed into New York City, where friends of Oleg's from theatre and film held a memorial gathering. The following day, Oleg was buried.

While at the viewing, just prior to closing the coffin, I made my way through the thick crowd, crying to see Oleg once more before they sealed the casket closed. Pushing, shoving, I made my way for a final glimpse of my dear friend. Part of me expected to see somebody else inside, but that was not the case.

On the way back from the funeral, I went to see Chad. Deep into the night, I was in his stall, my eyes puffy and my voice hoarse. Hours passed before I managed to gather myself and head back to my new empty apartment.

The road was dark and winding along the riverfront. An oldies song about happiness was on the radio. A curve was ahead, the road was slick, and the minivan glided freely on its own, out of my control, as it smashed into a guardrail before the steep cliff drop. The minivan came to a sudden halt. I opened the door, went around the front of the vehicle, saw the headlight hanging out, and pushed it in. Back in the minivan, the happy song was still on the radio, and in a haze of utter surrender, I drove away, onward toward my apartment.

The minivan went to the repair shop, and I was given a small rental car. Back and forth from the farm to the apartment, apartment to the farm. I emptied the horse trailer and filled my new apartment with all my things.

I was alone, broke. My life savings, over $30,000, was gone, and my credit cards charged up in the thousands. I needed to find some means of income to pay my rent and Chad's board.

Having no initiative to do anything, I applied for a position at a convenience store located three minutes from the apartment I rented. When I completed the application, listed my education and work history, the store manager told me, "No." He would not hire me. He said I was overqualified and wanted to know why I would be interested in working at a convenience store. "I'm looking to slow down and relax more," I told him. "I don't want to be in charge right now, and I'm looking for something less stressful, close to home." He expressed his concern that I would grow bored and quit the job in a week. I assured him that would not be the case. He gave me the job.

Immediately, I began working at the convenience store earning minimum wage. However, my paycheck did not cover my expenses. To help with the difference, on weekends when I was not working the cash register at the store, I took my belongings to sell at the flea market.

I made attempts to call Camille and Drew. Drew would not answer my call. Camille answered once. She was cold and distant and did not want to talk with me.

Jezbah and Loocia lived with me in the apartment. Jezbah had taken to chewing all the paper he could. Pets were not permitted in the apartment and considering the landlord lived in the apartment next to me, I had to find a good home for my bunnies. It was imperative that Jezbah and Loocia not be separated, ever. A coworker from the convenience store said she would take my two little ones for her kids. Packing up Jezbah and Loocia, I gave the woman my bunnies.

All the windows in my apartment made it extra cold during winter on the shore. I required an additional space heater to stay warm. The electric power went out when I turned on more than two appliances at a time. Often, I called the landlord to flip the circuit breaker back on; the breaker box was inside their apartment next door. Sometimes, I just went the night without any electricity at all.

A guy in town wanted to take me on a date. I tried to tell him I was not interested. He persisted. I did not want to go with him to have drinks; I didn't have the funds to buy a $5 cocktail if I needed to. I was not going to be indebted to anyone. I missed Drew. I missed Oleg. I needed Oleg.

Christmas rolled around. The minivan was still in the repair shop; I still had the rental car.

Christmas Day I spent working at the convenience store. Being rather busy, I rang up quick and bagged fast. A man came in and made a purchase totaling less than $20. He handed me a hundred-dollar bill; told me to keep the change.

New Year's 2002 was spent quietly, alone at the barn with Chad, missing my Simon and bunnies. I needed Oleg. I couldn't believe he was gone.

I made trips back and forth to my parents' house to see Simon. Since pets were not permitted in my apartment, when I did bring Simon to spend a night or afternoon with me, I had to make extreme efforts so my landlord would not see him.

The woman from work called; she wanted to return my bunnies. Happily, I picked up Jezbah and Loocia at her house and brought them home, back to me; their cage set up in the living room.

My email was flooded with eBay responses from the items Oleg had listed in the online auction. I tried my best to manage the shipping and payment process without him. Oleg was supposed to be there helping.

Another day came when the burden of the madness was raging, and while driving on the winding river road, I slammed the gas pedal, racing the rental car down the hills and around the curves while screaming for the end. Then, thinking how Chad, Simon, and the bunnies depended on me and needed me, I slowed the vehicle to a safe speed, gaining control of the rental car.

It wasn't until February 2002 that my minivan was finally repaired and restored from the accident, and I could return the rental car intact at last.

My folks were taking a trip out of town. I went there to house-sit, bringing the bunnies with me. I let the bunnies roam about in the guest room. Then, with Simon curled under the covers beside me, I welcomed a good long sleep in my own bed; the air mattress at my apartment was cold.

The following morning, I woke peacefully in my bed to the playful squeaks of Simon with his toys. Going into the guest room to check on the bunnies, I stepped on something that went POP! When I looked down, I screamed as I realized it was a baby bunny! Panic and horror came over me. The baby bunny was still alive, and he was busted open. All I could do was get a clean towel to wrap him in and pray his suffering would go fast. I searched the room for the nest Loocia had made, and I found six more baby bunnies! I cleaned the mess and prepared a nursery box. Packing up the bunnies and bidding my dear Simon goodbye, I left my parents' house before they arrived home.

On the drive back to my apartment, it was getting dark. I looked in my rearview mirror and saw flashing lights signaling me to pull over. My heart raced, and my blood heated with intensity and fear. I made my way to the shoulder off the road, where an officer came up to my window. "Your lights are out in the back," he informed me.

"Oh, I didn't know," I replied. "I'm almost home, just a mile away." I was relieved that he let me go on. The following day I brought the minivan back to the body shop, where it was discovered that they had disconnected a fuse.

Back at my apartment, the bunnies chewed papers and wires. I ate assorted sweets from the convenience store where I worked and ice cream by the pint. I rapidly gained weight.

At the convenience store, I was promoted to lottery ticket agent and cigarette sales. I played the scratch-offs whenever a spare dollar was worth the sacrifice for the moment of hope or luck. Locals would come in and talk with me, telling great stories of their beach town lives. I listened and talked, finding them therapeutic in my trench of deep despair. Other than my bunnies and Chad, they were all I had.

One particular afternoon, I recognized an old acquaintance from my high school days. Feeling uneasy, I could not explain to him how I was doing while I rang up his groceries and gave him his change. I smiled and wished him well. He had a look of pity on his face.

Drew would not return my calls. The pounds were packing on, and I was nearing 148. I could not get Florida off my mind. The multiple attacks were too much to bear, and I was angry about the injustice done to me. Oleg was supposed to help. My pink pill was supposed to help.

I contacted the attorney service seeking help in filing a complaint. "What is your complaint?" they would ask. I didn't know how to tell them. "I was attacked," I said, "assaulted by an officer for singing *New York, New York*." My pleas made no sense to any of them. My attempts at representation to file a case were crushing. I made notes. I wrote letters. I gave copies of my records to various attorneys, the ACLU, and nobody would help me to understand what happened to me. Still, something was not right.

Late one night, I went to the horse farm to see Chad. It was quiet and dark as it usually was. I had put a little nightlight in the outlet near Chad's stall so he wouldn't be afraid in the cold, dark concrete barn. That night, I walked into the stall and Chad was soaking wet. Realizing his stall was also saturated, I spent the next four hours cleaning it. Rats were roaming and running through the stalls next to the sleeping horses. It was an old cow barn, and, beautiful as it appeared, the walkways were barely large enough for the horses to turn around, and the ceilings were extremely low. The wiring and cobwebs were ancient; continuing to clean in the night, I feared a potential fire.

There was a horse boarder at the barn who I talked to on occasion. He was preparing to move his horse to another barn about thirty minutes away. I discussed with him the idea of also moving Chad; I wanted to get Chad into a safer barn. I also started to consider that my four-month apartment lease would be ending soon.

Early March 2002, my thirty-second birthday and Chad's first birthday arrived. Chad and I celebrated in the barn with fresh carrots and my frozen friends, Ben & Jerry.

The night shift became available at the convenience store; the manager offered me the position, and I gladly accepted. My workday hours ran from 11 p.m. to 7 a.m. I took to wearing my pajamas to work.

A punk kid, early twenty-something, worked the night shift along with me. He worked in the deli section and napped on the floor behind the deli counter. Since the convenience store was generally quiet through the night, I amused myself creatively: I colored the punk kid with marker pens, put lettuce on his head, and plastic-wrapped him like a cocoon. He just slept.

One day the punk kid mentioned pills; I told him about the bottles of prescription pills I had been given from Florida and had stored away. I would not take those pills they forced on me. The kid lit up like a firework and asked if he could have some.

The following night at work, I brought the kid some of the pills. After taking the prescription drugs, the kid ended up paralyzed in the emergency room. Panicked because he did not have health insurance, when he was finally able to move again, he jumped up, ran out of the hospital, and disappeared. It was three days before the punk kid showed up at work again. He was freaked out.

The baby bunnies were ready to be weaned. I placed an advertisement in the classified pages of the newspaper. Phone calls began, and dozens of messages a day poured in. Eventually, all of the babies were placed in good homes. Then, it was just Jezbah and Loocia again.

With my apartment lease expiration date approaching quickly, I planned to return to my parents' house. My dad made it firmly clear that Jezbah and Loocia were not welcome there. I had to find my bunnies a loving forever home. After much screening on the telephone, a woman and her children came to my apartment. I kissed my Jezbah and Loocia goodbye, and the woman put my bunnies in her car and took them to her home a good distance away. Grieving, I felt like a mom giving away her children, never to see them again.

Once more, I loaded Chad into the horse trailer and moved him to another barn. Unfortunately, that barn was significantly more expensive and forty-five minutes away. However, it was a beautiful brand-new barn with wide walkways and an indoor riding arena. As an added bonus, Chad had his own light and ceiling fan in his stall!

My one-year prescription for my SSRI had run out. I was mentally, physically, and emotionally depleted. Exhausted. I would not return to any doctor; that was not an option for me. I was fearful. There was no choice but to move forward on my own; no pink pill. When body zaps flooded me, I was too tired for their communication.

Loading up the minivan, I packed my belongings that had taken over the beachfront apartment. Trip after trip, I brought everything to a storage unit near my parents' house. My dad had rented a space for me there. I cleaned the apartment the best I could and taped the wires that Jezbah had chewed, including the refrigerator. I left my apartment keys on the kitchen counter, then returned home with my mom and dad. I curled up in my own bed, in my own room where I grew up. Simon snoozed alongside me while I slept deeply for two days.

15

New Tires

Living back at my parents' house, I continued to work at the convenience store down the shore. What was a three-minute ride to work became a thirty-minute commute, and from work, it was another forty-five minutes to the horse farm where Chad lived. Completing the triangle, another thirty minutes from the horse farm back to my parents' house. So many miles, the radio played on.

As spring began to blossom, my depression sank deep, and my losses hit hard. I no longer had my pink pill. Yet, despite it all, I was still alive. I made more attempts to call Drew. One day, he answered the telephone and told me he was dating someone new.

A letter came in the mail. It was from Camille. I knew about her letters. Camille wrote all her thoughts and feelings about a situation, then she released them by giving the letter to the intended recipient. I began to read the pages upon pages that Camille wrote in anger, love, and deep expression. In great detail, she told how I destroyed her home and invaded her environment. Camille had been evicted because of me; she moved out of the house where I had stayed with her. Still, Camille thanked me for the strength and insight I brought to her and wished me well, as she told me she never wanted me in her life again.

Simon and I took long walks around the old neighborhood where I grew up. I cried on the playground at my elementary school and walked past the familiar childhood homes of former schoolmates, friends, and neighbors. I recalled one having a wishing well in the front yard; I had made many wishes in that well. Things that once seemed so perfect were now destroyed, and all was lost. Yet somehow, I was still alive; scarred, scared, but alive. Buried below starting point, I needed to rise, regroup, and redirect, on my own.

A letter came in the mail from the landlord at my beach apartment. Apparently, Jezbah had eaten so much of the apartment rugs and wires my deposit would not be returned.

I was growing tired of driving miles upon miles from my parents' house to the convenience store, back to the barn, and around. My thoughtful twenty-five-cent pay raise did not relieve the amount I spent having to constantly fill my gas tank. One spring day, I was on the full-time schedule to work at the convenience store. I had been there months by then and long past the week that the manager thought I would last. I had proven my reliability and dependability. That particular day I decided, no more. I called the convenience store and told the shift manager I would not be coming in that day. It was the first time I had called out. I never returned.

The season was gearing up at the local concert venue located just fifteen minutes from my parents' house. Years before, I worked at that particular venue when I was selected to go on my very first music tour, Janet Jackson. Often, I returned to work locally at that venue whenever I was home in Jersey and off the road from touring. Needing employment, I called Mike, the production manager I knew there. I told Mike that I would be home in the upcoming summer and was interested in working the season backstage if any openings were available. Happy to hear from me, Mike invited me to come by the venue.

Mike's concern in having me work the summer concert season was that I would pick up and go on tour in the midst of the season's series of shows. I assured Mike that would not be the case. Knowing I was dependable and knew my gig well, Mike hired me to work that upcoming season of concerts backstage.

At home, I spent much of my time walking Simon around my old neighborhood. Confined to my childhood bedroom at the house, my dad and I argued and fought whenever we spoke. My parents thought it best to forget the whole ordeal that happened to me in Florida and simply move on. But, for me, that was not possible. My experience was very real; I had to live with the devastating effects of my experiences, not knowing at this point what had caused them.

Continuing to seek legal representation for my injustices, I made serious attempts to reach out for help. I contacted attorneys about how I was attacked, assaulted, shackled, stripped, beaten, caged, and sodomized by a catheter. A few told me they were not able to help because I didn't actually commit suicide. I thought not committing suicide was a good thing.

The phone rang while I was at the farm one day. It was the woman with my bunnies. Apparently, between her kids, husband, dog, and house, the bunnies were too much for her to handle, and she needed to return them; I immediately drove to the woman's house and picked up Jezbah and Loocia.

I took the bunnies back to the barn where Chad lived, and the barn manager there graciously allowed me to keep Jezbah and Loocia in an old pen out back near where her pig lived. It was a good size bunny pen next to the pig's pen, and I was able to put a few huts inside for bunny housing and protection; they had always been house bunnies and were not accustomed to living outdoors. I was comforted by having Jezbah and Loocia back with me again.

The summer concert season began at the venue, and the musicians came to play; my regular sixteen-hour workdays were back in full swing. Faces of fellow road crew came through, filled with greetings and gossip from the touring bubble.

As the season went on, I inevitably saw roadies from the tour rehearsals I interrupted in Florida. It was unsettling to bear their looks. Awkward and uncomfortable, I attempted to explain to them that I was unsure what had happened to me. I told them I was getting myself back and vowed to find out why it all occurred. I apologized for my out-of-character behavior; most were forgiving, but others shunned me. At least the body rushes, zaps, and eye zigzags had finally diminished.

I was grateful for the opportunity to work again and in the comfort zone of a world I knew and understood. Working sixteen hours a day for five or six days a week backstage was more normal and satisfying than one hour of work in any office or at the convenience store. It was good to be around people with whom I was comfortable and who had high expectations of me.

As autumn rolled in and the summer season of shows came to a close, Mike asked me to be his production assistant on another show at another venue in New Jersey. Naturally, I welcomed the opportunity and accepted his offer.

It was September 2002; I was home in New Jersey as the one-year anniversary of the September 11 attacks approached. My mother read the newspaper and noticed an obituary; it was for the father of my dearest friend from elementary school. His body parts had been identified from the rubble of the Trade Center site. A funeral was scheduled for September 10, 2002. My parents and I attended the service. My childhood friend and I were reunited again; I was glad to have her in my life.

In Brooklyn, the French girl still lived in Oleg's apartment; his belongings still remained intact. I went to visit. The French girl, Oleg's family, his young son, and I all sat together and watched one of the last films Oleg ever acted in. It was one of the greatest short films I had ever seen, and it was silent! Oleg was hilarious as he played multiple characters, each to perfection; how far he had come in his acting abilities in such a short time. He had been taken from us far too soon. I missed Oleg every day.

Mike called asking if I would work another show with him at the New Jersey arena. Again, I was on board to do it. Starting the show day at the usual 7 a.m. load-in, I again saw familiar faces and many road friends. By the time midnight rolled around, the day had wound down, and load-out was halfway finished.

Mike and I were in his production office when the tour's production assistant, Lynn, entered. She and Mike had known each other for a very long time. They discussed an upcoming tour that Lynn would be going on next. Lynn explained to Mike she was looking for a wardrobe girl to go on the tour; she asked Mike if he knew anybody who could do it. Suddenly, right before my eyes, Mike expressed faith in me and my previous experience working on tour. He pointed my way and told Lynn that she had just walked into the perfect person. Mike recommended me for the position! Lynn took my phone number and said she would call me. Two days later, she did.

I made arrangements at the barn for Chad and the bunnies, then packed my suitcase. My parents, myself, and my Simon drove to the airport. Early November 2002, one year after my Florida escape and many months pill-free and normal again, I finally flew out onto my next concert tour.

On the road, I worked for a musical artist who was a straightforward, tough cookie. He sure was good, one of the greatest American musical artists ever. Every day he, his band, and tour crew had me smiling and wanting to do the best job I could. Though he was unaware of my Florida nightmare and loss of everything, his confidence in me and appreciation helped me to recover from the devastation. That artist showed he was a star through and through. I was filled with gratitude.

The short five-week tour came to a close; I went home again to my parents' house. After greeting Simon, I made my way to the farm to check on Chad and the bunnies. While visiting the barn, I received a phone call from Mike. He was organizing a very special upcoming event at the stadium in New Jersey. The production manager with whom I had just toured would also be there and requested my help. Naturally, I accepted the gig.

Soon thereafter, I found myself driving a fifteen-passenger van and parking at the stadium heliport, waiting to pick up and transport another road crew belonging to a dream rock star team. Upon completing that job, within days, I received word that the dream rock star team was going on a major world tour. I was offered a crew position with their wardrobe department; I accepted the gig.

The tour would take us overseas; I was required to submit my passport for a visa. That made me nervous and fearful. Considering my Florida experience, I worried if I would be permitted to leave the country and enter another.

I sent my passport to the appropriate visa administrative address. Soon afterward, I received a phone call from the tour production office. The Consulate had called the production office questioning my passport; the corner on the back page was torn and chewed. As a result, my passport was considered defective. To complete the visa process, I was required to write a letter to the Consulate explaining how my bunny, Jezbah, had eaten my passport. Thankfully, my visa request was granted.

Prior to leaving for the road once again, I made arrangements for additional care for my animals, and I was assured Chad, Simon, Jezbah, and Loocia would be well tended to in my absence. Gearing up for an extensive world tour, by early January 2003, I boarded an airplane headed for Japan.

16

Road Map

After four weeks touring around Japan, we headed back to the United States for shows in North America. Coincidentally, in the United States, Drew was on tour with the band scheduled as our opening act. For four months, Drew and I toured together once again. Things between us were different and forever altered in a broken friendship. For me, it was a sad relief when we finished the U.S. leg of the tour and took on a different opening act for our next eight weeks in Europe throughout the summer.

All the while, memories of my experience in Florida haunted me. A dark cloud loomed above; I suppressed emotions into a hidden disguise of well-being. The madness that had occurred made no sense. Grateful to have survived; I was expected to forget.

The dream team tour wrapped later that year; I returned to my parents' house, where Simon was overjoyed to have me home. Chad and the bunnies had also fared well. I sat in the living room, having morning coffee and reading the newspapers with my parents. My mom noticed an article on the inside page of the local press. She handed the newspaper to me and suggested I read it.

The story I read was about a teenage girl prescribed an anti-depressant drug for symptoms resembling Lyme disease. Upon daily intake of the drug, the young girl soon entered into a state of psychotic mania and proceeded to slash herself with razors, on multiple occasions, in attempts to take her own life. The symptoms the girl exhibited led doctors to diagnose her with a multitude of disorders, including bipolar, attention deficit disorder, ADHD, depression, and suicidal ideation. They gave her more pills.

Through much devastation, hospitalization, drug changes, and dosage escalation, the girl's mother began questioning the drugs the doctors administered. Through her research online, the mother saw similar cases of individuals who experienced identical side effects resulting from the same drugs her daughter had been prescribed.

The mother and daughter agreed the girl would stop taking the prescription pills. Upon discontinuation of the drugs, and after much time suffering the aftermath of their physical withdrawal effects, the daughter returned to her normal teenage self. Still, she continued to live with the cutting scars that covered her body. The mother sought an attorney and filed a lawsuit against the pharmaceutical manufacturers.

Shocked and intrigued, I immediately went online and searched for adverse reactions resulting from psychotropic pharmaceutical drugs like the Selective Serotonin Reuptake Inhibitor/SSRI I was first prescribed, my pink pill. I discovered a checklist of answers for me:

Nervous System effects included: Depersonalization (feelings of existing outside oneself), Derealization (feelings of existing outside of reality), Hallucinations, Heightened Feelings of Grandiosity, Mood Swings, Mania, Anxiety, Violent Tendencies, Aggression, Agitation, Chills, Trembles, Convulsions, Alcohol Abuse, Drug Abuse, Amnesia, Lack of Coordination, Lack of Emotion, Manic Reactions, Paranoid Reactions, Abnormal Thinking.

More drug effect symptoms continued: Insomnia, Akathisia (urge to move about constantly with an inability to sit still), Extravagant Spending, Religious Preoccupation, Severe Weight Change, Akinesia (paralysis of the muscles causing intense pain), Hyperkinesia (abnormally increased mobility, motor function, and activity), Hypertonia (excessive tone and tension), Difficulty in Coordinating Muscles, Irregular Muscle Action, Conjunctivitis, Ear Pain, Eye Pain, Mydriasis (extreme dilation of the pupils), Pain, Fever, Hearing Abnormalities, Deafness, Tinnitus, and Vertigo.

Reading that and recalling the body rushes, zaps, and eye zigzags I experienced, I felt more disgusted. I quickly realized the flood of spiritual communication I had so desperately and psychotically believed in 2001 was nothing more than chemical reactions attributed to the prescription drug toxicity in my system. That was far worse than any headache, dry mouth, nausea, or yawn mentioned in the colorful pamphlet I received—the pamphlet the doctor handed me when he initially prescribed me the SSRI and included a one-year prescription.

Taking note of the attorney's name in the newspaper, the one the mother had attained for her daughter, I located his phone number and made the call. To my great relief, the attorney invited me to the office where we would discuss my case.

There, in the attorney's office in early 2004, I learned many more people lived stories like mine. I was not alone. Class action lawsuits flooded the courts with hearings that the media would not report. Media companies received millions of dollars for pharmaceutical drug advertising campaigns, all the while, silently, thousands upon thousands of normal, average Americans experienced similar drug reactions like I endured. Most sadly, not as many had survived. Astounded, discovering I was not alone, I set out to network with others who battled the traumas associated with psychotic prescription drugs.

I drove to Washington DC and attended a rally on Pennsylvania Avenue outside the White House, organized by other American citizens harmed by pharmaceutical psychiatric drugs. There, I met parents of children who had been prescribed medications for so-called "mental health disorders" that included attention deficit and social anxiety. Others took the drugs simply for the "high" they gave and because they were readily available to them in school. Many of the children committed suicide in horrific ways. Many were drugged for simply being kids with childhood or puberty disorders.

Another man was there with his two teenage boys. He described to me how his beautiful, happy wife shot and killed herself in front of their children. She did so after only one week of taking a medication; she had gallbladder disease and was prescribed Wellbutrin.

Another young survivor was there. He was a creative boy from a broken home who was diagnosed with depression. He made the rounds through doctors, hospitals, and mental facilities. Each visit brought about a change in medication, increase in dosage, or combination of a few: over 300 milligrams prescribed a day! That young boy found a gun, put it to his head while in the boys' bathroom at his middle school, and pulled the trigger. The gun fired, jolted the boy, causing the bullet to strike the bathroom door. The loud sound alerted teachers, who stormed into the bathroom stall, and the police took the boy into custody.

I spoke with a survivor from Columbine, Mark Taylor. He was shot multiple times and taken to the morgue, where they eventually discovered he was still alive. He remained tortured. Detained. Forcibly drugged. Who cared? I did.

Husbands, wives, widows, parents—they each wanted to talk to me, asking questions about my experience. They wanted to know what I felt and thought at the time of my prescription intoxication—moreover, how I survived it. How did I survive when their loved one did not? It overwhelmed me as I tried to comfort their loss, explaining to the families how their loved ones experienced no pain in their final moments of life. From my personal experience, the deceased would never have rationalized death while in their drug-induced state and condition. It was a manifested delusion.

I described how during a toxic prescription psychosis, separation of self and reality distorted the individual in such a way that, for example, an induced individual may believe they could slice themselves open, pull out their heart, set it on a table, and step back to look at it, all the while, still breathing. All things were possible. Moreover, anesthetized in the psychotic prescription drug-induced state, any escape from the insanity was welcomed without any remorse, regard, or pain. Somehow, as sad as it was to me, the families seemed comforted. They were assured that their loved ones passed on with peace, even if it was a tormented delusion.

September 1, 2004, I wrote to First Lady Laura Bush, a schoolteacher. In my letter, I expressed my discontent with the lack of attention or concern surrounding the mass labeling of children as having mental health disorders, accompanied by the mass-prescribing of psychotropic pharmaceutical drugs. I emphasized to her how many children were tortured and committed suicide as a direct result of pharmaceutical drug toxicity. Even more, drug companies themselves had admitted that most psychiatric drugs had never been tested long-term or on people under the age of 18. Worse, pharmaceutical drug advertisements prevented the media (who profited from the revenue of the ads) from reporting on the prescription drug-induced psychosis, suicides, and homicides that jeopardized the health and safety of children, adults, our communities, and society. I asked First Lady Laura Bush to take a stand on the issue to help save lives. She remained mute.

In 2005, an open stall became available at a horse farm near my parents' house. It was the same farm where I used to ride when I was a young girl. Knowing the time and money it would save me, plus the beautiful fields it had for Chad to run, I once again loaded Chad into the horse trailer and moved him to another horse farm, Pioneer Stables, only ten minutes from my parents' house.

More time passed. More tours rolled.

In 2006, with all my heart, I thanked God I was home from touring when a dreaded day came to be; my Simon had to be rushed to the hospital. Simon had been suffering from bone cancer. Unable to speak through the grief in detail, earlier that year, Simon had his front right leg amputated and had undergone chemotherapy treatments. He was a trooper. But the bone cancer had returned in his back leg, and the doctors said nothing else could be done.

I took Simon home to spend a last night with him. Unable to walk, I bought Simon a puppy stroller and placed him inside. Together with my boy, we took our last stroll around the neighborhood. We listened to the birds and squirrels and visited all of Simon's dog friends in their backyards along the way. The neighbors came up to us and gave Simon their affection. He was loved and adored by so many. Eleven-year-old Simon had a sparkling twinkle in his eyes despite his circumstances. His zest for life was still inside him. Simon and I lay together on the front lawn in the sun, like Simon loved so much to do. It was warm; we slept. I did not want to ever get up. My broken heart cannot bear to share any more on that...

One workday on tour in some city, USA, I was going about my usual work when my wrist began to throb in a familiar way. My finger became numb and tingly as it did when I was at Camille's house in Florida. I could not pick up the iron. I took advantage of a moment with our tour Rock Doc and explained the sensations to him while backstage. He informed me I was likely experiencing Carpal Tunnel Syndrome and suggested I take supplements of Omega 3s and Vitamin B-6, plus wear a special support band on my arm. I followed his advice, and the pain subsided quickly without any escalation or further treatments. Carpal Tunnel Syndrome. Who knew. Obviously, not the doctors in Florida.

September 13, 2006, my "Pharma-Harmed" network and I made another trip to Washington, DC. That time, we walked Capitol Hill. We stopped in the offices of Congressional representatives who were on the governing committees related to health, including drugs, pharmaceuticals, and the FDA. We had a forty-five-minute meeting with Robert Clark in the Office of Congressman Frank Pallone of New Jersey. Another meeting with Marcus Rayner, in the Office of Congressman Mike Ferguson of New Jersey, who was Vice Chairman of the Health Subcommittee. Another hour meeting with Emma Palmer in the Office of Senator Robert Menendez of New Jersey. And a meeting with Brandon Clark, in the Office of Congressman Nathan Deal from Georgia, who was the senior policy maker for the Subcommittee on Health.

Our goal was to get prescription psychotropic drug warnings out to the public. That included drug warnings, not cautions, on all drug bottles, ensuring each and every person subjected to a psychiatric prescription drug would be fully and completely warned of any and all side effects from that drug. In addition, a full-disclosing handout must accompany the prescription and the pill bottle. Informed Consent; that was our goal. The women I accompanied needed no map for the Capitol; they were mothers fighting for their children and had been around The Hill many times before. I, on the other hand, should not have worn heels.

Surprising or not, one of the representative assistants was particularly attuned to the prescription drug cause because he, too, had a friend who had experienced the psychotic adverse drug effects. The ladies who were with me played a heart-wrenching video for him; it included footage from the FDA hearings in 1991, including a woman who testified how her father, an elderly man, fell victim to the effects of his prescribed medication. That woman found her father in the kitchen with a butcher knife, repeatedly stabbing himself in his stomach until he died.

My quest for justice driving me, I sought more answers and knowledge. October 7-9, 2006, as a victim of the pharmaceutically harmed community, I was able to attend a conference outside Washington, DC. It was hosted by ICSPP, the International Center for the Study of Psychiatry and Psychology. The big conference included presentations from world-renowned doctors, authors, researchers, professors, lawyers, medical directors, psychiatrists, and psychologists. Also welcomed were victims like myself and loved ones of those whose lives were taken before their time due to pharmaceutical drug toxicity and adverse effects from pill discontinuation.

At the conference, I listened and took extensive notes from speakers and graduates of Columbia University, Oxford, Penn State, Johns Hopkins, and Brown University, to name a few. The conference was three full days, with topics including adverse reactions to ingesting pharmaceutical psychotropic drugs, toxicity and trauma from discontinuation of the drugs, law, civil rights, human rights, legal rights, history, science, chemical composition, school systems, and criminal accountability. There, I learned how American society was forever altered when drugs like Ritalin were introduced into our homes some- time in the late 1980s.

Some of my notes from the conference:

Prozac hit the market in 1988. 1989: the first recorded case of an individual taking prescription psychotropic medications, experiencing severe behavioral change, and murdering his family.

1990: the pharmaceutical companies defend their territory, spinning doctors with the belief that violent aggressions and mania are not produced by the drugs but rather by the depression and disorder itself. Prescribe more. Increase patient dose.

1991: Due to public concern and outrage, the FDA held its first Psycho-pharmacologic Drug Advisory Committee Hearing on the subject of suicidal thoughts associated with prescription antidepressant drugs.

1997: Suddenly, pharmaceutical manufacturers were permitted to engage in Direct-to-Consumer Marketing of prescription drugs to the American public. Soon, cartoon commercials began flooding the television; magazine pages filled with advertisements of man-made prescription psychotic drugs that promised to help depression, anxiety, and panic attacks. Pharmaceutical sales soared.

The tragedy of Columbine High School was blamed on gun laws and poor parenting. More psychotropic drugs flooded the markets.

More lawsuits were quietly filed and more innocent lives silently destroyed: Forsyth vs. Eli Lilly, March 1991. Tobin vs. SmithKline, June 2001.

In 2004, public outrage again forced the FDA to hold a Psychophar-macologic Drug Advisory Committee Hearing. As a result, a Black Box Warning noting danger and caution was given for psychotropic drug use in children and adolescents.

May 2006: Pharmaceutical companies were forced to acknowledge suicide causality associated with their products. Preemption, TORT Reform, tainted test study reports, suicides, homicides; drug sales flourished, and the country crumbled.

It was a very enlightening conference and a comfort to be with others who understood my trauma well. I found their knowledge and empathy healing.

October 10, 2006: The woman and her daughter, whose story I initially read about in the newspaper, along with a few others from our pharmaceutically harmed community, were invited to a sit-down meeting with Congressman Mike Ferguson in his Warren Township, New Jersey office. The meeting was also attended via conference phone by Senior Legislative Assistant-Lead Healthcare Policy Advisor, Tom Fussaro. They listened as the young girl with scars of slashes covering her arms and I told of our terrifying and near-death adverse reactions to the prescription drugs. For an hour and a half, the Congressman listened and asked questions. He vowed he would research the subject and address the issue and crisis at hand.

I continued touring, working, missing Simon, enjoying home with Chad and the bunnies between gigs for a few days here and there. I continued remembering what happened to me in Florida and pursuing my quest for justice. Not only was I seeking truth for myself, but even more so, grace for those who no longer had the same luxury of life. My strength was to always remember I was not alone.

Headline news began reporting and exposing case after case of Catholic priests molesting young boys. I recalled my 2001 visit to the priest in Florida. He thought I was frightful. Maybe his fears really had nothing to do with me.

Thankfully, I knew myself best and was doing fine with no incidents and no "medications." Life without the pink pill was back to normal for me on the road.

On the road and out of nowhere, I received an email from Camille! It had been years since we last spoke. Camille wrote that she and Jerry had been married almost two years by then. They had a romantic wedding on the beach, and Native American prayers were read. Camille was still in Florida. Helen had since passed away. Camille went on to thank me for the experience that had terrorized her home and traumatized me so. She said it took a few years for her to get to that point, but she wanted to thank me. Elaborating on that, Camille attributed the experience to the evolution of her own personal self-development and the strength it gave her to be the woman she yearned to become. After I was taken from her home, Camille resisted believing Jerry was 'The One,' but the traumatic experience had also altered Jerry into his own personal growth, and he soon became her rock.

I responded to Camille's email, sharing all the information I had discovered. I told her about the efforts I had made regarding pharmaceutical drug safety, warnings of prescription drug side effects, and drug-induced deaths they had caused. Hoping to assure her, I directed Camille toward information on the Internet. Knowing the reality of the drug-induced destruction I crazily caused upon Camille, her friends, and her community, I felt there was no way to apologize enough: so much sorrow and shame. I was grateful the road to our lifelong friendship was on its way toward restoration. Our Sisterhood lived on.

All day on television, on nearly every channel, commercials for antidepressant drugs pitched their song. Women's magazines and ladies' journals, all drowned in drug advertisements with cute critters and pretty pictures painting the pages with promises of peace – take this drug, and too will live in a beautiful world of happiness and bliss. The direct-to-consumer marketing of prescription drugs was everywhere. All the while, I pictured the banned and prohibited Joe Camel slumped in a bar sitting next to the illicit Marlboro Man and ordering a Budweiser with the forbidden dog, Spuds MacKenzie. The news reported a grandma was jailed for growing a natural cannabis weed created from earth, seed, sun, water, air: she trusted in God.

A "Teen Screen" program took the scene in American schools. Kids were classified and diagnosed as having mental health mayhems, disorders in the classrooms: ADD, ADHD, Bi-Polar, and Schizophrenic. More disorders were compiled in the big book, the DSM, Diagnostic and Statistical Manual of Mental Disorders. More children were labeled, diagnosed, and drugged. Prescribing "off-label" became the norm. Mental health drugs expanded: restless leg syndrome pills; toe fungus pills; even asthma pills required daily, in addition to the asthma breath inhaler formerly used on average only twice a week.

December 2006, I was once again preparing for my next tour when I received a phone call informing me the FDA was planning to hold another Psychopharmacologic Drug Advisory Committee Hearing mid-month. It was scheduled exactly one day before I had to leave for the road. Even though the hearing was in Washington, DC, plus I had a flight scheduled from New Jersey to California early the morning after, I submitted my name to speak. There was a lottery to bear witness; most fortunately, that was a lottery I won! With only two weeks to prepare, I would be given exactly three minutes to testify before the panel of the FDA.

I quickly realized three minutes was a very short amount of time to tell all that had happened to me. Spending days at the horse farm with Chad and my bunnies, I did my best to prepare a speech that would fit into such a short period. On the days leading up to the hearing, I cut words and sentences from my speech while I timed the reading repeatedly for length. I recruited a friend from the barn, Debbie, and the farm owner, Jewell, to listen and give their thoughts. I appreciated their patience.

December 13, 2006, I went to Washington, DC once more. That time I was going to share my adverse pharmaceutical drug experience before a committee of the FDA! I wore a black pencil skirt and heels, and I had designed a special T-shirt for the event: a black T-shirt with the word "SURVIVOR" embroidered on the front. The "R" had a line drawn through it, indicating Rx. I also compiled a folder of information about my experience, including a copy of my FDA testimony. I made enough folders, which matched the T-shirt, to give to every member of the FDA Advisory Hearing Panel there that day.

My T-shirt and the folder provided at the
FDA Psychopharmacologic Drug
Advisory Committee Hearing, 2006

All morning I watched scientists, medical professionals, and pharmaceutical drug company representatives give presentations of evidence, both pro and con. Various research work, marketing studies,
grants, graphs, and tables were viewed, and test studies riddled with
payoffs exposed. Lunchtime came, and we broke for an hour.

The second part of the day consisted of public testimonies. One by
one, story after story, many were ruthless and grueling. One mother,
Mathy Downing, stood at the podium to speak about her eleven-year-
old daughter, Candace Downing. A group of loved ones stood silently
beside Mathy, each holding up various posters and pictures of a very
happy and adorable Candace doing the many things she loved in life.
That mother testified to the FDA that her daughter had been given
a blue pill antidepressant for test anxiety at school. As the doctor
increased her dosage, Candace began experiencing hallucinations, fever, elevated heart rate and blood pressure. Hospitalized, the doctors
administered even more of the anxiety and antidepressant drugs to
Candace. Released and at home, the mother walked into her daughter's
bedroom days later and found that while in a drug-induced psychotic
state, Candace had hanged herself from her canopy bed.

A wife, Kim Witczak, testified how her husband, Woody, who was not struggling with depression and had no history of suicidality, was given Zoloft for difficulty sleeping. Soon thereafter, Woody experienced akathisia, anxiety, tremors, and was heard screaming while in the fetal position, "Help me, help me! I don't know what is happening to me. I am losing my mind! It's like my head is outside my body looking in!" Woody was found hanging from the rafters of his garage. His wife, Kim, testified, "It wasn't Woody's head. It was the drug." Woody mattered.

With bullet remnants still inside his body, Mark Taylor, a student shot multiple times in the 1999 Columbine High School massacre, testified that day. Mark previously sued Solvay Pharmaceuticals, claiming their antidepressant drug, Luvox, made Eric Harris psychotic and violent.

Food and Drug Administration
Psychopharmacologic Drugs Advisory Committee
December 13, 2006

**Open Public Hearing
Speaker # 63**

The speaker ID sticker provided to me by
the FDA in order to testify that day

Another number was called; number 63! It was my turn to speak! Rising from my seat and walking to the podium where the microphone was, I faced the panel and presented them with my story. While others thanked the panel for listening, I began my testimony by thanking MYSELF for the miracle of my being here today. With every spoken word, my passion grew; I felt relief knowing I would finally be heard. I spoke with clarity and conviction, wanting to ensure that the FDA Committee truly understood the severity of these drug dangers and what I was trying to express. December 13, 2006, before the

Psychopharmacologic Drug Advisory Committee of the FDA, directly from the transcript that day, I testified:

0266

1   (Applause.)

2   DR. PINE: Thank you.

3   The next speaker is Dawn Jeronowitz.

4   MS. JERONOWITZ: I would like to thank

5 myself for the miracle of my being here today. In

6 2001, healthy, thirty-one and with no troubled

7 history, I went to a doctor concerned about pain in

8 my finger.

9   Finding nothing broken, his diagnosis was

10 anxiety. He prescribed an SSRI for one year. Upon

11 intake, I became high, high developed into

12 euphoria, euphoria intensified to grandiose, until

13 mania overtook me.

14   I lived delusions, paranoia, insomnia;

15 endured radical, obsessive, irrational antics; fly-

16 on crazy. Oblivious, other people noticed.

17   Within weeks, having lost 22 pounds, I

18 was taken into police custody after running and

19 screaming through the neighborhood. I kicked out

20 the police car window barefoot, then dove through

21 the shattered glass.

22   The emergency room described, "Impaired,

0267

1 disheveled, impulsive, combative, threatening,

2 depersonalization, derealization, acute

3 psychosis."

4   Held in four-point restraints, I was

5 committed to a mental crisis facility. Days after

6 my release, law enforcement came again when I

7 myself called 911 twelve times repeatedly. Police

8 arrived to find me locked in the house, razor in

9 hand, screaming to kill myself while begging police

10 to do it for me.

11   I was forced into total appendage

12 restraint position. Again, I was committed to a

13 mental crisis facility for suicidal ideation. My

14 words on an antidepressant, "I will sacrifice my

15 living breath and return to the sea of my

16 Mother Earth, drown, car off bridge. Drugs?

17 Death."

18   "Prescription suicide" is simple: A

19 delusion manifested to actualize an escape from

20 madness. Optimum because induced insanity is so

21 horrific that living as such is more petrifying

22 than death itself -- comparatively, a relief.

0268

1   Make no medicinal mistake, SSRIs are

2 hardcore, mind-altering legal drugs --

3 overprescribed, addictive, and deadly.

4   Unlike illegal drugs, however,

5 prescription high does not subside, rather it

6 swells higher to toxic levels masking itself in

7 diagnosis while deflecting culpability. To end it:

8 withdrawal, suicide.

9   Victimized, I filed a lawsuit against a

10 pharmaceutical manufacturer mass marketing such a

11 treatment knowingly, criminally failing to warn

12 doctors, patients and the FDA of lethal consequence

13 and poor efficacy.

14   Offered a settlement and gag order, I am

15 able to speak today because I rejected that

16 proposal. My case continues onward. I stand

17 before you the powers that be giving you my

18 experience. Now alerted and informed, I trust the

19 policies you produce will be epic.

20   I appreciate your time. Thank you.

21   (Applause.)

22   DR. PINE: Thank you.

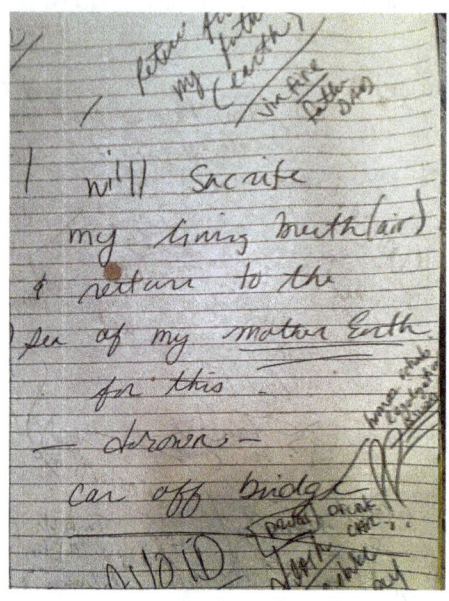

Pharmaceutical Drug induced suicidal ideation, 2001

Completing my testimony, I turned, saluted, and returned to my seat. The speaker called out the next number. One man took a stand and walked to the microphone for his three minutes of time and testimony. Surely his wife would have liked to testify, such as I had the opportunity to do, but her husband was there that day, and these are the words he spoke:

0269

1   The next speaker is Allen Routhier.

2   MR. ROUTHIER: This is a circus sideshow.

3 The FDA has known all about antidepressant-induced

4 suicidality at least as far back as the hearings in

5 '91. This is the third time I'm doing this. And

6 for what? I don't expect the FDA to do the right

7 thing. They have had plenty of chances, and their

8 record is abysmal.

9   My beautiful 40-year-old wife of 18 years

10 was murdered. She was sick with undiagnosed

11 gallbladder attack and the doctor she sought help

12 from poisoned her with an unmarked, free sample of

13 Wellbutrin.

14   After a week of severe adverse effects,

15 she took her own life in a toxic psychosis. I

16 blame Glaxo and the FDA. You invaded my home

17 insidiously. These twisted mercenaries have been

18 hiding suicides and homicides for years.

19   The FDA's own head of Drug Safety,

20 Dr. David Graham says it seems the FDA has declared

21 war on the American people and has now become the

22 number one threat to their health and safety.

0270

1   Black boxes only cover financial

2 liability and attempt at preemption. How do you

3 put a price tag on someone's life? This can't be

4 covered up any longer. Too many lives have been

5 and are still being destroyed.

6   We all know antidepressants cause

7 suicides by their terrible side-effects. It's all

8 there in the "PDR." The same dubious benefits that

9 can be achieved with crack can never outweigh the

10 risk of killing innocence.

11   The time for secrets is over. The word

12 is out. Any idiot advocating the use of poison is

13 part of the problem. The young, sick, old, or

14 simply genetically unsuited can be especially

15 vulnerable to the toxic effects.

16   We are told these toxic chemicals may

17 balance something, although there is no measure,

18 yet they admit they don't even know how

19 antidepressants work. People who think they are
20 being helped by staying high are facing serious
21 health ramifications.
22   We are being lied to by killers.
0271
 1 Clinical trials are riddled with suicides even
 2 though suicidal people are excluded from
 3 participating. We all know people hurt by these
 4 drugs. This is huge.
 5   We need to shine light on this
 6 unspeakable darkness to reveal it for what it is.
 7 Drug company cheerleaders are being paid to
 8 perpetuate this nightmare. Pushers keep spewing
 9 that it is dangerous not to drug people. It's all
10 about the billions in profit.
11   The FDA is bought out. Prove me wrong.
12 Do something now. Sorry if you can't handle the
13 truth, but the poisoning of my wife has left me
14 bereft and bitter.
15   This should not be a civil matter; this
16 is criminal. We need new Nuremberg trials. This
17 is all old news and just the price of doing
18 business.
19   Why are we here? What kind of b.s. do
20 you have for us victims this time? What kind of
21 black box to cover your liable asses this time?
22 What kind of obfuscations for the media? How
0272
 1 manipulated is this entire proceeding when we have
 2 a lottery to be allowed to speak with a few weeks
 3 notice to deliver our three minutes less than two
 4 weeks before Christmas?
 5   (Cheers and applause.)
 6   MR. ROUTHIER: Kill one person, you're a

7   murderer. Redeem yourselves. Get the warnings

8   out. Let the media report it. If you think we're

9   going away, you are on drugs.

10   (Applause.)

11   DR. PINE: Thank you.

Following testimony upon testimony of victim stories, and after another short break, the FDA panel then discussed the evidence before them. One dilemma the panel faced was knowing that, due to continued and increased public outrage regarding prescription drugs, they must do something pertaining to the drug warnings.

The FDA panel was hesitant to add drug warnings, alluding that if they did, it may, in turn, deter the public from seeking 'treatment' for disorders and depression. Certainly, they emphasized, the depression disease could produce suicidal and homicidal tendencies and, if not treated with the medications, may become a problem. One panel member actually suggested the FDA could include a "White Box Warning" next to the "Black Box Warning," thus insinuating that the white box was not as bad as the black box but should be heeded with caution. As if a warning could be anything else.

It was painful for me to watch the members of the FDA panel go on without any sense or wits about the words they spewed while trying to protect themselves and monetary interests. The full transcript available in the FDA archives was well worth the read, but the video would surely be something to watch.

The panel began to consider age limits. As the Black Box Warning stood, children and adolescents should be warned. To satisfy the work of the day, the FDA then suggested they could increase the age warning to "young adults, under twenty-five." Bemused, sitting there in the front row, I watched as the FDA panel wanted to put another age limit on how a drug would affect a body. Absolutely outrageous. Objecting, I stood up, and the words came out. "Thirty-one. I was thirty-one!" The looks turned in my direction. I sat down.

Appalled, I could not believe the very same FDA panel had spent the entire day witnessing victim stories that included a man of sixty-five, a woman of forty-nine, another seventy-eight, thirty-eight, six, twenty-two, fourteen, fifty-nine, thirty-one—all who committed unspeakable acts of violence and madness against themselves or others due to the effects of psychotropic prescription drugs prescribed to them by their health care provider, and advertised on TV. Now the panel was talking about age limits? My goodness, the drugs didn't care if they were inside the living body of a mouse, chimp, rabbit, dog, horse, or human, much less mind their age. The drugs did their neurological chemical work, regardless.

Time was ticking; I had to catch the train back to Jersey and prepare for my early morning flight to California.

The panel was still in discussion when I had to leave for the train. Along the ride home, another attendee from the hearing called me with the news. Apparently, after I left, the FDA panel voted to extend the prescription psychotropic drug Black Box Warnings that included changes in thoughts, moods, and behaviors, plus suicidal thoughts and actions up to the age of twenty-four: children, teens, and 'young adults.' That was especially concerning because the psychotic drugs were neither tested nor approved for young consumers and were being prescribed to them off-label. *How many more drug advisory committee hearings would it take?* I wondered.

USA Today Newspaper reporting on the FDA expansion of Suicide Warnings, Black Box Warnings on pharmaceutical antidepressant drugs.
© *Marilyn Elias – USA TODAY NETWORK December 14, 2006*

The following afternoon, December 14, 2006, and a couple of time-zone changes later, I found myself inside a California rehearsal studio talking with the performing artists I would be working with. My phone rang. Excusing myself from the performers, I stepped outside and listened as my attorney, who also attended the FDA hearing, told me how the pharmaceutical drug manufacturer was furious about my testimony in DC the day before. Well now. I, too, was pretty darn mad about the whole ordeal I had been subjected to, so I simply responded, "I am at work with an artist right now and am not going to discuss the subject at this time. All I have to say is, me too." I hung up the phone, turned off the ringer, and went back to work.

Time passed. Tours rolled.

2007, Britney Spears' year of meltdown happened; the footage of her antics, police encounters, and hospitalizations was especially disturbing to me as they were plastered around every supermarket, newsstand, television station, web page, and coffee house I encountered. My own bizarre pharmaceutical drug-induced experience was virtually mirrored before my eyes.

April 16, 2007: A Virginia Tech college campus massacre left thirty-two people dead, thirty-three including the suicide of the shooter. The perpetrator was twenty-three-year-old Seung-Hui Cho, revealed to be a patient in and out of psychiatric facilities, and prescribed pharmaceutical psychotropic drugs. According to an *NBC News* article by M. Alex Johnson, "Gunman sent package to NBC News," Cho had sent a disturbing manifesto that included videos and photographs to news networks. The *Wikipedia* page for Seung-Hui Cho, and, an *ABC News* article by Terry Moran, "Inside Cho's Mind," report Cho had struggled with mental health issues since his childhood. The *ABC News* article said: "His family and others had gotten him help – including counseling and medication." It also reports about the psychiatric medication Cho had taken, which eerily reminded me of my own 2001 experience with my pink pill. Although officials said no drugs were found in the toxicology results from Cho's autopsy, a *NY Times* article by Manny Fernandez and Marc Santora, "Gunman showed signs of anger," reports prescription medications related to the treatment of psychiatric problems were found with Cho's belongings. Even more, his roommate said he saw Cho take a prescription medication, but did not know what the medication was for.

That same year a gorgeous yet heavily pharmaceutically-drugged TV reality star, Anna Nicole Smith, died, as did her son. Both were senseless, needless prescription drug-induced deaths.

My Jezbah bunny and I also lost our dear Loocia in August that same year. My poor baby Jezbah was heartbroken at the loss of his companion; he mourned and grieved after I presented him with Loocia's body, allowing him to understand she would not be returning home to him. I got Jezbah a stuffed bunny to help with his sorrow. Soon, I discovered an old barn friend had found a domestic bunny underneath a car. I adopted that bunny into our family; Jezbah missed his Loocia partner but found a little comfort in his new Indie bunny friend.

January 2008, I was on tour, working in Australia. News reports flooded in. The hometown hero, Heath Ledger, had died. A *Teen Rehab* article, "Heath Ledger's Prescription Drug Abuse Equals a Wake-Up Call," reports that the toxicology analysis of Ledger's autopsy revealed "acute intoxication by the combined effects of oxycodone, hydrocodone, diazepam, temazepam, alprazolam, and doxylamine." While I was coincidentally in his hometown of Perth, Australia, at the time of Heath Ledger's death, I had a conversation with a taxi driver who drove me around town. I told the driver about the prescription drug epidemic plaguing America. Shocked and appalled, the taxi driver could not accept that prescription drugs were so easily and widely administered and obtained in the United States, moreover, used for recreation. He said that did not happen in Australia. There were no commercials that advertised drugs. He said in Australia, their doctors talked to them. They had real doctors, not merely prescribers. I told the taxi driver this joker was no joke.

Valentine's Day: February 14, 2008, I was working in rehearsals on the campus of Northern Illinois University in Dekalb, Illinois, when we were suddenly ordered into a lockdown. Word spread quickly that a gunman had entered a classroom and was gunning down fellow students. Instantly, as the shooting unfolded on campus, my instinct sensed it was another case of prescription drug-induced insanity.

In the backstage catering area where I was seated, students stared at the television in astonishment. The news reported the happenings just a few hundred feet away from us. We remained inside a building, hoping it was safe. Shock, horror; students were silenced into mourning. Their questions and disbelief filled the air. The shooter killed five people that day. He then committed suicide.

It was cold and snowy, but the students still gathered in outdoor memorials and candlelight vigils. My heart broke for them. I talked with a few students there, alerting them to the symptoms associated with psychiatric medication-induced insanity.

In the following days, news reports, including a *CNN* article by Abbie Boudreau and Scott Zamost, "Girlfriend: Shooter was taking cocktail of 3 drugs," confirmed my intuition. The shooter, twenty-seven years old, Steven Kazmierczak, had been diagnosed with a 'mental health disorder' and was reportedly under the influence of Xanax, Ambien, and Prozac.

My parents called me one day while I was on the road. "We bought ourselves a birthday present," my mom stated.

"Really!" I said. "What did you get?"

"A house," my mom replied.

A house? Fortunately, I came off the road just in time. My parents had sold my childhood home and were moving to South Jersey. Packing and reminiscing, I remembered to check all the hidden nooks and crannies but failed to find my childhood time capsule.

Not wanting to move Chad again or have a long drive to see him when I was on a short pitstop at home, I opted to accept Jewell's offer, and I moved into a deserted 1960s mobile home permanently nestled in the woods located at Pioneer Stables; the farm where Chad and the bunnies lived safely. I would then be able to fully care for Chad when I was home from touring. Bonus: we could ride on the trails all day! At seven years old, Chad loved his saddle. To ride, I simply clipped reins to his halter; no bit or bridle needed.

The outside of the mobile home appeared as an old, dirty trailer. But, on the inside, I created a masterpiece! I even impressed myself with the demolition and design I turned out. I actually bought my first coffee table and couch. Living on the farm saved a lot of time and money when I only had a week off the road at home. More time spent with Chad.

17

Another Mile

It was August 2008 when I found myself at last sitting on my own couch inside my little trailer hut tucked into a back field at Pioneer Stables and enjoying a little time off tour. I could simply wake up, walk a minute to the barn, and feed Chad—a welcome delight. Jezbah and Indie inhabited an old empty stall and had quite the bunny setup. Jezbah especially loved coming inside the trailer hut. He adored watching TV and human conversations; a social bunny indeed! Relaxing afternoons on the farm were spent lazing in the meadow. My next tour was not scheduled to begin for a few more weeks.

At last, summer in New Jersey with friends and off the road again. Debbie and her daughter, along with Jewell, her toddler, and I went to enjoy a relaxing weekend down the shore. Jewell's in-laws had a beach condo where we could stay.

We were having a fun time splashing in the ocean, watching the toddler delight in feeding swarms of seagulls when Jewell said she was taking the toddler back to the condo for a diaper change. Debbie and I remained on the beach. Over an hour passed, and still Jewell and the toddler had not returned. Packing up beach towels and toys, we headed back to the condo to check on them.

Entering the condo, Debbie and I discovered Jewell passed out on the floor. Sitting beside her and softly tapping her mother was the toddler uttering words, "Okay, Mommy." Debbie and I looked at each other with concern, then proceeded to shake Jewell and call her name. Jewell woke disorientated, saying she had just fallen asleep.

Back at the farm, Chad was enjoying having me home almost as much as he enjoyed his large grassy paddock and horse friends. One of the mares belonging to a distinguished gentleman, Cliff, was pregnant and expecting very soon. We were all looking forward to the birth of the foal.

One morning, I walked to the barn in my usual routine, fed Chad, and checked on my bunnies. In the bunny stall, I saw Jezbah lying still; immediately, I knew. Jezbah had passed over; my baby blue eyes had gone to reunite in Heaven with his Loocia girl. I was thankful that each passed on while I was home and off tour.

That evening, I had the very sad task of digging up the box where I had buried Loocia the previous year. At that time, I had prepared the little bunny coffin for this day, all the while knowing eventually, Jezbah would need a space beside his life partner. The day had come; we buried my bunny boy beside his love. The following morning, we woke on the farm to a foal; a baby colt had been born, Sparky.

News spread of Sparky's birth, and by late morning a celebratory gathering at the farm had assembled. Removing mom and baby Sparky from the same paddock where Chad lived, Cliff walked them to a fenced field area in the back, closer to my hut. Sparky had such wobbly legs! Each morning when I woke, on my way to feed Chad, baby Sparky greeted me with big eyes of wonder and mischievous play. I made sure to keep extra cookies in my pocket.

Early fall had rolled around; evening campfires were in order. Jewell, her husband, their many friends, and even some family relaxed in a circle of flames to keep warm. Music, laughs, conversation, an occasional drunk ride on a horse; I began to notice a pattern of Jewell escaping inside the house only to return sometime later, seemingly jumpy. I continued to observe.

I received a phone call from the production manager of my upcoming tour and learned that the position would not happen after all. My plans for that tour were instantly over; I would have more time at home in the hut.

Debbie would come to the farm early in the mornings; she took complete care of her horse, Moosie. Moosie and Chad were the best of friends; we often let them roam freely around the farm together. Chad was a black beauty by that time in his life, and Moosie was a slim blue-eyed girl, mostly white with brown paint horse markings. The two horses would graze and roam while Debbie and I talked and discussed our concerns about Jewell and her husband. As the two had been a perfect, beautiful young couple in their late twenties, lovebirds with a gorgeous child to boot, I noticed lately that Jewell and her husband were displaying many peculiar behaviors.

After spending much time working on tour and missing daily goings-on at the barn, I quickly began to see a view of the Pioneer Stable that I had never been exposed to before. Often, I would notice shortages of feed, hay, and bedding. Many mornings Jewell slept in, I supposed, as the horses remained locked and unfed in their stalls. Debbie and I began to feed, water, turn out, and clean stalls. Unnerved, by October, I knew I had to have a talk with Jewell. Apparently, the behavior had been going on for some time.

Debbie came to the hut; we called Jewell to come down. Expressing my concerns about the farm and horses, I continued the conversation regarding my suspicion of drug abuse and disgust, knowing my board and rent money would be utilized for such a purpose. Given all that I had survived already, I could not stand the thought of my hard-earned dollars supplying drugs that would jeopardize the safety and well-being of my horse. Jewell confirmed my suspicions but assured me it wasn't that bad; she would do better with her management of the farm.

As winter months began, things did not improve. Jewell was a skeleton of her former self, and her husband appeared slightly de-ranged and went unshaven for weeks. Passing their house on my way down the driveway to the hut, I would often see the toddler staring out alone from the window. Inside, her parents were likely still asleep; her diaper not changed for days. There was no childproofing done, and electric sockets were certainly within reach. When Jewell's heavily medicated father shot a bullet into his jacket over a broken zipper, I knew the problem was seriously deep.

Christmas Day 2008 was not a very merry day for sure. Thank God I was staying onsite in the hut. While Jewell never came out of the house, I spent the entire day alone with the horses, tending to all the chores on the farm. While the horses grazed peacefully in the field, I cleaned the stalls and thought about all the filth and addiction. Finally, there came a point where I just had had enough; buckets flew as I kicked them inside the barn. This was bullshit. I vowed to get myself and Chad away from that place.

The very next day, December 26, 2008, I began my search to buy a home. The country was at the height of a recession, and the banks had stopped their generosity with loans; however, a first-time homebuyer rebate was available, and I was prepared to take advantage of that. So, having saved enough money for a healthy deposit, I went to see houses that very day, knowing I only had until spring to seal the deal; another tour was lined up for then.

Given the desperate situation of increasing drug-induced madness at the farm, I was relentless in my search for a home. New Year's Day, snow and all, I dragged the realtor and my folks to see an old farmhouse on nine acres in the heart of New Jersey horse country. New Jersey had lots of horse country. Inside, while checking out the attic space, I noticed an unusual object there. It was a petrified bat! I took its picture. The farmhouse was a short sale; I made an offer but rapidly discovered that short did not imply quick.

Moving onward, I recruited Debbie in my house hunt, often bringing her along for opinions on properties. Most importantly, there had to be space for Chad. If the house was going to be our forever home, it should best accommodate him. Additionally, as Chad was a herd animal, I would have to get a second horse as his companion. Naturally, Sparky came to mind; I made no secret to Cliff that I would love to move Sparky with us when he was weaned and ready.

February 2009 was approaching; time was pressing. One day I saw pictures of a promising small ranch on an eight-acre property, but it was somewhere too far away. Finding a nice home on a two-acre lot, I made an offer, but the seller did not consider it. Hours upon hours I spent searching, driving, photographing, looking for a home that Chad and I could call our own. All the while, the drama at the Pioneer Stables was worsening; violent fights were soon overheard coming from the main house. I feared for the life of the toddler inside.

February 16, 2009, a friendly fourteen-year-old, well-socialized, animal actor chimp named Travis, who was being treated with Xanax, suddenly attacked his keeper's friend. Travis violently mauled the woman's face, blinded her, and severed several body parts. His long-time friend and keeper then stabbed Travis the chimp with a butcher knife, and ultimately the police shot him dead. The tragic story of Travis is included in his *Wikipedia* page, as well as a *Fox News* report by *The Associated Press*, "Tests Show Chimp Had Anti-Anxiety Drug Xanax in System During Vicious Attack."

Jewell was rarely seen. She, her husband, friends, family, and others passed in and out of the house. They were all partying, fighting, drowning in drama. As I sat in the hut, my own experience in Florida haunted me. I knew the capabilities of a psychotic prescription drug-induced mind; I knew them better than I cared to consider. Drawing upon the revulsion surrounding me, I knew I needed to write my story. Gathering all the medical, police, and mental health records I had collected, sprawling them out over the floor of the living room, trying to make sense of it all, I began writing my story from 2001.

While off the road, I decided it would be a good time to finally get health insurance. I researched something affordable, purchased the insurance, then made an appointment for my first mammogram. I kept in mind that early detection was key. Though I tried hard to live for prevention and hoped never to require a cure, to my great misfortune, the doctor saw something; surgery would have to be done. I scheduled an appointment for early April, concerned about what that meant.

Cliff came by the farm one afternoon to check on the mare and Sparky. It amazed me how every time Cliff was there, he managed to stay clean while dressed in his khakis and long-sleeved button-down shirt. He sure could ride, though! He had perfect posture. And his horse training techniques were wise. Telling Cliff about my quest for a home, I mentioned the small ranch on eight acres located rather far away. Without hesitation, Cliff responded, "Far away from what?" *Good question,* I thought. I decided to make the trip.

The following day I drove the hour it took to get to the small ranch house. It was actually only twenty-five minutes from my parents' new house, and the infamous Jersey highways were accessible. As I pulled down the long, tree-lined driveway, a feeling came over me. Having never been married and only hearing stories of a love match so true, this property, well, I knew. I called the realtor immediately. Make an offer; make it happen.

While I roamed the grounds of the park-like property I was determined to make my own, a car pulled down the driveway. Out of the car came an older couple and a man who was clearly their realtor. Kindly, the realtor asked if I would like to accompany them inside the house as he had the key in hand. Absolutely I would, and I did!

Inside, the house was a throwback to 1973; original harvest gold stove, wood paneling, and shag rug. Made no matter to me; it had eight acres, paddocks, and a barn. The man walked through the living room, heading toward the back of the house, while the woman remained near the kitchen. It did not take but a few steps inside before the woman exclaimed, "This house needs to be torn down." Hearing that, I knew it was going to be mine.

My realtor spoke to the seller, whose name was Dorothy. That made me chuckle. Certainly, there was no place like home and no humor the likes of our God. Dorothy's sister, Mary, had lived and passed on inside the house only recently, the day after Christmas. The house would be sold with Mary's belongings in it, as is. My offer was made and miraculously accepted; there really was no place like home. I prayed the inspection would go well.

March was underway; Debbie and Cliff were excited about the news of my farm purchase. I hoped for a quick closing that left me enough time to settle before the tour. While I packed and prepared for my home purchase and move, I continued writing about my 2001 prescription drug ordeal in Florida. Each day, looking out the windows of the hut, I recalled the once happy farm filled with hope, dreams, and friends. Sadly, it had become the shell of all that might have been. Rainbows replaced by dark clouds.

I should have just bit my tongue and held my patience until I signed on the bottom line for my new home, but only through hindsight could such wisdom be achieved; what happened next was astounding.

Between all the factors, my frustrations grew fast. Finally, a day came when I stormed from the hut to the house and demanded Jewell come out to talk. She did not. My anger with her regarding the dangerous situation her addiction had created escalated. I screamed that she come out of the house. She did not. I wanted Jewell to know the destruction she and her husband's addiction caused and brought upon the farm, the horses, her friends, her family, her child, herself; I blasted curses and screamed with gusto about the disgust, disappointment and betrayal I felt. Still, Jewell and her husband remained inside the house. I could not wait to get out of that place and into the safety of my own home.

I walked down the long driveway toward the road to check the mail; I was expecting papers regarding my home purchase. The mailbox was empty. Wondering if the mail had already been delivered that day, I crossed the road to peek inside the neighbor's mailbox. Seeing that it, too, was empty, I turned, crossed back, and began walking up the driveway toward the house. Passing the house, I screamed once more to Jewell as I walked back toward the hut, cursing all the way. The rain began to fall.

When I arrived at the hut, I noticed a police car coming down the driveway. It passed the house, the barn, Sparky's paddock, and was nearing the hut. I was wearing a yoga top, so as it was raining and felt chilly on my skin, I reached into the mudroom, grabbed a wrap to cover up, and began walking to meet the police officer.

Stepping out of his car, the officer questioned me; he asked if everything was all right. He said he heard I was running in the road, hoping to be hit by a car. I assured him that I neither ran in the road nor hoped to be hit by a car. I told the officer I yelled at Jewell, wanting her to come out of the house, and then went to check the mail; I was expecting a piece of mail regarding the purchase of my new house. The officer did not accept that as enough reason to call the police. I agreed. Glancing up toward the house in the rain, I was skeptical, fearful of how much to tell him.

Distressed and frustrated over the circumstances, I was worried that if I told the police officer about the drug abuse and child endangerment in Jewell's house, it would jeopardize Chad's safety. I did not want to risk any revenge or insane vengeance against him; I vividly recalled how the broken zipper on the jacket belonging to Jewell's father did not fare well. I was upset and knew it showed. Also, I was scared.

There was a strong odor of cat urine. I realized that the wrap I had grabbed from the mudroom and thrown over my body to protect me from the rain had been sprayed by the barn cats. It smelt horrid. Promptly, I removed the cloth and tossed it in disgust. The officer then suggested I was undressing, behaving unusually suspiciously. He asked me to follow him; naturally, I did.

I was led to an ambulance that had pulled in while I spoke to the officer. I sat down in the back as directed, and the vehicle began driving away. I suspected we were headed toward the police station, where I awaited the opportunity to clarify the farm situation while in a safe environment. I engaged in conversation with the first responder in the back of the ambulance with me; we laughed and were friendly, but we did not go to the police station as I had anticipated.

At a small local hospital, I was taken into a room and held, doors locked. My parents soon arrived. They knew I had been stressed about the purchase of the house and was unhappy with the management at the farm, but were unaware of Jewell's family drug use, amounting to hundreds of pills a month. They were also unaware of the weapons that had become commonplace toys to the drug-dependent Jewell and her family.

While talking to my parents, a nurse entered the room to inject me with something. I objected, yet I had no choice. She stuck the needle inside me. I was held another hour; my mom told me she would check up on Chad at the farm. Soon thereafter, I was transported to another hospital.

When I arrived at the big hospital, I was taken to a floor with a familiar arrangement, including a nurse's station, community room, and pay phone. Unfortunately, I understood exactly what was happening: a seventy-two-hour psychiatric hold supported by no judge, no rights, and no say. There was zero point in telling anyone at the facility about the dire dealings back at the farm. I tried to find humor in the irony of it all. What else was there to do?

Bored, I arranged the furniture nicely in the community room. Scattered furnishings and utter disarray, their setup was least conducive to their community and group-counseled gatherings. Such facilities should consider their environment more thoughtfully for patient needs and healing. I took advantage of the time to help other people there while I remained in custody against my free will.

Line up. Pill time came; no choice, no voice, just take the drug. Being well informed about the dangers associated with psychiatric drugs, I had a problem ingesting them. I didn't want to cause confrontation and attempted to hide the pill under my tongue, but the nurses were wise to the trick; it did not work at all. Swallow.

Problems arose the following afternoon when a young nurse's assistant came by with a wheelie drug cart and handed me a cup of pills with some water. Gathering the courage to take a stand, I politely explained to the girl I was not comfortable taking the drugs. The girl emphasized it was mandatory, not an option. Respectfully, and for the love of my life, I rejected the pills again. I told her I felt strongly that they were a danger to my health and well-being. The assistant returned to the nurse's station, filing a motion of complaint against me.

Following the young girl to the nurse's station, I continued defending my position of rejecting putting drugs inside my body. Moreover, I asked the nurses to provide me with my paperwork and grounds for involuntary hold. The nurses grew angry with me and refused to comply. They insisted I be forced to take the drugs. Defiant, I told the nurse I was going to make a phone call and get in contact with my attorney.

Knowing she would have access to my phonebook in the trailer hut, I went to the pay phone and called Debbie. Thankfully she answered and was at the farm. After addressing her genuine concerns about how the police and hospital ordeal came to be, I then asked Debbie to retrieve a phone number.

While I directed Debbie to where the information was located, I looked up and saw a pack of people in white coats walking toward me with determination. Fearful, I desperately told Debbie what I saw and implored I needed the attorney's help. Then, hearing Debbie frantic on the other end of the line, in panic and concern, I screamed to her as I was grabbed, but I was quickly hauled away by the herd of doctors; the pay phone handset left dangling by its wire.

I screamed while I was dragged into a hospital room, and my life flashed before me as once again I stared into the face of death. Six white coats held me down, wrestled me, and repeatedly jabbed needles all over my body, jabbing, stabbing needles over and over while I shrieked in horror in fear for my life. It's a wonder my heart did not explode with a coronary attack.

When they left the room, I slowly rose up, trembling, a distorted, mangled mess.

The following day, the facility arranged to relocate me to a more permanent institution. Prior to the transfer and while in a psychotic, drugged state, I kicked a hole in the bathroom wall of my room. Hours upon hours, I filled a garbage pail with water from the bathroom sink, then poured bucket upon bucket of water into the abyss. I listened to the water fall.

After another ambulance ride, I found myself in the next institution—same shit, different spot: nurse's station, community room, patient rooms, telephone, same smoking cage, and same clothes in a cardboard box. Line up and take your drugs—medication. No judge, no due process, no rights, and definitely no questioning the authority. I was classified as non-compliant.

Concerned about what was happening with my home purchase and inspection, my parents assured me they would take care of things and be there when the inspector did his job. Meanwhile, at the mental health facility, I took on an inspection job myself; the place was filthy.

Many patients in dismal circumstances were there of their own free will, while others like myself were not. Making the best of my time in the institution, not only did I get patients talking, laughing, dancing, singing, and exercising, I also counseled many who needed support. I even helped get an anorexic patient to eat.

One nutty boy always followed me around. I listened to his woes and helped his self-confidence grow, though I sometimes wished for a silent moment of solitary peace and quiet; I was very much exhausted and just wanted to get Chad and me into our new forever home.

One normal day in the mental health facility, I made a call to Debbie. She told me Cliff had passed away. Unbeknownst to us, Cliff had cancer, and he had been suffering for some time in silence. Such a dignified man, Cliff wanted no pity or sympathy for his life-threatening disease. He crossed over, leaving behind the image of the strong, stately gentleman he was. I was not able to attend his funeral services, and I wondered what would become of the mare and Sparky.

Another glorious day in captivity, held by the superpowers of their own might, I sat on the couch in a state of drug-induced numbness and despair. Suddenly I felt overwhelmingly lightheaded and hot. Then, growing in intensity and panic, I felt myself losing consciousness. As I fought to remain aware and conscious, I called out for help. The nurse's station was twenty feet behind me; I called to the nurse on duty that I needed help. I told her I was going to pass out. The nurse repeatedly responded, "I'm not running, I'm not running, I'm working." The nurse never got out of her chair, nor did she come to my assistance.

Desperate to remain conscious, I occupied my brain by counting numbers and slowly articulating them aloud. I focused intensely on the numbers and repeated them, calmly with clarity, over and over. It worked. I felt my body respond; strength and blood flowed again until I could finally manage to stand. Then I drank water until I cooled and calmed down.

At pill time, I had to find a way to save myself from the frightening drug effects imposed upon me; there was not a single chance in the highest heaven I was going to allow another man-made psychiatric pharmaceutical drug to poison my bodily system, my vessel. So I drank lots and lots and lots of water. So much so I could barely finish a cup of water before needing to return to the restroom. No sooner water went in, it was flowing out. Dilution filtered the pollution.

In the community room during a group meeting, I felt the daily crayon drawings depicting our feelings grew old. At the point in the group session where everyone described their colored picture and thoughts, when my turn came, I stood and recited the greatest poem my seventh-grade English teacher ever taught me, *Invictus* by William Ernest Henley: I am the Master of my fate; I am the captain of my soul.

At last, the day came when I could leave. Once again, I was provided bottles of dangerous psychiatric drugs and prescriptions for pills I would never take. My parents and Debbie picked me up at discharge.

Though grateful for my parents' assistance in ensuring the home inspection went well, I was extremely disappointed in them. Assuming I must have done something wrong, my parents trusted whatever story Jewell manically professed, and the police officer and doctors were justified in their actions. It never occurred to anyone that had I genuinely run in the road hoping to be hit by a car, I would have been hit by a car. But I did not; I checked the mail and walked back to the hut in the rain that desolate day. I harbored no interest in suicide; on the contrary.

My parents dropped Debbie and me back at Pioneer Stables, where I began to clean up the mess.

Mere days after my detainment release, it was closing day on my house at last. I signed and signed. Whatever stack of paperwork was necessary to secure my home, I signed. Dorothy was there; she handed me my keys.

Following the house closing, like any good New Jersey family would do, my parents and I went to The Diner. As I sat in the booth looking at my mom and dad, and before our food even arrived, I stood up and declared, "I'm going home." I excused myself from the table, got in my car, and drove home, to MY home.

18

Parking Lot

April 3, 2009: pulling down the tree-lined driveway for the first time, knowing it was all mine, produced a feeling I wish everyone in the world could experience; nothing shy of incredible. I had purchased a home on my own, eight acres with a barn!

With an overnight bag packed in the car, I immediately dropped my stuff in my own house, then headed into my own barn for cleaning. I needed to have the barn ready for Chad and his horse friend in only two days. Wow, there sure was a lot of work to be done. A deep breath of fresh air; the oxygen increased the high.

Along my way to get barn supplies at the tack store, another canine finally found me to make her own. She was at a local zoo and was a little mixed breed of something unknown. She was a tiny, little black fluff with enormous ears that stood up. When I looked at her, I laughed at a funny-looking little dog who reminded me of Toto. Certainly, there was no place like home. I named her, Ollia. She was a barker.

Two days later, Debbie hitched the trailer to her truck; my minivan had been long gone by that time. Hauling Chad and a barn buddy of his I borrowed, we made the hour-long trek to our barn. Chad immediately took to his new surroundings. With head and tail held high, he paraded around the property as though he knew it was all his!

We met the neighbors; our neighbors. They had a slim blue-eyed mare just like Moosie. At last, we could unpack and settle in. We made it; we made it. At last, we were home sweet home.

A few days later, I prepared for breast biopsy surgery. I drove an hour, checked in, completed the paperwork, and noted my allergies: cold medicine and prescription drugs. I was provided with a special allergy-warning bracelet to wear.

When I awoke after surgery, I ate the cookies provided while the nurse called a taxi to satisfy my discharge approval. Because of the general anesthesia, I was not permitted to drive myself home. After an hour of waiting and despite the allergy-warning bracelet, I was discharged with a prescription for pain medication attached to my discharge papers. The pills were neither wanted nor needed.

I paid the cab driver twenty dollars to take me on a two-minute taxi ride around the building and to the parking garage. There, I got into my car, drove myself down the NJ Turnpike, and to my very own home, a home where my horse, Can You Imagine, would live in a barn on my own property, along with me. That was something most spectacular.

While unpacking and settling in, I came across a letter written on yellow notepad paper and handwritten in 2001. It was a letter from Camille, but it was not addressed to me. Instead, the letter was one Camille had written to a woman I believed was a nurse, Elaine. She wrote it when I was pharmaceutically induced and first taken into involuntary custody on September 13, 2001. How I came to have the letter, I really did not know. But the letter read:

"Personal Facts – 31 years old, Theatre Degree UNC Charlotte. Present job – roadie, 9 yrs friend, 5 months roommate. Panic attack May 23/2001 SSRI, mid-June – erratic behavior slowly – loopier & loopier. Late July, early August started writing a lot – messages from God – word plays + numerology making all coincidences seem substantial – stopped making sense. Exactly one month ago, August 13 or so, really started having delusions about her role in the world – purpose/divine plan, said she was a prophet like Jesus – got steadily worse – concerned about state of our world. Started reading the Bible

& studying other religions, pagan. Martyr - thinks she will be executed fighting for what she believes in. This week since Trade Center incident – delusions of grandeur – manic behavior laughing hysterically at what God is "telling her," then sobbing uncontrollably. Called FBI – went to see them w/ info passed on to her by God about the terrorists and where she believes they are hiding etc. Faxed speeches + plans to Pentagon, White House, NBC, ABC, CBS + local FBI. Started talking in "code" – didn't make any sense – paranoia. Fits of rage – no sleep, rarely ate. Normal behavior – cleaning her room, stopped. She, over the last two months, has become increasingly inconsiderate – like a tornado – leaving crap all over the place. She has tunnel vision only talking & writing & saving the world is important – not everyday duties. She has in a sense lost her social skills – people she didn't know called the house and she would scream at them – how dare they be concerned with day-to-day life issues when there is a war going on. The mellow side of Dawn is gone. Now she demands the attention of everyone –singing loud, talking about really wacky stuff and not letting you get a word in. I am very worried that she will just be "let go" without anyone finding out what is wrong with her. She is NOT the person she was 4 months ago. She thinks she is normal and sane & that everyone else is crazy. She thinks people are after her and that's why she ran from the cops. Even though she is calm now, she hasn't changed her opinion about the FBI + people following her – it's like Conspiracy Theory. She has blown about $15,000 in the last 4 months and has practically nothing to show for it. She's a shop-o-holic, but, the sweetest most caring individual I've ever met. She is normally not a slob though lately she has become a horrible one. I know she either had a chemical reaction to the SSRI, or that something has gone chemically wrong in her brain because this is not the best-friend I've known for 9 years."

How I came to have that letter in my possession, I may never know. It was an emotional letter to discover, difficult to read, but enlightening all the same.

A few weeks after moving into my home, it was time for Chad's barn buddy to return to Pioneer Stables, Jewell's farm where he normally lived. Once again, Debbie hitched up the trailer. It was dreadful knowing that horse had just spent a few weeks in paradise, and now, through no fault of his own, he had to be returned.

Fortunately, the old barn manager from where Chad had stayed, way back when I worked overnight at the convenience store, had called. Due to trying times, she needed a permanent home for her aging quarter horse, BG. The stocky, chestnut mare came to live with us. She and Chad were overjoyed to reunite. BG reminded us we really were staying alive.

Luckily, the surgery results came back negative; no breast cancer. Health insurance paperwork and bills began rolling in. It was overwhelming; at least a dozen different invoices for one procedure. What a headache that was. I could not keep up with the insurance, so I eventually dropped the health care and went back to self-pay.

Also, nearing the time to hit the road again on tour, another blessing came; God provided me with the best babysitter I could ever dream of having! In addition, a wonderful roommate moved in, so no worries about home while I headed out on the road for work.

As the tour rolled on, I often thought about Jewell and her daughter. I thought about all the medicated children, some living, others not. When did childhood become such a disorder? Seemingly any curious, mischievous, innocent child with imagination and energy could quite easily become labeled with an attention-deficit disorder, social anxiety disorder, or hyperactivity disorder. Parents were being forced to drug their own children or face the child's removal by the state. Forced drugging of kids was mandated. Millions of children were drugged; their numbers rose like the federal deficit. Not long ago, when I was kid, Mr. Rogers said, "I like you just the way you are." I wondered if kids today had ever heard anyone say that to them.

Thousands of creative, focused individuals who mastered objectives meticulously were diagnosed with obsessive-compulsive disorder, a bipolar disorder that required pharmaceutical drugs to 'cure' their behavior. Many of them may have been creating and doing incredible things, perfect, unaltered, and wonderful as God intended them to be. Instead, they were drugged.

Life events brought normal anxiety, stress, and depression. However, there was no need to cope anymore. Drug companies claimed a pill would fix it all. Fry up those eggs, Nancy Reagan; breakfast is served.

I went to a church one day to sit in prayer and cry there. A woman came over to comfort me. I expressed my fear to her that mass shootings and killings would escalate to where one day, a person would walk into a church like where we sat, and begin shooting wildly. No place would be safe. Putting her arm around me, the woman assured me that would never happen.

September 2009. One wonderful day on the road in somewhere, USA, I received a most welcomed phone call with great news: Cliff's widow was going to give me Sparky! During a work break at home, Debbie and I loaded up the horse trailer just one more time. When Sparky arrived at my farm, I don't know who jumped higher, whinnied louder, or ran faster, but oh boy, Chad and Sparky sure were happy to be reunited again! Brothers!

Time passed; tours rolled.

Pharmaceutical companies were spending billions of dollars each year advertising their prescription drugs to the public. Drug commercials told consumers: "Talk to your prescriber." I saw the mind-altering pharmaceutical drugs given to me in 2001 advertised on TV. In the 1980s and 1990s, Budweiser's party dog, Spuds MacKenzie, and Camel cigarettes', Joe Camel, were eradicated from marketing after they were deemed 'bad influences on children.' Yet, in 1997, under President Bill Clinton, the United States became the only country to adopt Direct-to-Consumer Marketing of prescription drugs. America approved commercials and advertisements for prescription drugs, even those with psychotic and suicide side effects. Doctors were demoted to drug dealers.

Healthcare insurance did not cover holistic care, natural care, nutritional care, preventative care, homeopathic therapies, animal therapies, herbal treatment, and alternative health options, not even through what would become Obamacare.

General practitioners and pediatricians were encouraged to prescribe drugs off-label. They routinely diagnosed people with mental illness, per the ever-evolving DSM, Diagnostic and Statistical Manual of Mental Disorders. Children, teens, young adults, older adults, and even infants were customarily drugged with psychiatric pills.

Our food supply was polluted with antibiotics, fillers, hormones, pesticides, factory-farming filth, and GMOs, all producing contamination and fueling the diseases and disorders that defined us. Artificial colors, artificial flavors, artificial food, artificial people; surrounded by the artificial and losing sight of what was natural, real, and good.

A nice update informed me Jewell and her family encountered enlightening revelations. After intervention by Child Services, they underwent rehabilitation and were on the road to recovery, restoring their beautiful family. Unfortunately, under the influence of mental health drugs, Jewell's father, who had shot his jacket because of a broken zipper, had turned his gun on himself. He took his own life. Worse, in a separate incident, Jewell's drug-using brother-in-law was ill-fated as well. He died alone in the dark of night after losing control of his car. Thankfully Jewell, her child, and her husband were well and even welcomed a new baby.

Time passed; tours rolled.

As headlines reported more fatally tragic news, the horrific memories of trauma I experienced in 2001 haunted me. My story, which I began writing when I lived in the hut at Pioneer Stables, loomed over my head like a dark cloud.

Never forget the American mom, Andrea Yates, who was given multiple mind-altering pharmaceutical pills, including Effexor. On June 20, 2001, she systematically drowned her five young children in their bathtub at home. The tragedy was widely reported and has a *Wikipedia* page. A *Chron* article by Angela K. Brown, *Associated*

Press, "Group warns of drug Yates took before Deaths; Antidepressant Effexor found to possibly raise risk of homicidal thoughts in users," details the dangers of the pharmaceutical drug prescribed to Yates. Also, in *Oprah* magazine, "A Cry in the Dark" by Suzanne O'Malley details extensive mental health treatment and drugs, including Zoloft, prescribed to Andrea Yates.

Never forget Susan Smith, a South Carolina woman, wife, and mother who blamed a black man for drowning her kids in 1994. All the while, the white mom was the lone killer of her two boys herself. Did drugs influence her actions that fateful day?

I remember December 5, 2007, when a nineteen-year-old kid, Robert Hawkins, gunned down eight people at Westroads Mall in Omaha, Nebraska. Then, he killed himself. It was reported that Robert Hawkins had a history of mental health treatment. *Associated Press* and *Fox News,* "Autopsy Shows Valium Only Drug in Omaha Mall Gunman's System," reported the anti-anxiety drug diazepam, known as Valium, was present in his system at the time of the shooting.

I remember September 24, 2008, when a man with a history of mental health care, treated with psychotropic medications, Inman Morales, was naked while he screamed from the fire escape of his third-floor Brooklyn, New York, apartment. Inman was tasered by police and fell to his death. A *Daily News* article by Kelly Burke and Alison Gendar, "Naked man falls to his death after tasered by cops in Brooklyn stand-off," and, "Stop the Insanity," by *Daily News* Editorials, reported Inman Morales received appropriate mental health care and medication. One week later, on October 2, 2008, the initiating officer, NYPD Lieutenant Michael Pigott, committed suicide by a self-inflicted gunshot. I wondered if he chose suicide over the distress of Morales' death. Or was the lieutenant prescribed any medication to help him cope?

I remember March 10, 2009, when Michael McLendon, twenty-eight years old, killed his mom, then burned down her house in Kingston, Alabama. Michael then drove to Samson, Alabama, where he killed his grandmother, uncles, cousins, and others when he fired his gun at random while he drove. He killed ten people before he killed himself. According to reports, including *Wikipedia* and a *CNN* article by Saeed Ahmed and Dave Alsup, "Gunman in Alabama slayings was briefly a police officer," the Coffee County District Attorney Gary McAliley said medical supplies were found inside McLendon's Kinston home. Were medications included in those medical supplies?

Time passed; tours rolled.

Poor judgment raided and invaded American society. Random acts of violence increased: A medicated teen jumped from a dorm window and plunged to his death. Medicated children committed suicide, while other medicated kids erupted into mania and caused bloody massacres of innocent victims.

Warning: drug side effects may include suicidal thoughts or actions, such as mall shootings, school shootings, flight attendants who erupted into psychotic episodes as they emitted demonic screams, and psychotic passengers who went mad.

Now, I did rock 'n' roll wardrobe, but there was no malfunction here. Traveling, working, music playing, crowds singing, people laughing; overseas streets were still safe to stroll. Time passed; tours rolled.

January 8, 2011: twenty-two-year-old Jared Loughner shot US Representative Gabrielle Giffords and killed six people in Tuscan, Arizona. His history of drug and alcohol abuse was widely reported, along with his contorted speech, inappropriate laughter, bizarre public behaviors, and delusions of persecution. A news article, "Loughner, at 17, was treated for a behavioral-health issue" by Fernanda Echavarri and Tim Steller for *Arizona Daily Star* reported that as a teenager, Jared was treated for mental health issues by Dr. Thomas Brittain at Sonora Behavioral Center Hospital in Tucson, and at Northwest Medical Center. Jared was diagnosed as paranoid schizophrenic and drugged. At the time of the shooting, was Jared still using pharmaceutical drug treatments?

In Detroit, Michigan, psychiatrist Daniel Zak from The New Oakland Center had prescribed the anti-psychotic drug Risperdal to thirteen-year-old Ariana Godboldo. Ariana's mother, Maryanne, observed her daughter daily. After a few months of taking the Risperdal, the mother believed the medications caused harm to her daughter. She reported that the side effects of the drug had caused concerning changes in her daughter's thoughts, moods, and behaviors. In an effort to protect her daughter, Maryanne felt it was in her daughter's best interest to stop taking the drug. Ariana was safely weaned off the pills. Still, Health and Human Services and Child Protective Services insisted Ariana be forcibly drugged and accused her mother of neglect because she chose to stop giving her daughter the psychiatric medication.

On March 24, 2011, Maryanne Godboldo and her daughter, Ariana, were at home preparing dinner when police, an entire SWAT team, and a tank arrived at their house. Police illegally forced themselves inside the home without a warrant or judge's order. Because Maryanne had defied the Social Service authorities and safely stopped giving her daughter, Ariana, the anti-psychotic drug Risperdal, police sought to remove Ariana from the home.

What resulted was a ten-hour police standoff with Maryanne and Ariana terrified, barricaded inside a bedroom at their home. After ten hours, Ariana was forcibly removed and taken to Hawthorn Center, a juvenile psychiatric facility, where she was held captive and force-drugged. Maryanne was assaulted, arrested, jailed, and charged with illegally resisting and assaulting police by allegedly firing a gunshot while barricaded inside her home.

After a lengthy legal battle, a judge finally dismissed all criminal charges against Maryanne and ruled the order to remove her child was invalid. Fighting to regain custody of her daughter, Ariana was finally reunited with her mother on September 29 of that year. The heart-wrenching story was widely reported by news sources, including *Associated Press, Fox News, CCHR International, Freedom Mag, The San Diego Union-Tribune,* and many more.

July 22, 2011: I was on tour in Europe when thirty-two-year-old Anders Breivik, a man with a manifesto, "*2083: A European Declaration of Independence,*" set off an explosive car bomb in the center of Oslo, killing eight people. He then went on to gun down sixty-nine kids who were enjoying summer camp on the Norwegian island of Utoya.

Anders Breivik had received psychiatric care since childhood. According to *The Famous People* article, "Anders Behring Breivik Biography," Breivik was diagnosed as a paranoid schizophrenic and later described as suffering from narcissistic personality disorder and antisocial personality disorder. More on his mental health was reported by *The Independent* in an article, "The psychiatric disorders that might have driven Anders Breivik to kill" by Clare Allely, and, *The Guardian* article, "Anders Breivik was a challenging and aggressive child, court hears." Many news outlets, including *Wiley Online Library, The Local NO, The Telegraph UK,* and *Israel National News*, reported Breivik had an androgen and anabolic steroid called stanozolol, ephedrine, caffeine, and aspirin in his system when he massacred 77 people.

September 6, 2011: thirty-two-year-old Eduardo Sencion entered an IHOP in Carson City, Nevada. He shot twelve people and killed five. Many news outlets reported on the tragedy, Eduardo's mental health, and his compliance with medications. A *Huffington Post* article by Sandra Chereb, "Eduardo Sencion, IHOP Shooter, Was Convinced Demons Were After Him," reported that Eduardo had been diagnosed and treated for paranoid schizophrenia since his teenage years. He was pharmaceutically medicated, voluntarily and involuntarily committed to psychiatric facilities throughout his life. Even more, the article reported: "Sencion's medications were changed this summer. About a month later, he approached a priest in the street and asked him for help, telling the priest, 'They're telling me to do bad things.'" Eduardo took his medications at 10 p.m. the night before the shootings.

While home in New Jersey, on March 8, 2012, I attended a Governor Chris Christie Town Hall Meeting in Roebling, NJ. At the meeting, I happened to sit next to a man who initiated a heated exchange with the governor. After the man asked his question, he returned the handheld microphone to the governor's assistant, then sat down to hear the response. He suddenly grew angry and rose from his seat.

My concerns grew. The man's voice intensified, louder and louder; I could feel his hostile energy and see the crazed look that filled his eyes. I began considering a plan of action in case the man started to shoot. Unfortunately, there were no metal detectors upon entry.

The media quickly began swarming around us, and the flashes from the cameras were blinding. Unfortunately, it got worse when Governor Christie called the former Navy Seal an 'idiot.' The man was escorted outside by police. It was cordial. The police asked me if I wanted to go with the man, but I assured them we were not together.

The incident proved very well to my advantage. I had previously attended other Governor Christie town hall meetings and observed that he never called on people sitting together. Instead, Christie worked the room when taking questions. But on that particular day, I suspected Governor Christie also thought I was with the 'idiot' man because the governor called upon ME! Grateful for the opportunity, I expressed my concerns about pharmaceutical psychiatric drugs and mental healthcare. I asked the governor a question about how he would address the escalating violent, pharmaceutical psychotropic-drug-induced epidemic.

Governor Christie replied to my question; he stated that more pressure needed to be placed on the federal government to put strict warning labels on prescription drugs. I thought we did that in 2006 when I and many others testified to the FDA and Black Box Drug Warnings were expanded. However, Governor Christie continued his reply to me:

"People need to realize how powerful and dangerous these drugs can be. And I know how hard it is for people who have gotten hooked on them to get off. I think that's why we need this treatment program."

Christie continued by stating that the State Attorney General's Office was working with the Board of Medical Examiners to bring more disciplinary action to doctors. He said:

"The physicians that give out prescription drugs like candy need to have their licenses pulled, and that's what we're looking into doing across the state."

The Governor also invited me to provide my information to his Director of Constituent Relations, Jeanne Ashmore. I did. I also included my 2006 FDA testimony for the Governor's review.

Despite the Roebling Town Hall Meeting being overshadowed by the disruptive 'Navy Seal idiot' and subsequent media-hyped coverage about that, I was pleased that the governor's response to my question was also picked up, and reported on by our NJ news radio station, NJ101.5; *Christie Continues Crackdown on Prescription Drug Abuse.*

A few weeks later, on March 27, 2012, a forty-nine-year-old exemplary commercial airline pilot for JetBlue Airlines, Clayton Osbon, had a psychotic episode in mid-flight. The pilot attempted to correlate unrelated numbers like radio frequencies, left the cockpit, and ran through the cabin while he yelled about Jesus, religion, and terrorists. In an *ABC News* article by Susan Donaldson James, "JetBlue Pilot Rage Likely Not Panic; Drugs or Brain Tumor Possible," Una McCann, director of the Anxiety Disorders Clinic at Johns Hopkins Medical Institution, said, "Osbon's behavior looked more like a drug-induced toxic reaction." According to the FAA.gov website and reported by news sources, including *Fox News*, "FAA Changes Rule to Allow Pilots to Take Antidepressants," and *CBS News*, "FAA: Pilots Can Take Antidepressants on Job," despite drug warnings and side effects, the FAA permits pilots to fly while under the influence of SSRI drugs, Prozac, Zoloft, Celexa, or Lexapro.

That summer, on July 20, 2012, people were enjoying a lovely night at the movie theater in Aurora, Colorado. Suddenly, twenty-four-year-old James Holmes entered the theater and wildly fired his weapon. He shot and killed twelve innocent people; injured seventy. It was extensively reported that James Holmes had been under psychiatric care. An *NBC News* article, "Psychiatrist warned of Holmes threats before shooting, documents show," reported that a University of Colorado at Denver psychiatrist, Dr. Lynn Fenton, treated James Holmes. She warned police one month prior to the movie-theater shooting of "homicidal statements" Holmes made. A *Los Angeles Times* article by Jenny Deam,

"James Holmes' psychiatrist warned he may pose threat," reported that District Judge Carlos A. Samour Jr. made public the arrest affidavit and 12 search warrants. The search warrants revealed James Holmes was taking Clonazepam, a benzodiazepine drug sold under the brand name Klonopin, and Sertraline, a drug commercially known as Zoloft.

Winter rolled around. Nearly six years to the day following my FDA testimony, on December 14, 2012, a twenty-year-old boy named Adam Lanza killed his mother at home. Adam then went on to massacre twenty children and six adults at Sandy Hook Elementary School in Newtown, Connecticut. Next, Adam took his own life, all just two weeks before Christmas.

In the aftermath, even though the State of Connecticut and prosecutors spent the years that followed attempting to block the release of records, journals, and evidence found inside the Lanza home, it was through the persistence of the *Hartford Courant* news organization, help from the non-profit group, AbleChild, and the Connecticut State Supreme Court who finally ordered police to release the incident records to the *Hartford Courant* newspaper as the journalists requested. A *Pressreader* article by John Ferraro, "Courant honored for Lanza records release," describes how the *Hartford Courant* was awarded a top Freedom of Information Award for its successful five-year legal battle to win the release of the documents seized from the Lanza home, including Lanza's writings and psychiatric evaluations.

The official narrative claimed Adam Lanza's mother, Nancy Lanza, refused to give Adam psychiatric medications; she was non-compliant. Since her son had shot and killed her, Nancy was no longer alive to contribute her testimony. However, a *Hartford Courant* article by Alaine Griffin and Josh Kovner, "Lanza's Psychiatric Treatment Revealed In Documents," reported Adam Lanza "was seen at the Yale Child Study Center in his early teens and was prescribed the antidepressant Celexa." It was reported that Nancy Lanza took her son off the medication after her concern about side effects grew.

Prior to the Sandy Hook massacre, due to charges of inappropriate relations with a female patient, Adam's psychiatrist, Dr. Paul Fox, had relinquished his license to practice and moved to New Zealand. A *Fox News* article, "Sandy Hook shooter's former psychiatrist surrendered license over alleged misconduct," also reported that Dr. Paul Fox told investigators he had destroyed Adam Lanza's medical records.

An *AbleChild* article, "New Information About Adam Lanza's Mental Health Treatment Reveals Multiple Drugs," reports about another drug, Lexapro, that was prescribed to Adam Lanza by another psychiatry specialist at Yale Child Study Center, Kathleen Koenig. Notably, there are conflicting statements about whether Koenig prescribed the anti-anxiety drug Celexa to Adam Lanza, as police investigators reported in their summary of an interview with her following the shooting. The *AbleChild* article references information from *The New Yorker* article, "The Reckoning: The Father of the Sandy Hook killer searches for answers," by Andrew Solomon.

Though a *CBS News* article, "Report: Adam Lanza Had No Drugs, Alcohol In His System During Newtown Massacre," reports that Adam Lanza "was not under the influence of any drugs or alcohol, according to the results of toxicology tests," within the article, it also states: "It is unknown if Lanza, 20, was on medication or took illegal drugs."

Considering my own experiences, combined with those of mothers such as Maryanne Godboldo, it was challenging for me to believe that any doctor, child services, or state would not have forcibly drugged Adam or involuntarily committed him to a psychiatric facility to do so, despite his mother's apprehension about the medications. But again, Nancy Lanza was no longer alive to attest to her experiences with her son and his medications or provide her statement and testimony.

Even though Adam Lanza had a long history of mental health care, diagnosis, and treatment with a psychiatrist, Dr. Paul Fox, and Kathleen Koenig at Yale Child Study Center, ultimately, guns were blamed for the Sandy Hook bloodbath.

My life evolved into a beautiful mix where I cleaned horse stalls at home and dressed rock stars on the road. I mowed the acreage of lawn on my property and set up backstage dressing rooms around the world while on tour. I stacked feed and hay in my barn and organized backstage catering logistics for a hundred road crew. Thankfully luggage was made lighter to meet rising travel weight restrictions and fees. Thankfully music still played on.

Unfortunately, catastrophe struck again; a Connecticut woman, dental hygienist, and mom, thirty-four-year-old Miriam Carey, had been treated with an anti-psychotic drug, Risperidone, for postpartum depression. She subsequently developed delusions, obsessive ideas of grandiosity and believed President Obama was communicating, stalking, and electronically surveilling her. Miriam Carey believed herself to be the 'Prophet of Stamford' and was pharmaceutically medicated for bipolar disorder, schizophrenia, and mental illness.

On October 3, 2013, while on a paranoid, delusional rampage, Miriam Carey drove from Connecticut to Washington, DC. There, as she drove erratically, Miriam attempted to ram her vehicle through a White House barricade and led officers on a high-speed car chase. Miriam was shot multiple times by police and killed on Capitol Hill. Her one-year-old baby was found safe in the back seat of the Infiniti G37. No weapons were found inside her vehicle. The tragedy was widely reported in the news media, including *The Chicago Tribune, New York Magazine, ABC News, The Daily Beast,* and *Wikipedia.* A *CNN* article by Michael Pearson, Lateef Mungin, and Deborah Feyerick, "Source: Mental health paperwork found at home of Miriam Carey after Capitol chase," reported that when searching the home of Miriam Carey, law enforcement found discharge papers from a mental health treatment center and medications including Risperdal and Lexapro.

Another attempted murder-suicide happened on November 19, 2013. That one involved a Virginia state senator, Senator Creigh Deeds; he was stabbed multiple times by his son, Gus. His son had a history of mental health care, but the hospital was unable to provide him with a bed that day. For him, the hospital had no bed. While for me, in 2001,

I was made to sleep on metal chairs in a waiting room until a bed was available. After the son repeatedly stabbed his father, scarring him for life, the son then took his own.

The mental diagnosis, years of medications, personality changes, and behaviors of Gus Deeds are detailed in an *ABC News* article by Abby D. Phillip, Serena Marshall, and Jim Avila, "Friends Saw Creigh Deeds' Son Struggle With Bipolar Disorder Before Killing." The high-profile case was widely reported by many news outlets. When I read a *CNN* article by Trish Turner, "Creigh Deeds: 'No reason to believe there would be any violence,'" I was reminded of my own 2001 pharmaceutical drug effects. The article reports Creigh Deeds' recollection of his son's behavior: "Gus' whole attitude, his delusions had taken over. Delusions of grandeur that he was a demi-god. Gus' delusions often took on religious overtones." The article also reported how Senator Creigh Deeds "sat at one end of his dining room eating a sandwich; Gus 'writing furiously in his journal' at the other end, no interest in dinner." I wondered if Gus' journals looked like mine did.

Time passed; tours rolled.

Still, psychotic drug effects increased; their usage and prescription popularity grew. Millions of people were prescribed psychiatric medications, antidepressants, and anti-anxiety drugs. Too many experienced side effects that may include: suicide, homicide, massacre by gun, truck, airplane, knife, machete, hanging, drowning, bombing, or worse. Shh-hhh. Thoughts and prayers to the families, our politicians said. Political leaders invested even more millions of dollars into mental health treatment. Pharmaceutical drug advertisements pushed even more pills; pills to add to other pills, pills for the side effects of other pills, and pills for problems people never even had. Drug warnings were not heeded on Capitol Pill. Profit was power.

On March 24, 2015, twenty-seven-year-old co-pilot Andreas Lubitz intentionally flew a commercial airplane, Germanwings flight 9525, into a mountain in the French Alps. News worldwide reported that Andreas was previously treated and pharmaceutically medicated with psychotropic drugs for insomnia and mental health conditions. Psychotropic pharmaceutical drugs were found in his home.

An *NBC News* article by Andy Eckardt, "Germanwings Crash Co-Pilot Lubitz Had 'Psychosomatic' Illness," reported that police found "clear" evidence of a "psychosomatic illness" and found several psychiatric medications in the co-pilot's apartment. A *Newsweek* article by Max Kutner, "Final Germanwings Crash Report Says Co-Pilot on Medication, Referred for Hospitalization," reported that the French Civil Aviation Safety Investigation Authority report on the plane crash confirms that Lubitz crashed the plane as an act of suicide because of a mental health condition. Even more, it reported a toxicology examination on Lubitz's remains found the antidepressant SSRI drug citalopram, sold under the brand name Celexa, and the antidepressant drug mirtazapine, sold under the brand name Remeron, plus the sleep-aid medication zopiclone, sold under the brand names Zimovane or Imovane, in Lubitz's remains. He intentionally flew a commercial airplane into a mountain. A delusion was manifested to actualize an escape from madness. All one-hundred-fifty crew and passengers onboard that airplane were killed.

On April 23, 2015, we lost our beloved Sparky. He had been taken to an equine hospital after falling ill. Though improving nicely, I received a shocking late call from the vet informing me the situation had become suddenly dire. Immediately, I drove to the equine hospital thirty minutes from home, but Sparky did not make it. The doctors determined the cause of death was attributed to a neurological crisis. I uploaded a video to YouTube, *Sparky Lyle: In Memory of My Horse*. We all grieved deeply. Sparky rejoined Cliff in Heaven. Chad and BG still had each other for comfort.

Crazy or not, the day finally arrived that I was assured would never come. But, as I suspected, most unfortunately, it did. On June 17, 2015, twenty-one-year-old Dylan Roof entered Emanuel African Methodist Episcopal Church in Charleston, South Carolina. He shot wildly, crazily. Dylan massacred nine people in Mother Emanuel church that day.

Like so many others, Dylan also had an extensive history with mental health care. He had been diagnosed with multiple mental health issues and prescribed psychotropic drugs. Dylan was known well by his friends as a 'pill-popper' who heavily used Xanax and Suboxone.

The Charleston church tragedy was widely covered by news outlets worldwide, including an *International Business Times* article by Philip Ross, "What Drugs Was Dylan Roof On? Suboxone, A Powerful Narcotic, Found On Charleston Shooter in February Arrest." According to an *Inside Edition* report, "Shooter Dylan Storm Roof's Friends: He's a Pill-Popping, Gun-Toting Loner Who 'Made Racist Comments,'" a classmate of Dylan Roof, Adam Martin, said: "Pills, I mean if I'm being honest with you, that's what I heard were his drug of choice. Xanax."

As my heart wept and soul mourned, I could not help but think about the woman who sat with me in church just a few years prior. I wondered what she may have thought about that most sorrowful day in Charleston. Despite her assurance that such a church shooting would never happen, it did. As I knew then, it eventually would.

August 26, 2015: While conducting an interview on live television during a morning news broadcast in Roanoke, Virginia, newscaster Alison Parker and the accompanying photojournalist, Adam Ward, were fatally shot. Journalist and gunman, forty-one-year-old Vester Lee Flanagan II (aka Bryce Williams, his on-air, professional name), then committed suicide by gunshot.

Vester Lee Flanagan's history presented hostility, paranoia, violent outbursts, racial aggression, and bizarre behaviors. He had also faxed a twenty-three-page manifesto to the *ABC News* office. An *ABC News* article, "After Shooting, Alleged Gunman Details Grievances in Suicide Notes," reports disturbing details in the twenty-three-page document that Vester Lee Flanagan faxed to the news station. In it, Flanagan claims the reason for the shooting was his reaction to the racism of the Charleston church massacre. He also expresses his strong admiration for the killers from the Virginia Tech and Columbine shootings.

According to a *WSLS 10* article by Trish Bradle, "Warrants show Flanagan sought mental health treatment same year as being fired," prior to the homicide and suicide in 2013, Vestor had sought treatment at the Blue Ridge Behavioral Healthcare facility. What diagnosis did he receive? Were any medications provided to him? Was a toxicology analysis completed on Flanagan after his act of homicide and suicide? Vester Lee Flanagan II shot and killed a newscaster and photojournalist on *live* TV. Can you imagine?

As I felt helpless and troubled about the epidemic of pharmaceutical drug-generated violence, I sought other ways to help share information. So, after the New Year rang in, on January 2, 2016, I uploaded a short video I made to YouTube: *A Pill 2 Kill.* I hoped it would provide insightful information that could help save lives.

Seemingly there was no end or limit to the escalating violence and massacre madness. Frustrated, disgusted, and saddened, I contacted the office of my New Jersey representative, Senator Cory Booker. I wanted a meeting with him to discuss the psychosis and mass casualties that pharmaceutical psychotropic drugs had perpetuated for decades. However, rather than meeting with Senator Cory Booker, for whom I voted in his first term as senator, his office permitted me a meeting with his deputy counsel in Newark, NJ, Hanna Mori, Esq.

In preparation for the meeting, I organized a red binder filled with information I had compiled related to my personal adverse experiences with pharmaceutical mental health drugs. I included my 2006 FDA testimony, as well as the testimony of the man who spoke after me that day. I also added information from other pharmaceutically harmed people, plus news reports and information related to suicidal and homicidal acts committed by pharmaceutical drug-induced people. Also, information related to FDA studies and medical findings about the so-called mental health drugs. The new opioid drug crisis was also taking hold, so I included information on that pharmaceutical drug crisis. I prepared to give the binder to Senator Cory Booker via his counsel, Hanna Mori.

On the day of the meeting, February 18, 2016, I left my house extra early to ensure I would not be late for my meeting in Newark, as it was a forty-five-minute drive without traffic. While I drove along the New Jersey Turnpike, my car began acting unusual. There seemed to be a problem with the transmission. I became concerned about whether my Chrysler PT Cruiser would even make it to Newark.

Putting safety first, I pulled into a rest area along the highway. There, I called my father and asked if he could pick me up and continue driving me to the critical meeting in Newark. Thankfully, my dad said he could do so, though it would take him an hour to get to where I was.

While I waited for my dad to arrive at the rest area, I reached out to Senator Booker's office to alert them. Speaking with Hanna, she asked if I wanted to postpone the meeting. I assured Hanna I did not; I would be there that day and about fifteen minutes late. Postponing the meeting was not an option for me. I had to prepare to leave for a tour, and the meeting was THAT important. If I had to, I would've called a taxicab to be there.

Upon arriving at the Newark office, Hanna and I sat at a conference table in a private room. For the next hour, I presented the contents of my binder to her. Going through it with her, I explained my experiences and concerns. In one visual effort, I attempted to convey to Hanna the potential for mass devastation. I showed Hanna a large picture of my work environment: a stadium filled with 80,000 people enjoying a huge rock concert. I expressed my serious concern, explained to Hanna how our entertainment venues were soft targets for people in a drug-induced psychotic condition and warned her that our concert venues would eventually become sites for major tragedies. Hanna stared at the picture I presented but said nothing.

Additionally, I emphasized to Hanna that guns and mass shootings would not be the only means of mass casualty; I vividly warned her that such people would eventually drive vehicles through crowds of people, explode homemade bombs, shoot at random from vehicles while driving down the road, or stab people at random in the streets and shops. Blank-faced, Hanna did not ask me questions. Instead, she expressed little alarm and seemed dismissive of my credibility. The only question Hanna did ask me was about the news piece related to opioids.

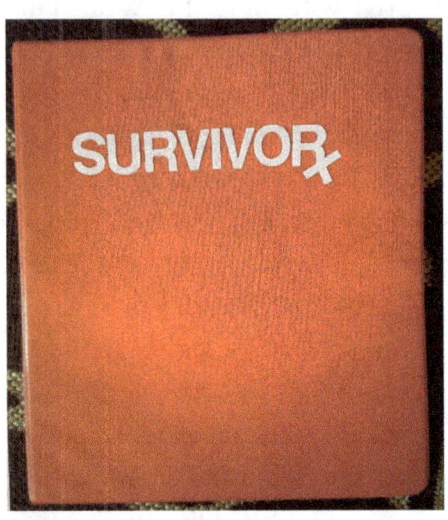

My binder provided to Senator Booker in 2016, via his counsel, Hanna Mori

Just two days after that Newark meeting, on February 20, 2016, a forty-five-year-old Uber driver, Jason Dalton, randomly opened fire on strangers between fares. While he drove around the city of Kalamazoo, Michigan, with his German Shepherd dog in the back seat, Jason, a father and husband, went on an hours-long shooting spree. The massacre included shots fired at a Cracker Barrel restaurant and a Kia car dealership. Six innocent people were killed that night in Kalamazoo.

Jason Dalton displayed bizarre behaviors; he claimed the Uber App was communicating with him. He said the devil took over his body like an 'artificial presence.' An article by Ryan Felton for *The Guardian*, "Kalamazoo shooter saw 'devil' on Uber app and blames visions for killing spree," reported that Jason Dalton described how the Uber app would give him an assignment, take over his body, and force him to go on a killing spree.

Though Jason Dalton denied any history of mental health problems or treatments, there were unverified accounts that he had been taking the anti-smoking drug Chantix. Chantix had been linked to causing mental health issues, including suicidal thoughts, delusions, hostility, and agitation. It also had FDA Black Box Warnings. Was any blood alcohol level test or toxicology analysis done on Jason Dalton when he was taken into police custody after the shootings?

Soon thereafter, on March 8, 2016, a thirty-year-old Idaho man and Marine veteran, Kyle Odom, shot an Evangelical pastor in Idaho. He then flew to Washington, DC. While there, Kyle was found throwing flash drives over the White House fence. All the while, he obsessed about aliens, mind-controlling Martians, and newspaper headlines with hidden meanings. He had written bizarre, paranoid coded manifestos, which he sent to his parents and television stations. Kyle had a history of mental health care, mental illness diagnosis, and medication treatment.

An article by Michael E. Miller published in *The Sydney Morning Herald*, "Kyle Odom's Martian manifesto is a window into an unraveling mind," provides many disturbing words and images found inside Kye Odoms' crazed manifesto. A *Los Angeles Times* article, "In Idaho, there's no insanity defense for accused shooter who says he was fighting aliens," reports how Kyle Odom believed the pastor he shot was part of an alien conspiracy and, after attempting suicide twice, plus seeking help at a local Department of Veteran Affairs hospital, Odom believed his only remaining option was to "go after the aliens." *The Washington Post* article by Michael E. Miller, "Idaho pastor shooting: Manhunt widens as police disclose Marine's mental illness," reports that Coeur d'Alene Police Chief Lee White confirmed Odom had a history of mental illness. However, White said, "The degree of it and the scope of it, I really can't speak about."

What comes to mind when one hears there's a big story about the wife of a pianist? Certainly not the events of March 17, 2016, when a thirty-one-year-old woman, mother, and pianist's wife, Sofya Tsygankova, suffocated her two young children, then tried to kill herself. According to a *Fort Worth Star-Ledger* report, "Wife of Cliburn Winner Found Not Guilty by Reason of Insanity in Daughters' Deaths," Sofya had been diagnosed with depression, anxiety, and mental illness and medicated with the anti-psychotic drug, Quetiapine, plus antidepressants and anxiety drugs. She experienced hallucinations, became suicidal, and was hospitalized after she jumped from a moving car and lay in traffic on a busy road. Sofya feared her husband had poisoned her and was controlling her through his cell phone. Ultimately, Sofya believed the devil had stolen her family's soul. She said she had no choice; in order to save her children, she had to kill them.

April 21, 2016: The musical artist, Prince, died from a drug overdose. In a news article, "Experts: Prince toxicology report shows very high drug level," Amy Forliti of *The Associated Press* reported fentanyl was the cause of death. Prince likely believed he was taking Vicodin, an opioid-containing painkiller drug, that was laced with fentanyl, as it was reported in an *NBC News* article by Daniella Silva, "Prince died after taking fake Vicodin laced with fentanyl, prosecutor says."

The very next day, I followed up on the meeting I had at Senator Cory Booker's office on February 18. I sent an email to Hanna Mori. I wrote to her that it had been two months since our meeting, and I had received zero response or reply from the Office of Senator Cory Booker regarding my critical psycho-pharmaceutical drug concerns and, consequently, lives killed as a result of the drugs. Also, I high-lighted that numerous more tragedies had occurred since we met in Newark: a pianist's medically-intoxicated wife brutally killed her two young children whom she loved, one medically-intoxicated New Jersey police officer crashed his car, another one took his own life with a self-inflicted gunshot, and Prince died. Hanna replied to me:

"Thank you for your email. We have been working diligently on drug regulation, specifically on the overprescription of opioids. Recently we convened a roundtable with federal, state, and local partners to discuss access, drug monitoring, treatment, and law enforcement angles to this epidemic. Your concerns are valid, and we are working diligently on opioid abuse right now." – Hanna Mori Esq, Dep. Counsel of Senator Cory Booker.

Nice. Or not? By the time summer rolled around that year, on July 14, 2016, a thirty-one-year-old man, father, and husband, Mohamed Lahouaiej-Bouhlel, deliberately drove a truck through crowds of people while they celebrated Bastille Day on the Promenade in Nice, France. After he killed eighty-four people, Mohamed Lahouaiej-Bouhlel was also killed by police that day.

A *Daily Mail* article by Fidelma Cook and Abe Hawken, "'Bring more weapons...It's good. I have the equipment': Terrifying final messages of Bastille Day killer sent MINUTES before he murdered 84 people," reports that Bouhlel was on multiple medications for schizophrenia, alcoholism, depression, and control of his violent rages. He had been medicated since the age of 12. An *International Business Times* article by Fiona Keating, "Nice attack: Lorry driver killer Mohamad Lahouaiej Bouhlel sent £84,000 to his family days before the massacre," reports that Bouhlels' father, Mohamed Mondher Lahouaiej-Bouhlel, said his son was not religiously motivated or an Islamic State militant, rather, he said about his son: "He had some difficult periods. I had to take him to a psychiatrist who gave him medicine. He had a very serious illness."

As the Nice attack happened, I checked social media to see if my colleagues on tour, who were staying in a hotel along that route, had checked in and marked themselves "safe." I took a moment to wonder if Hanna Mori believed me now or even cared. After all, depression drugs were not opioids.

Eighty-four people were killed that day in Nice, France. Plowed down. Hundreds more were injured on that horrific day. I had tried to warn of such an incident and was told numerous times that it would never happen. It did. The tragedy in Nice was the first of many more vehicles driving through crowds to come.

Just in time for back-to-school, on September 23, 2016, twenty-year-old Arcan Cetin killed five people while randomly shooting instead of shopping at Cascade mall in Burlington, Washington. An *NBC News* article by Andrew Blankstein and Corky Siemaszko, "Arcan Cetin, Accused Cascade Mall Shooter, Faces Five Counts of Murder," reports that court records showed Cetin had a history of mental health issues. He was diagnosed and treated for anxiety and depression. Arcan killed himself by hanging while in jail. Who talked to his prescriber?

When I talked to people about the adverse psychiatric drug effects, they often asked for my source; my source was me. I knew firsthand. The drugs flowed through my blood and distorted my brain. I had also attended the 2006 FDA hearing and listened to other victims with stories similar to mine. I testified then. Pharmaceutical drug advertisements warned: side effects may include changes in thoughts, moods, behaviors, and suicidal thoughts or actions. In 2006, FDA expanded Black Box Warnings for children, teens, and young adults, people under twenty-five. Still, prescribers doled out drugs to that age group without any regard for drug warnings.

Headlines reported one pharmaceutically-intoxicated father stabbed his wife to death, then shot and killed their two children before he killed himself. A pharmaceutically-intoxicated local neighbor near me shot his wife, their kids, the family dog, then himself. Did he talk to his prescriber? A United States senator was gunned down at a congressional baseball practice by a sixty-six-year-old man, James Hodgkinson. Was any toxicology analysis done on Hodgkinson? A New Jersey man jumped from an overpass into the traffic below on the Garden State Parkway. Was he pharmaceutically medicated? Is he cured?

Another horror happened on March 7, 2017, when an eighteen-year-old boy in North Carolina, Oliver Funes-Machado, made a 911 call to the police. Oliver called to report that he had beheaded his mother. When police arrived, Oliver walked out of his home in North Carolina brandishing a butcher knife in one hand and his mother's decapitated head in the other. He was taken calmly into police custody after he put down his mother's severed head.

Oliver Funes-Machado was just one week out of a mental health institution when he beheaded his mother. A *People* magazine article, "NC Teen Accused of Decapitating Mother Tells 911 Dispatcher 'She Made Me Mad,'" reports that, according to warrants, Funes-Machado was under the influence of four different psychiatric drugs. The initial *People* report identified the four pharmaceutical drugs; however, the drug names have since been removed from the article. A *CBS News* article, "Teen decapitated mother 'because I felt like it,' affidavit says," reports that in court, officials said that Funes-Machado was taking medication to treat psychosis and schizophrenia. Fresh out of a mental health institution and under the influence of four psychotropic drugs, the boy beheaded his mother. Crazy, or not?

Once again, I was reminded of my meeting at Senator Cory Booker's office when, on May 22, 2017, a twenty-two-year-old suicide-bomber, Salman Ramadan Abedi, detonated a backpack filled with homemade explosives during an Ariana Grande concert at the Manchester Arena in the UK. I knew that arena well and had worked there on multiple shows. Salman was addicted to painkillers and had previously attended anger management classes after he assaulted a female. That was reported by Duncan Gardham in a *Sky News* report, "Manchester Arena inquiry: Bomber Salman Abedi 'addicted to painkillers and had anger management classes.'" I wondered if a toxicology analysis was done on the remains of Salman Abedi. Despite the apathy of Hanna Mori and Senator Cory Booker, twenty-three people were killed at that music concert; over a thousand were injured, including children. Can you imagine?

Imagine, on July 26, 2017, the BBC program, *Panorama*, released an in-depth documentary report on James Holmes, the kid from Colorado who shot people inside a movie theater: *The Batman Killer – a Prescription for Murder?* by Shelly Jofre. The documentary was forthcoming about the pharmaceutical drugs prescribed to James Holmes and even included images of his journals, which frighteningly resembled the crazy pharmaceutical drug-induced journals I, too, had scribbled back in 2001.

Only a few months later, in the United States of America, on October 1, 2017, sixty-four-year-old Mesquite, Nevada resident Stephen Paddock opened fire on concertgoers attending the Route 91 Harvest Music Festival in Las Vegas, Nevada. From the 32nd floor of his Mandalay Bay hotel room, Stephen Paddock fired bullets into the crowded audience. He killed sixty people and injured hundreds more. He then took his own life with a self-inflicted gunshot.

According to a *Las Vegas Review-Journal* report by Paul Harasim, "Las Vegas Strip shooter prescribed anti-anxiety drug in June," the records from the Nevada Prescription Drug Monitoring Program show that Stephen Paddock's physician, Dr. Steven Winkler of Henderson, Nevada prescribed Paddock fifty 10-milligram tablets of the anti-anxiety drug Diazepam in June of that year. It was reported that Paddock refilled that prescription the same day of the shooting while he was in Reno, Nevada, over 460 miles away from Dr. Winkler in Henderson. Dr. Winkler admitted it had been a year before the shooting since he last saw Paddock. A *lalate news* article by Lucy Paresh, "Stephen Paddock Medication: Doctor Steven Winkler Diazepam Prescription," reports: "It remains unclear why a Henderson doctor prescribed the Mesquite resident. Moreover, Paddock reportedly filled the prescription with cash/credit, not via insurance coverage, not in Las Vegas, but in Reno." *Did Paddock receive a one-year prescription as I had been given in 2001?* I wondered.

Diazepam is a benzodiazepine with the brand name, Valium. Three metabolites of diazepam are nordiazepam, temazepam, and oxazepam.

The drug is known to interfere with a person's judgment, thinking, and motor skills and could induce hallucinations, psychosis, agitation, aggressive behavior, anxiety, suicidal thoughts, or actions. Diazepam has an FDA Black Box Warning.

The toxicology analysis conducted on Stephen Paddock during his autopsy found the drug. Many news outlets reported the toxicology results. One was an *Oxygen* article by Sowmya Krishnamurthy, "Las Vegas Shooter Stephen Paddock's Autopsy Results Are Finally Released: Stephen Paddock was on anti-anxiety medication, but no neurological abnormalities were found." Another article by Tania Hussain for *popculture*, "Las Vegas Shooter Had Anti-Anxiety Medication in System, Autopsy Reports," states that: "Amounts of nordiazepam, oxazepam, and temazepam, which are consistent with the anti-anxiety drug Valium, were discovered in his urine."

Crazy. Or not? I was horrified, saddened, and disgusted about the October 1 massacre at a music concert in Las Vegas on October 4, 2017, so I sent another email to Hanna Mori. I wrote:

"It's been reported Stephen Paddock was given mental health drugs in June. I went to you and Senator Cory Booker in February 2016, giving you extensive Rx Drug Warning information, evidence, pictures, and even excerpts from my Rx drug-induced personal journals... you did NOTHING. In the time since we spoke, my friends have been killed, my workplace attacked at numerous times and locations in US & Europe, thousands dead. Multiple vehicles have rammed through crowds of people, killing many like I told you they would. People randomly shot from cars like I told you they would. And this Rx drug-induced Las Vegas shooter who killed 58 people at a concert... it's on you. You and Senator Booker won't even support abolishing Rx drug advertisements with psychotic Black Box Warnings for suicide and homicide... how many more dead before you do anything to help, Hanna?"

Despite all, even as a constituent, neither Hanna Mori nor Senator Cory Booker replied to me. Enough was enough. On November 1, 2017, I contacted a self-publishing company, Dog Ear Publishing.

Then, I signed a contract to publish my personal, humiliating, and most harrowing story.

Imagine, only four days later, on November 5, 2017, a former member of the US Air Force, twenty-six-year-old Devin Patrick Kelley, entered First Baptist Church in the small rural community of Sutherland Springs, Texas, and began shooting. Ultimately, after being shot by a church attendee, he fled in his truck and committed suicide with a self-inflicted gunshot.

It was reported that Devin had a history of mental health disorders, psychiatric treatment, violence, and assault. He had previously escaped from Peak Behavioral Health Services in 2012. Numerous news sources reported on his stay and escape, at Peak Behavioral Health, including a report by Christal Hayes for *Newsweek*, "Texas Church Gunman Devin Kelley Escaped Mental Health Facility After Making Death Threats."

Available to view on *Scrib*d, the toxicology results in Devin Patrick Kelley's autopsy revealed multiple tranquilizers and anxiety drugs in his system, including benzodiazepines: Alprazolam, commonly sold under the brand name Xanax, Clonazepam, widely sold under the brand name Klonopin, 7-aminoclonazepam, barbiturates, Cyclobenzaprine, commonly sold under the brand name Fexmid, and Butalbital. Devin massacred twenty-six people in that small-town church. Luke Barr reported in an *ABC News* article, "Court finds US Air Force 60% responsible for Sutherland Springs, Texas, shooting." The US Air Force was 60% blamed for the tragedy.

They say, "If you see something, say something." I would have preferred to spend all my time at home with Chad, but between tours and over many years, I attended meetings, conferences, town halls, and hearings. I went to DC, Capitol Hill, and the New Jersey State House. Whether via testimony, telephone calls, email, social media, letters, or petitions, I reached out to each of my presidents, governors, congressmen, senators, and representatives, plus the FCC, FDA, and FBI. Yet, try as I might to help save lives from the deadly prescription drug side effects that were still advertised on TV, neither Democrats nor

Republicans, local or federal, expressed any interest in taking action to relieve the deadly psychotic pharmaceutical drug epidemic and consequential violence. They could not even commit to helping abolish America's new-age commercial advertisements for pharmaceutical drugs, even drugs with psychotic and suicide side effects.

Over many years, I logged incident after horrific incident. Still, my database of drug-induced violent tragedies paled in comparison to those of leading experts like Ann Blake-Tracy, Ph.D., executive director of the International Coalition for Drug Awareness. Ann Blake-Tracy testified at the 2006 FDA Psychopharmacologic Drug Advisory Committee Hearing. She also testified on the subject at the FDA hearings held in 1991 and 2004. She had spent over three decades documenting pharmaceutical drug-induced cases and assisted law enforcement in numerous drug-induced violent crimes and suicides. She appeared on various news programs, local and national, to discuss psycho-pharmaceutical drug dangers and side effects. She also wrote and published a book in 1994, *Prozac: Panacea or Pandora*, and had categorized and logged thousands of pharmaceutical drug-induced homicide and suicide stories in a database on her websites: SSRIStories.net and DrugAwareness.org.

Also, Dr. Peter Breggin, the 'grandfather' of psychiatric drug warnings, is a Harvard-trained psychiatrist, a former full-time consultant at NIMH, and a private practitioner in Ithaca, NY. Dr. Breggin was also a speaker at the International Center for the Study of Psychiatry and Psychology Conference I attended in Washington, DC, in October 2006. He testified at the FDA hearing that year, as well as the previous 2004 and 1991 FDA hearings regarding psychotropic drugs, and assisted law enforcement in psycho-pharma drug-induced suicide and homicide crimes. He has published numerous scientific articles and over twenty books on the psychiatry subject that include: *Toxic Psychiatry, Talking Back to Ritalin, The Antidepressant Fact Book,* and *Medication Madness: The Role of Psychiatric Drugs in Cases of Violence, Suicide, and Crime.* Dr. Breggin is the founder and director of The Center for the Study of Empathic Therapy, Education, and Living. He is a hero.

The *Citizens Commission on Human Rights International* report, "Another Mass Shooting, Another Psychiatric Drug? Federal Investigation Long Overdue," lists dozens of violent crimes committed by people under the influence of psychiatric drugs, as does a *Thought Catalog* report by Jerome London, "37 Mass Shooters Who Were On Antidepressants." Also, the *Los Alamos Daily Post* news article by Daren Savage submitted by Carol A. Clark, "A Brief History of Psychotropic Drugs Prescribed to Mass Murderers."

Michael Jackson, Prince, Chris Cornell, Chester Bennington, Carrie Fisher, Robin Williams, Whitney Houston, Bobbi Kristina Brown, Kate Spade, Naomi Judd, Amanda Peterson, Philip Seymour Hoffman, Kate Barry, Dave Mirra, Stevie Ryan, Anna Nicole Smith, Heath Ledger, Judy Garland, Tom Petty, Chyna, Marilyn Monroe; the list of celebrity deaths while under the influence of pharmaceutical pills was endless. Rest in peace, dear Elvis, our king of rock 'n' roll.

Blame a flag, gun, religion, or race. Prescription suicide was simple: a delusion manifested to actualize an escape from madness. Millions of people were prescribed psycho-pharmaceutical drugs in the name of mental health. Side effects may include suicidal thoughts or actions: the Colorado movie theater 12, Washington Navy Yard 12, Fort Hood 13, San Bernardino 14, Sutherland Springs Texas Church 26, Virginia Tech 32, Orlando Nightclub 49, and a fun night in Vegas turned concert massacre 60 +1.

Still, 22 veteran suicides a day.

The publishing process proceeded. It had plenty of bumps along the way. While that was happening, I headed back on the road for another music tour. At last, my book, *Crazy or Not, Here I Come*, was published through Dog Ear Publishing on April 18, 2018! Yee Haw!

Seventeen-year-old Chad, spokesmodel
Can You Imagine

19

Lemon

But wait, there's more?

There's always more.

Weeks before publishing my book, while my manuscript was underway with Dog Ear Publishing, another tragic Valentine's Day event occurred on February 14, 2018. It happened exactly ten years after I was on the campus of Northern Illinois University back in 2008, when a pharmaceutically drug-induced gunman, Steven Kazmierczak, massacred five students on that cold, snowy day. This time, it was a nineteen-year-old kid, Nikolas Cruz, who massacred seventeen high school students at Marjory Stoneman Douglas High School in Parkland, Florida.

It was widely reported that the gunman, Nikolas Cruz, had been in and out of mental health treatment for many years since his childhood. Between the years 2009 and 2016 Nikolas had been treated by Henderson Behavioral Health in Broward County for ADHD, autism, and depression.

Though the adoptive mother of Nikolas Cruz, Lynda Cruz, died from pneumonia in November 2017, only three months prior to the mass shooting, she had previously reported that Nikolas displayed symptoms that included rage, anger, aggression, violence, hostility, and homicidal ideation. Reportedly, in 2016, Lynda Cruz told mental health investigators at the Florida Department of Children and Families that her son suffered from ADHD and autism. Lynda Cruz insisted Nikolas did receive his necessary medication as prescribed.

After posting a Snapchat video showing he cut both of his arms and expressed his intentions to buy a gun in 2016, Cruz was evaluated for a psychiatric hold under the Baker Act. Henderson Behavioral Health clinicians chose not to hospitalize Cruz at that time because there were no issues with Cruz's medication; he was compliant with taking his medication and kept all of his appointments. Cruz was considered "low-risk."

As I reviewed that information, I recalled how easily I was placed under Florida Baker Act in 2001, even though I never threatened anybody or harmed myself. Even when I was simply broken down at a truck stop and my dearest Simon was having an epileptic seizure, I was taken into custody under Baker Act.

It was reported that only one month before the Parkland Valentine's Day massacre, on January 5, 2018, the FBI received a tip that Nikolas Cruz may attack a school. Someone close to Cruz reported concerns about his erratic behavior, gun ownership, desire to kill people and animals, plus, disturbing social media posts. The individual was worried that Nikolas Cruz may shoot up a school. The FBI ignored that warning.

I recalled my 2001 visits to the Tampa FBI office and the follow-up phone calls I received from agent Dean Smith, the 'Dean of Students.' Did the FBI somehow consider me more dangerous than a kid threatening to shoot up a school?

Nikolas Cruz, his extensive history with mental health treatment, medications, forewarnings about his behavior and subsequent FBI failure to respond, plus, statements by Lynda Cruz and reports by Florida Department of Children and Families can be found in many news reports, including: *The Washington Post*, "Red flags: The troubled path of accused Parkland shooter Nikolas Cruz," and, *NBC 6* article by Dan Krauth, "DCF: Parkland Shooting Suspect Was Receiving

Treatment, Medication When Probe Closed," plus, *MurderMeds* article, "Parkland Florida High School Shooting," and a *Sun-Sentinel* article by Megan O'Matz, "Mental health provider had long history with Parkland shooter. Was agency negligent?"

After the shooting, and while other high school classmates, politicians, and media blamed guns for the violent acts of horror, Dr. Peter Breggin wrote an article republished on *MadInAmerica.com*, "Psychiatrist Says: More Psychiatry Means More Shootings." Dr. Breggin wrote:

"Had Cruz been committed under existing gun laws, he would have become unable to legally buy a gun to carry out his murderous fantasies. Alternatively, if he had been carefully and safely removed from his psychiatric drugs while receiving good psychosocial therapy, his escalating violent impulses might have abated. Instead, he was left on his own to face the death of his mother and his expulsion from school, while his murderous impulses were fueled by drugs."

Even more, Dr. Breggin said:

"This is an irony of tragic proportions. Cruz was left unsupervised and free to buy a gun because he was faithfully taking psychiatric drugs that can cause or aggravate violence."

A month later, I was on tour when my book was finally published on March 19, 2018. Oddly, I discovered that my book was available on Amazon after a friend purchased it and texted me a picture of her reading it. It seemed like something the publisher would have alerted me to prior to its publication and availability for purchase. I expected to at least receive a hard copy of my book for myself before others were able to purchase it, but that was not the case. Regardless, I was happy my book, *Crazy or Not, Here I Come*, was finally completed, published, and available for purchase.

Being on tour did not permit me any time to focus on my book. I was able to make a post about it on my social media, but my job on the road was all-consuming. Maybe one day, I could share those much more fun, enjoyable and happy stories from all around the world. In the meantime, I realized that my backstage 'show-blacks' and comfortable roadie attire would not be appropriate for a professional and promotional book tour. In preparation for an exciting new book adventure, I began shopping for blazers and heels.

As the year pressed on, tours rolled, and a new year rang in: 2019. Many friends and colleagues had told me they bought my book, read it, and were educated by my experiences. It even helped save a few lives! Still, I had never heard a word from my publisher, Dog Ear Publishing; all correspondence went unanswered. I never received copies of my book as contracted or any author profits for my book sales. In fact, to obtain a few copies of my own book, I went onto Amazon and bought them myself.

Frustrated by the lack of response or action I received from my well-established publishing company, which had over 10,000 authors, I filed a complaint with the Better Business Bureau. I was surprised when I went onto the publisher's Facebook page. There, I saw a comment from another author expressing the same difficulty in communication and author payments that I experienced.

In a private message, I sent an inquiry to that author. She responded to me, and we exchanged email information. Within a few days, we discovered six other authors who experienced the same difficulty with Dog Ear Publishing.

As our group of authors scammed by the publishing company quickly grew, we decided to create an official Facebook group. We hoped to begin organizing and taking action for justice and retaining our files and the monies owed. *Dog Ear Authors Revolt* Facebook Page was established.

Every author filed a complaint with the Better Business Bureau. We also decided to each file a complaint with the Indiana Attorney General, Consumer Protection Division. On April 2, 2019, I did just that; I received a file number and complaint confirmation from Case Analyst, Leslie Gebby at the State of Indiana Office of the Attorney General.

By the summer of 2019, I was touring Europe again. I seized the opportunity to speak with many in that region about my book and the psychotic side effects attributed to pharmaceutical mental health drugs. Knowing Europe did not have commercials and advertisements for prescription drugs, I showed some people the print and video drug advertisements with suicide warnings from the United States—their shock and awe spoke volumes. I wished I had more of my books to offer, but I only purchased eight to give away.

While I worked in Europe, our Facebook group of disenfranchised authors had grown into dozens. Verified and victimized Dog Ear Publishing authors regularly joined the group. Some gained success when they attained more attention to our publishing problem. All authors were very hopeful when, on August 17, 2019, Nyssa Kruse of *Indy Star* newspaper in Indianapolis, Indiana, published a lengthy and in-depth news article about our Dog Ear Publishing circumstance, "We were scammed: a dozen authors say Dog Ear Publishing owes them thousands."

When I arrived home from Europe, I noticed Chad appeared to be walking peculiarly. The vet came to our barn for a checkup. On September 11, 2019, Chad was diagnosed with laminitis. Laminitis is a painful, potentially fatal hoof disease in horses. It was a very serious diagnosis that would require intensive care and attention.

The fear I felt, I could not bear to even describe. Every fiber of my being was filled with worry. Compounding that, I needed to pre-pare to leave home in three days for a two-week stadium tour around South America. There was no way to avoid the trip, so I had to make preparations for my parents to tend to Chad's special needs while I left for work outside the country.

It was a successful time in South America. I was grateful to run into many old roadie friends from years gone by, all united together at Rock in Rio. I ran into Drew there too! He was great! It warmed my heart and soul to be surrounded by so many friends while in Brazil, especially at a time when the news of Chad's diagnosis was catastrophic to my heart.

When I made it home from South America, Chad required hoof sur-gery. I arranged for the best equine foot doctor located in Kentucky to come to our barn in New Jersey to operate on Chad. The doctor took a 4 a.m. flight to arrive; he was in surgery by 8 a.m.

Chad was a trooper. I remained with him, sang softly to him, and reassured him. He stood calmly and quietly as the doctor and his team worked for hours. The surgery was successful, though recovery would be lengthy and unpredictable.

My book remained in limbo. The theft and fraud were unlawful; I owned all rights to my work. My book was still listed on all sales sites, despite silence from the publisher and not a penny in royalties paid.

The Better Business Bureau received 114 complaints against the company and downgraded Dog Ear Publishing from an A grade to an F grade. Numerous media reports within the publishing industry began warning about Dog Ear Publishing's practices and its owner, Ray Robinson.

Our author Facebook group neared one hundred members. No author had received their digital files, photos, or royalties. Finally, one author found an attorney in Indiana eager to take on our extraordinary publisher cases. On December 16, 2019, I retained attorney Aaron Harshman to represent me in a lawsuit against Dog Ear Publishing and its owner, Ray Robinson. So much for the blazers, heels, and book tour I prepared for.

As the holidays rolled around, another tragedy struck on December 28, 2019. This time it was reported that a thirty-seven-year-old man, Grafton E. Thomas ambushed the home of Rabbi Chaim Rottenberg in Monsey, NY. Thomas stabbed five people with a machete as they celebrated Hanukkah.

According to a *WCBI* article, "Hanukkah stabbings suspect allegedly searched 'Jewish temples near me,'" Thomas' family stated the attack was not motivated by anti-Semitism, but rather mental illness. They said: "Grafton Thomas has a long history of mental illness and hospitalizations. He has no history of violent acts and no convictions for any crime. He has no known history of anti-Semitism and was raised in a home that embraced and respected all religions and races. He is not a member of any hate groups."

A *Chicago Tribune* article by Ryan Tarinelli, Jim Mustian and Larry Neumeister, "New York Hanukkah stabbing suspect had anti-Semitic journals and researched Hitler online, officials say," reports court papers filed in a 2013 Utah eviction case show Thomas said he suffered from schizophrenia, depression, and anxiety, and his "conditions are spontaneous and untamed." At the time of the Hanukkah attack, Thomas' family claimed Thomas was hearing voices. They suspected he may have stopped taking his psychiatric medications. Michael Sussman, an attorney retained by the family, searched Thomas' home. Reminding me of my own manic writings in 2001, Sussman found journals described as "the ramblings of a disturbed individual," but nothing to indicate the attack had an "anti-Semitic motive." Rather, Sussman said, Grafton Thomas told him that "a voice talked to him about property that was in the rabbi's house." Ultimately, anti-Semitic behavior was blamed for the attacks. Grafton Thomas was found unfit to stand trial and remained confined to a mental health institution.

The new year 2020 finally rolled in. Despite everything, I was excited about the new year. I had been looking forward to 2020 for a very long time. After all, I was turning fifty in 2020! That was a huge milestone in life; a half-century!

Tour preparations began, but I wasn't scheduled to hit the road until Spring. Since Chad required extensive daily medical care, every moment spent at home with him was a gift. Thankfully, his mare, BG stayed with him inside the barn; she was a loyal, loving companion for Chad, too.

One day at home, I experienced unusually heavy chest congestion. While I cleaned the barn, I found myself gasping for breath. I stopped often just to focus on getting air into my lungs. It came to mind that the barn dust, and the extensive time I spent in the barn with Chad, had caused a problem in my lungs.

During the middle of the night, the difficulty breathing was so awful it caused me to wake up. I tried various things to relieve the symptom: I stood outside in the cold air, took a hot shower, and inhaled a dynamic mix of menthol eucalyptus essential oils that would generally clear up any congestion instantly. Plus, Vicks. Nothing worked.

Due to my severe adverse reactions to cold medicine, taking any commercial decongestant was not an option. Instead, I purchased a Primatene Mist inhaler to use. That worked great! The inhaler provided relief for my breathing. Soon, I could breathe again without gasping for air.

Over the years, I saw many artists benefit from chiropractic treatment, so I booked an appointment with a chiropractor. The chiropractic care supported my central nervous system and helped my body's natural ability to heal. I scheduled monthly chiropractic appointments as a routine part of my healthcare.

As I managed home projects, worked on videos, and made tour preparations, news grew about a coronavirus, Covid-19, that was infecting people. Slowly then quickly, tour after tour began to be postponed. Venues and businesses shut down. Ultimately, everyone was placed in a mandated lockdown to control the spread of Covid-19. "Flatten the curve," they told us.

Our music tour would not happen. Nobody's would. All work ceased. In a way, that was a blessing for me; it afforded me the time to stay home with Chad when he needed me most. Thankfully there was also pandemic unemployment available to relieve any potential financial concerns as well.

By mid-March 2020, unusual activity began happening on my social media, electronics, and even my credit cards, car, and banking. I received worrying text messages appearing to be from a friend, but when I reached out to that friend, it turned out they had never contacted me at all. Repeatedly I received text and social media messages identified as though they were coming from someone I knew; however, that was not the case. Some messages and images were quite disturbing and alarming and even included death threats. In a few instances, my credit card transactions and the dashboard in my car were displayed in a foreign language I did not know. At times, I was unable to access my banking accounts. I may be tech-challenged, but all signs pointed to my information having been compromised. I suspected I'd been hacked or was experiencing what was described by the United Nations as a Cyber-Torture attack. Too much tech...

The Covid crisis worsened daily. Lockdowns, masks, and quarantines were being mandated upon society. Fortunately, the feed stores and grocery stores remained fully operational. Chad's doctors were able to continue working and checking on him. He required extensive medications, intensive care, and monitoring, but Chad's spirits remained good; a determined trooper indeed!

While in Covid lockdown, instinctively, something about the pandemic smelled fishy. The virus symptoms included chest congestion, cough, fever, sore throat, and body aches. The symptoms paralleled any other common virus. It seemed easily treatable to me. At work, I had an entire road case filled with natural and pharmaceutical items to aid such symptoms.

I suspected the heavy chest congestion I previously experienced myself and remedied on my own was the coronavirus. Oddly, no treatments for the virus or basic healthcare were even being promoted. Any such mention of basic common sense healthcare or well-being on social media platforms got people banned from those platforms. Worse still, the virus seemed to take a very politicized turn for the worse. Something alarmed me like a red flag. Common sense began not being so common anymore.

Each day as the coronavirus pandemic intensified, I vocalized my discontent with the Covid measures the government was implementing in society. I articulated my opposition to the lockdowns, "woke" culture, cancel culture, and censorship that was brewing by the day.

The unprecedented government impositions and authoritarian measures spurred my passion for politics. I was reminded of my own political activism while attending the University of North Carolina at Charlotte. As a student there, I became very involved in the 1992 Presidential Election and produced what I called an 'Awareness Fest' smack in the heart of the university campus. My outreach to organizations and news outlets described my event:

"This day is aimed at alerting people of various social, political, and environmental issues. It is a day to ask questions, get answers, gain information, get involved, and help make a change. Various organizations, both on and off campus, will come to the Awareness Fest to provide literature and speak about existing problems, causes, and solutions in our country today. Furthermore, tables will be provided for those who wish to register to vote, learn to vote by absentee ballot, and donate (food/clothes/money) to the homeless. Speakers will be present for various discussions throughout the day. These include AIDS, Racism, Abortion, and the Environment. The event kicks off at 9:20am with a FLAG CEREMONY and introduction of representing organizations."

Not only did I have dozens of organizations participate in my 1992 event, plus registered hundreds of students and faculty to vote, I also had support from MTV Rock the Vote, made the *Charlotte Observer* newspaper, and delivered a powerful twenty-minute prepared speech that withstood the test of time. I remained proud of my bi-partisan accomplishment and activism for America.

A large color photo of myself, along with a group of students who were speaking at the microphone, appeared in the newspaper. Under the *Charlotte Observer* newspaper feature photo, "Rallying Young Voters," by T. Ortega Gaines, it read:

"UNC Charlotte student David Z. urges fellow students to stand up for America on Thursday during an Awareness Fair at Belk Tower on the UNCC campus. Organized by junior theater major Dawn Jeronowitz (at right, holding flag), the event was aimed at increasing voter awareness on campus, 'The purpose was to inform people that there are good candidates, that they need to get involved, and they need to vote,' said Jeronowitz. 'We don't have enough people voting in our country, especially college students.'"

My April, 1992 'Awareness Fest' at UNCC

Poster for my October, 1992 'Awareness Fest' at UNCC

My 1992 'Awareness Fest' at UNCC

Unable to do any promotion, my book remained in limbo. It was still available on Amazon and other book sales sites, yet it was listed for hundreds of dollars rather than the $16 price I had set. Our group of authors had successfully gotten Dog Ear Publishing shut down, but our files were still not returned, and monies were never paid. Many of us had active lawsuits in Indiana against the publisher. The Indiana Office of Attorney General had an open case looking into Dog Ear Publishing. Even the FBI had surprisingly opened a case on them too! Unfortunately, the courts remained closed because of Covid.

One March morning, I went to feed Chad and BG their breakfast in the barn. Chad was lying down, but not like his usual lying down. Instead, Chad was sprawled out flat, sweaty, and moaning. Worse, there were feces under his tail which indicated to me that Chad had not gotten up throughout the night, not even to relieve himself. Needless to say, that was not good at all. In fact, it was a dire situation. I was terrified and immediately called the Vet.

While waiting for the doctor to arrive, I desperately needed hay but could not go to the store and leave Chad. Distraught, I noticed neighbors, a husband and wife in their early thirties who moved in just four years prior, were outside with their ponies; I thought to ask them for a bale of hay, even though the neighbors and I had never before spoken.

Previously, there were community concerns about the neighbors firing guns for hours upon hours on their property in our residential New Jersey neighborhood. The neighbors were mad when the community complained about it and blamed me when they were made to cease firing. It was recommended to me by the township that I not engage with them. However, I was in a dire situation with Chad and needed hay for him.

As I walked to speak to the neighbors, I stepped ten feet onto their property while remaining a safe two hundred feet distance away from them. I called out, asking if I could please have one bale of hay, and expressed that I would graciously replace it as soon as I was able to do so. The neighbors never took any steps to walk toward me or offer any help. Instead, they stayed exactly where they were and just stared at me.

It was pointless; they were not neighbors to be counted on in a time of need. I went back to my house.

Eventually, the vet arrived. We managed to get Chad up and take X-rays of his hooves. I was provided with more pain medications for him. We scheduled another appointment with the farrier to come out and trim Chad's hooves. Thankfully, within a few days, Chad was standing again and remained hearty in his appetite and determination.

While home alone during the Covid lockdown, in addition to home improvement projects and taking care of Chad, I had been working on making a variety of political videos covering nearly forty different hot topics and issues. Most ideas I had fleshed out were developed over decades of life experiences from my college years, plus working and traveling throughout my country and the world. At fifty years old, and considering the turbulent times, I contemplated running for an elected political office.

In the late evening of March 30, 2020, I was working on speech writing, delivery, and projection. While home alone and passionately delivering the speech I had presented at my college Awareness Fest, I noticed two strange men walking down my long driveway and toward my house. Notably, there was a closed gate at the end of my driveway to prevent the horses from potentially going into the road. Clearly, the men had jumped my gate and were trespassing on my property. It was dark; I was alone and naturally concerned.

Unsure whether to immediately call the police, I stepped outside my door and remained on my front porch stoop. At that point, I could see the two men were dressed in plain green uniforms with darker pants and lighter green button-down shirts. I called out and asked who they were. I asserted they were trespassing on private property and asked them to leave. The two men said nothing; they just kept walking toward me.

Growing more frightened, I again stressed to the men that they were trespassing on private property. I told them to leave and informed them I would call the police.

The men then stopped walking. One called out to say they had heard me yelling. The men still did not identify themselves but asked what I was doing. As I told the men I was working on a performance-speaking project, I apologized if I was too loud and assured them that I would stop for the night. Again, I asked the men to identify themselves and warned them I would call the police. The two men said nothing more as they turned and walked away, back down my driveway toward the road and into the darkness of night.

It was a sleepless night, a scary night. And the following day, March 31, 2020, was a shitty day. Restless with worry about the two unidentified men in green, combined with cyber-attacks, hacks, and death threats I experienced online, plus growing pandemic politics and still caring for Chad in his compromised health condition, I needed company and support.

The vet and farrier were scheduled to come by for Chad that day. I asked my parents to come to my house and help with that. I also asked Debbie to come over and hoped she could offer another perspective on the frightening situations I faced.

After Chad's appointments were finished, my father ordered pizza. Feeling unsettled, scared, and unsure of my safety at home alone, I expressed my fears and concerns to my parents and Debbie. While Debbie remained quiet, my parents were far from understanding. Unfortunately, their dismissal of my experiences and the excessive worry they exhibited about my distress did nothing to calm my concerns. Instead, it rapidly became a source of heightened and escalated tension.

By evening, while we all sat in my living room, I had enough of my overbearing parents and asked them nicely to leave. They would not. They could see I was frustrated, but they kept insisting they were worried about me. I very much wanted my parents to leave so I could spend time talking with Debbie, but they still would not go. Repeatedly, I asked my parents to leave my house until, eventually, I had to scream at them over and over to "Get the fuck out of my house!"

Finally, at last, they left. But I was so drained by the drama my parents evoked that I told Debbie I was no longer up for having a discussion that night and asked her to leave as well. By then, I simply wanted to decompress from the day. Debbie understood, we hugged, and she left.

At last, the house was quiet again. Exhausted, I wanted to do a final night check on Chad before securing my home and property, then going to bed. As I stepped outside my house and headed for the barn, I noticed a lot of flashing lights down by the road. I could not see what was happening, but there was definitely a commotion that appeared to be from the identifiable lights of a tow truck.

I called out to see if anyone needed help but heard nothing. Instead, I saw the two men in green uniforms walking down my driveway again and heading toward me! Standing on my front porch stoop, I repeatedly called to the men asking them to identify themselves. The men said nothing and kept walking toward me. As they were nearing me, I warned the men I would call the police. Still, the men said nothing and kept walking toward me.

Terrified, I went inside my house to get my phone and call the police. But before I could even do so, while I was standing in my living room, the two unidentified men in green opened my front door and entered INSIDE MY HOUSE!

In absolute fear for my life that the men were about to shoot me, my immediate response was to pull my pink ski hat down over my eyes so I would not see the gun as I was killed. Without the immediate sound of a shot, I quickly pulled my hat up to see the two unidentified men in green still coming toward me, fully inside my living room and only steps away from me!

Unable to complete the call to the police, I turned to run out the back door of my kitchen and away from the intruders. When I opened the back door, I saw a large man in a dark-colored uniform. He immediately grabbed me while another man piled on and wrestled me. Absolutely petrified while being physically assaulted by strange men in the sanctity of my own home, I heard one man complain that my back deck was slippery. The two men, maybe more, restrained me and put me into the back of an ambulance that had pulled up near the front door of my house.

Secured to a gurney, beaten and battered, I lay there with four men surrounding me in the back of the vehicle. I asked for their identities, but none would comply. I inquired if any were the names of those who had threatened me online, but the men just laughed.

In pure terror, I remained calm and quiet as I was transported to some unknown place. When we arrived at the destination, I was wheeled into a small white cinderblock room and placed onto a cold, hard metal bed. The metal bed was the only thing inside the room. My hands and feet were tightly bound and strapped down to the table by a team of people wearing what appeared to be hazmat suits and masks. None of the team members spoke to me. Nobody asked me anything or told me anything. My personal being was not even acknowledged.

With no idea of their intentions, it took all my strength and courage to remain still, quiet, and calm as the team of people slowly injected multiple needles of something into my body. I silently watched in terror as though these were the last moments of my life. First, they injected needles filled with a clear fluid into each of my legs, then one needle full into each of my arms, and something into the bottom of my feet.

As soon as they finished injecting me, the team turned and left the room. I was left alone, bound, petrified. They never returned. I desperately tried to remain awake, but I soon lost consciousness.

When I finally awoke from the drug-induced blackout, it was days later. I was disheveled, bruised, confused, and dressed in different clothes that were not mine. I was unable to determine where I was, but it appeared to be a hospital room.

Slowly, as my senses returned, I began to become aware of my surroundings. Despite the fact that I had been home alone and preparing to go to bed, never caused any public nuisance, and never made any threat to harm myself or others, I suspected I was in a hospital under a psychiatric hold.

My concern immediately turned to Chad. I was allowed to make a phone call to my parents, who assured me he was ok; my parents would stay and care for him and my other animals too.

I was unconstitutionally detained in that hospital for six days. Despite it being the early days of April 2020 and a global Covid pandemic was in full progress, neither patients nor staff wore any face masks. Nobody practiced any social distancing. None of that was even mentioned. There was also no discernable overcrowding at the hospital.

Every morning and night at the facility, the nurses tried to forcibly drug me. They warned that being non-compliant would only permit them to keep me there longer. Aside from daily pill distribution and meals, the bulk of the day in their psychiatric program consisted of watching TV, coloring, doing puzzles, or talking with other patients. An hour-long group therapy session happened each morning and afternoon, which consisted of doing some stretches, having an open discussion with a single-page worksheet, then coloring. I found it shameful they called it healthcare at all. It was imprisonment. Dehumanizing seemed to be their objective; compliance their goal. The nurses seemed to excite themselves in asserting power over others at any expense.

Upon my release, I was livid and disgusted. My home and myself had been brutally violated. Regardless of the Covid lockdown, I spent the following weeks in isolation, not wanting to speak to anyone at all. Instead, I focused my days on taking care of Chad, repairing fencing, and remodeling my house interior in hopes of cleansing all of the horror and violence that had planted a presence in my sacred home.

In mid-April, I received a letter from one of the vendors I worked with while on tour. The letter explained that their company recently became aware of a data security breach incident beginning in February. An unauthorized party had accessed their computer server and the accounts of personnel. Our compromised information included names, addresses, email addresses, birthdates, social security numbers, and financial account information. They assured me a cyber security firm was engaged to assist with the investigation. Receiving that letter brought a little relief for me. The information revealed that I may not have been targeted in an isolated cyber-torture attack; others too may have experienced such disturbance. Not knowing what corruption may have been living in my electronics, for additional precaution, I decided to get a completely new computer, email, cell phone, credit card accounts and internet service.

May rolled in, and so did the bills. Adding insult to injury, I began receiving thousands of dollars in invoices from the hospital and doctors. Plus, I received an $852 invoice for a three-mile ambulance ride from the medical transport company. The chance I was going to pay the invoices was zero.

Gaining the strength to begin my inquest into the unidentified men in green who illegally entered my home, I sought answers. Upon calling the hospital, unbeknownst to me, I discovered there was a police report for the 3/31 incident. Of course, I obtained that report and was shocked to read what was written. The narrative in the police incident report alleged:

"Daughter is having a mental breakdown and threatening to harm herself/Neg Weapons. Dawn was suicidal and in crisis; the mother believed Dawn was a danger to herself. Upon arrival the officers were met by the caller who advised the subject had a history of bi-polar disorder. She had not slept in several days and reported that she was hearing voices that were telling her she needed to die before the sun rose. Upon contact with the subject, she was outside the front door of the home, she had a flashlight in her hand and a lantern at her feet. The subject was screaming however, we were unable to decipher what she was saying. She retreated into the home and asked us to leave. Several times she stated she was going to call the police and we were trespassing. I asked her to call the police to confirm our identity's. After several minutes of attempting to de-escalate the situation, Ms. Jeronowitz pulled a hat over her face (in an attempt to hide from officers) the caller had previously advised she (Ms. Jeronowitz) ran into the woods to escape the police. Ms. Jeronowitz ran out the back door. She was stopped by officers and began to fight. She was subdued with compliance holds and taken into custody."

There was so much falsehood in that police report I wanted to gag. Considering we had been in Covid lockdown and I was home alone every night, alleging that I had "not slept in several days" was a fabrication that struck me oddly. I know I slept. I was there. I did it. And thankfully, each time I did sleep, I woke up too. The only sleepless night I had was after the frightening experience when two unidentified men in green came down my driveway, then retreated back into the night.

Also, I neither reported nor experienced "hearing voices," and especially not voices telling me I needed to "die before the sun rose." The police report narrative acknowledged that I was on my front porch and called to the men in green, but it claimed the men could not decipher what I was saying. Still, the report then acknowledged the men clearly heard me asking them to leave, as well as when I had stated several times that they were trespassing and I was going to call the police. The unidentified men wore green uniforms, not police uniforms. They were NOT police; they never identified themselves as police or identified themselves at all.

Also, the incident report claimed that the men asked me to call the police to confirm their identity. *Confirm their identity as who?* I wondered. The two men never provided their identity, despite my repeated requests.

I was extremely curious about the "several minutes of trying to de-escalate the situation" claim. Did they believe following a woman into her private home and assaulting her while she attempted to call the police on two unidentified, strange male intruders in green uniforms was "de-escalating" a situation?

The narrative reported I ran out the back door of my house; it recognized a police officer was outside there. That must have been the man in the dark uniform, a police officer uniform, that I saw when I exited my back door on that terrifying night. As much information as that police incident report offered, it also opened the door to A LOT more questions in need of answers.

I had not spoken to my parents since I returned home from the hospital. Upon reading the narrative of the police incident report, I texted my father for answers to my many questions. In contrast to the record of the police incident report, my fathers' response to whether my parents told anyone that I was 'bi-polar' or 'suicidal' was no.

While the police had my parents remain at the end of my driveway, near the road, on 3/31, they seemingly also told my parents a different story about what had occurred in my home that wicked night.

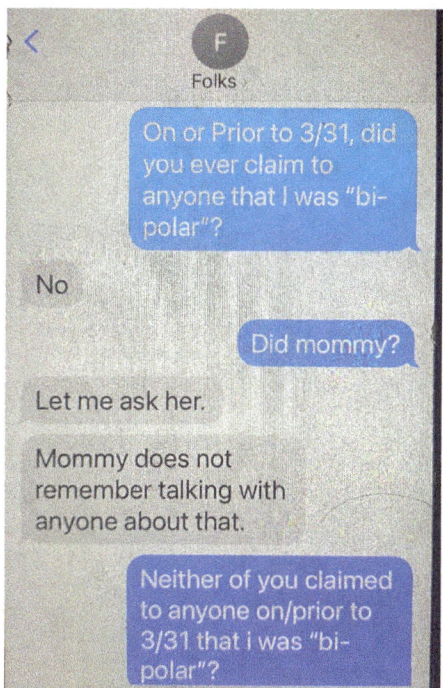

Text with my Dad

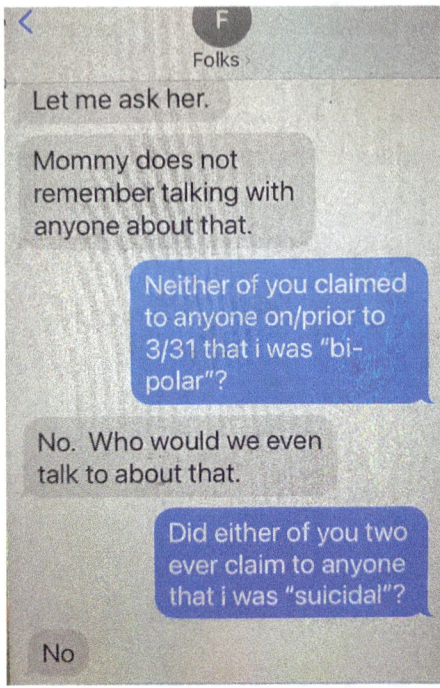

Let me ask her.

Mommy does not remember talking with anyone about that.

Neither of you claimed to anyone on/prior to 3/31 that i was "bi-polar"?

No. Who would we even talk to about that.

Did either of you two ever claim to anyone that i was "suicidal"?

No

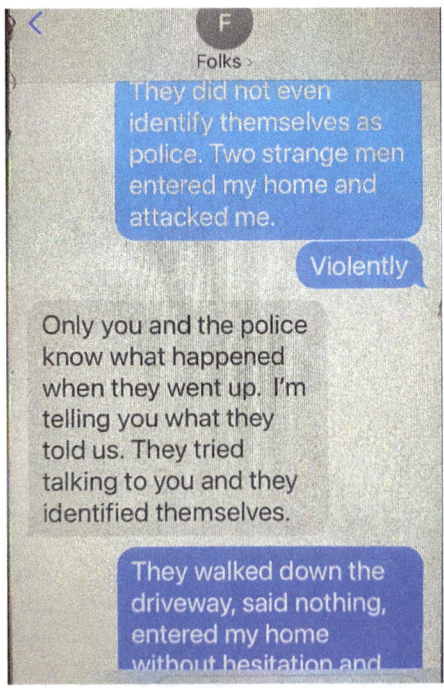

They did not even identify themselves as police. Two strange men entered my home and attacked me.

Violently

Only you and the police know what happened when they went up. I'm telling you what they told us. They tried talking to you and they identified themselves.

They walked down the driveway, said nothing, entered my home without hesitation and

Also, I had not spoken to Debbie since that 3/31 night. Wanting to get answers from her, I texted Debbie questions. She also denied hearing me say I wanted to kill myself or "die before the sun rose." From what I gathered, after they left my house, Debbie and my parents were still at the road at the end of my driveway when the police and men in green arrived. Debbie mentioned a tow truck was there, too; that confirmed the lights I saw that night which attracted my attention. It struck me as strange that the police did not want to speak to Debbie at all, especially considering she was a friend of mine who had just spent the day with me and was present on the scene.

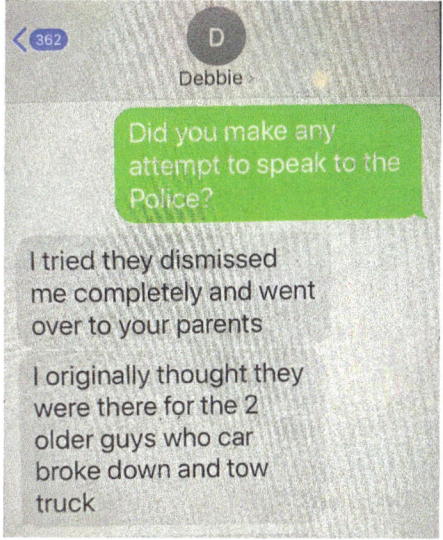

My Text with Debbie

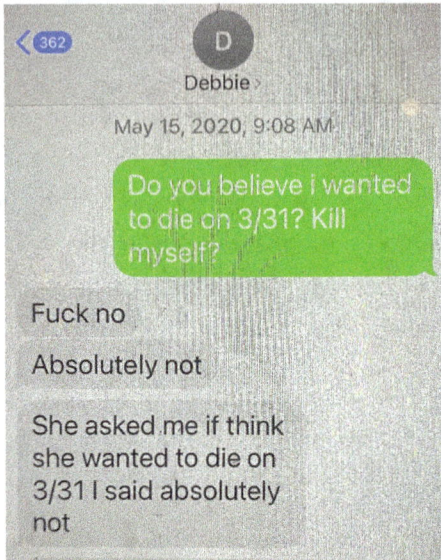

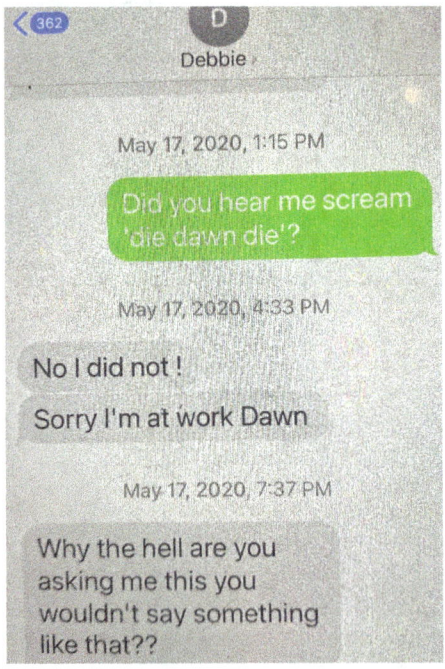

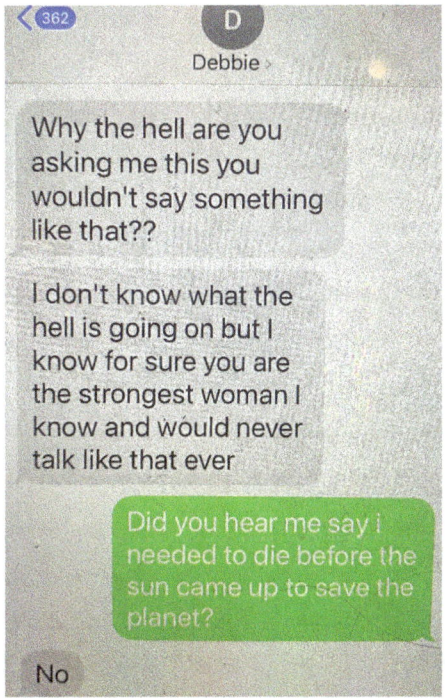

> Why the hell are you asking me this you wouldn't say something like that??
>
> I don't know what the hell is going on but I know for sure you are the strongest woman I know and would never talk like that ever

Did you hear me say i needed to die before the sun came up to save the planet?

> No

Did you hear me say i needed to die before the sun came up to save the planet?

> No

This is what my parents claim i was screaming when you were all here. Die dawn dawn to save the planet

Die dawn die

> They are out of their fucking minds...Im so upset and pissed at their bullshit right now

Of course, I followed up by going to the medical transport company to gather those records as well. The Endeavor Emergency Squad, First Agency Unit report included the language:

"Chief complaint: exhibiting strange behavior; acting strange and screaming randomly, Father states patient is bi-polar and is non-compliant with any medications. Medical history: Bi-polar; Obtained from Family."

The neurological exam of the report continued:

"AAO x 3 (person is orientated to person, place, time), Event Memory Intact, Appropriate Behavior, Gag Reflex Intact, Clear Speech, PERL (pupils equal and reactive to light). Level of consciousness – Agitated: no. Loss of consciousness: no. No known drug allergies reported by patient."

Stop. Seriously? Had they asked me about any allergies I had, I certainly would have told them about my allergic reactions to cold medicine and pharmaceutical drugs. It was not something I was known to be silent about; on the contrary. I had my FDA testimony, a lawsuit against a pharmaceutical drug manufacturer, and a published book that detailed my adverse experiences with pharmaceutical drugs. Plus, I had a breast biopsy bracelet. For my best health and safety, I needed only to be compliant with myself.

It confounded me that no medical mention was made relevant to my menstrual cycle or menopause. I was, after all, a fifty-year-old woman. As a female, the menstrual cycle inquiry was always part of any medical examination. In 2001, I was told I experienced numbness in my finger and anxiety and needed an SSRI pink pill because of low serotonin due to my menstrual cycle. Despite this, nobody inquired about it; no medical mention was made. Even more, at no point did anyone ask for the name or contact information of my personal doctor. Nobody asked if I had a doctor at all.

I also obtained the medical records from the hospital where I was involuntarily taken and held in captivity. Intake language there included:

"History of non-compliance with medications. No known allergies. No known drug allergies. No known food allergies. Voice paranoid thoughts about being hacked but she is coherent."

I was determined to confirm the identities of the men in green, so I sent an email to my township police department on June 5. I inquired about obtaining the police body camera video from the 3/31 horror at my house. The township police records officer, T. Hartman, replied to me in a single sentence:

"Our officers DO NOT have body cams."

Two weeks later, on June 18, I took a quick trip to the grocery store. Gone only thirty minutes, upon nearing my house on the way home, the road was blocked and filled with over twenty emergency vehicles. The sky was filled with black smoke from a blazing fire! Desperate to make my way through the firetrucks, police vehicles, and first responders, I was terrified that it was my house or barn on fire. Thank God, that was not the case.

The fire was coming from the neighbor's property, the one I previously asked for a bale of hay. Despite their six acres being an agricultural and farm-assessed property, that neighbor was not farming. Instead, they had been operating a commercial recreational vehicle rental business on their property in defiance of township zoning and ordinances. On that day, one of their ten motor homes was ablaze. The fire burned for hours, and the incident even made the newspaper.

Fortunately, I was able to make my way home safely; the fire had not spread to my property. But considering the RVs were parked along our property line and near my trees, the fire did provide much caution and concern.

Days later, on June 24, I contacted a member of my Town Council. First, I explained to him my concern regarding the neighbor's fire and the illegal operation of their RV rental business. What was once a beautiful crop field for soy and corn had been covered with a driveway and a large parking lot to accommodate a dozen large motor homes by the neighbor. That had since become my view outside my kitchen window. Secondly, I explained to the councilman what had happened to me on 3/31 when my home and myself were violated. Finally, I informed him that I was seeking the identity of the two men in green who entered my home illegally and then assaulted me. The councilman took my information.

Later that same day, late afternoon, I received a phone call from that councilman. He was at the gate of my property! I walked down the driveway to meet him and another man who accompanied him and was introduced to me as his son. For the next hour, the two men walked with me around my sprawling property while I explained in great detail all that I had experienced on 3/31, as well as the ongoing problems with the neighbor and the fire.

Throughout his visit, the councilman frequently looked toward the neighbor's house, seemingly making assessments. I presented the councilman with the police, hospital, and medical transport reports I had thus far acquired, as well as the letter I received from work that alerted me to the data security breach. The councilman confirmed that the two men in green were from the Endeavor Emergency Squad. They were not police.

When I explained to the councilman about the thousands of dollars of invoices I received from the hospital, doctors, and Endeavor medical transport, the councilman agreed with me and told me that if it were him, he would not pay those bills either. With concern, he suggested that certain parties would be seeking to discredit me. I explained I was not concerned about that; people who knew me, knew me well. Others could believe what they chose.

Still wanting confirmation from my police department as to the true identity of the two men in green who entered my home, the following day, I went to my township police department. There, I spoke with two officers, one of whose name appears on the police incident report from 3/31. Neither officer would confirm the identities of the men who entered my home that night in March. Instead, I was simply offered a piece of paper to provide a Voluntary Statement. That day, I submitted a brief account for the record. I wrote:

"*On the evening of March 31, 2020, approx. 11pm, two men wearing light green uniforms came down my dark, gated, private driveway. When I saw the men, I asked who they were. They did not respond. I told the men to leave again as they were trespassing. I told them I was going to call the police. When I entered my home to get my phone, the two men followed me inside my home and began assaulting me. They then dragged me from my home & took me away. I was no danger to myself or others, made no threats, was unarmed, had asked the men to leave. My house was broken into by these strangers who then assaulted me without any warrant.*"

Before leaving the Police Department, I pointed out to the officers the irony and sheer hypocrisy of the mass destruction, violence, vandalism, rioting, looting, tearing down of statues, and burning of cities that was transpiring across our nation that summer of 2020, that was continuing unabated, with little or no interference by any law enforcement.

On July 2, I sent another email to the Police Records Officer, T. Hartman. I told him the police report from 3/31 clearly stated that the police could confirm the identities of the two men who entered my home and assaulted me. The police incident report stated: "*I asked her to call the police to confirm our identity's.*" Again, I asked T. Hartman to please confirm and provide me with the identities of the two men who entered my house on 3/31. For transparency, I copied the township clerk and councilman in all my police department communications.

The reply I received to my inquest came from the township clerk, who replied to me:

"*Under OPRA laws, we are only required to produce written records that are on file which has been provided to you. If you wish to discuss the content of the report provided, you will need to contact the Sgt or Officer who took and prepared the report directly. We have provided all documents on file regarding this incident and deem this request fulfilled.*"

To say the least, I was not feeling fulfilled, and responded to the township clerk:

"*The police incident report states: "I asked her to call the police to confirm our identities." I am doing exactly as instructed per the police report: I am asking Township Police to confirm to me the identities of these two men. Please provide me their identification as they and I have both requested.*"

Additionally, I sent an email to officer T. Hartman stating:

"*I am understanding that the Township Police Department is UNABLE to confirm to me the identity of two men who entered into my home, assaulted me, dragged me away from my home on March 31, 2020. How may I best proceed with filing a criminal report and investigation into who these intruders were who broke into my home and attacked me? In order to report this crime during pandemic time, must I file a criminal report at the Police Station? Or is this done via internet, phone or an officer sent to my house to file a criminal report? Please advise.*"

Again, T. Hartman replied to me in one sentence:

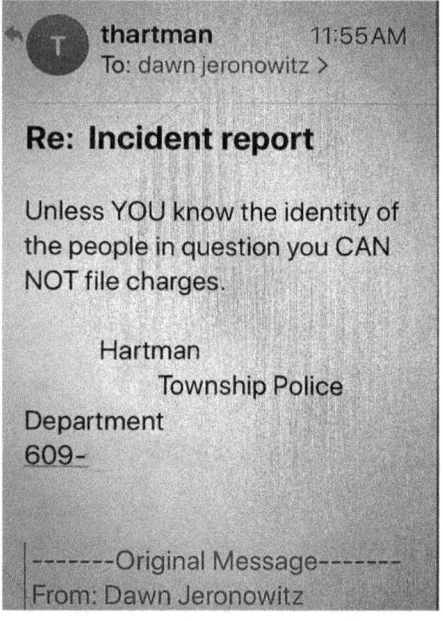

T. Hartman, Township Police Department, reply to my inquest.

"Unless YOU know the identity of the people in question you CAN NOT file charges." Despite the police statement in the incident report, my township police department would not confirm the identities of the two men in green after all.

All efforts to contact the police officers went unanswered. None would return my phone calls or respond to emails.

Two days later, on July 4, I went to my police department. I met two officers outside police headquarters and hand-delivered a letter to them. In the letter, I asked the police to please obtain a complete statement from my friend Debbie regarding the events of 3/31. Providing them with her email address and phone number, I informed the police that Debbie had been a friend for fifteen years and was present at my house before and during the police-involved events that night. I asked the police to please collect her witness statement and include it in the incident report. Without a verbal response, the officers took my letter then retreated inside the police building, where the public was no longer permitted to go.

Additionally, I asked my parents to provide their statements to the police. They assured me they would do so.

A few days later, on July 10, when I walked down my driveway to get the mail, I noticed the neighbor husband was outside. In an earnest effort to make amends with him, I called out to him and asked if he had a moment to talk with me.

He came over to our property line, near a telephone pole at the road. He was a small, thin, scrappy man in his early 30s, with dark hair, grungy. Knowing the gunfire on his property was a source of contention, I apologized to him for yelling about it a few years earlier. I expressed how I strongly supported the Second Amendment; I had no objection to guns. In fact, I fired a pretty good shot myself and been told I have good form. I apologized for any turmoil I may have caused.

The neighbor seemed eased, so I proceeded to engage in a brief conversation about our farming community. We talked about the neighborhoods' potential, and I suggested we landscape the area near the road where our property lines met. That area was wholly overgrown and could certainly use maintenance and sprucing up.

I thought the neighborly meeting went well, so I offered to exchange phone numbers. Not having a pen or phone on me, I told the neighbor if he and his wife were inclined to work together on the landscaping project, he was welcome to leave their phone number in a spot near my property sign. Before we departed, I asked him if he had any helpful recommendations. He told me: "More rice." As I laughed and asked what that meant, he smirked and walked away.

In the following days, I went about my business doing home improvement projects, caring for Chad and BG, tackling 3/31 paperwork, and getting out of the house for some shopping and food. Though many stores remained open, the world was still in Covid lockdown; my roadie gig remained shut down. Fortunately, unemployment benefits covered my home expenses.

The hospital, doctor, and medical transport company were still sending invoices to me; I was still not paying them. Chad's medical expenses were growing by the day but well worth every dollar and cent.

On July 13, after putting my little Ollia dog in a crossbody sling pouch, we headed out to the store. When I pulled out of my driveway, I saw the neighbor was outside. As I drove past their house, I tooted my car horn with a friendly hello. Realizing I had forgotten my face mask and would not be permitted inside the store without it, I turned the car around to retrieve a face mask from home.

Before doing so, I'd been thinking about the landscaping project the neighbor and I had previously discussed, so I decided to first stop at their house to inquire if they would be interested in splitting the cost of an eight-foot-tall colorful metal rooster being sold at the Tractor Supply. Not only was the rooster a fun piece of art for the roadside area, but it could also serve to attract customers for the eggs the neighbor had recently been aiming to sell.

Taking a moment, I pulled ten feet into the neighbors' long driveway and respectfully stopped my car there. As I opened my car door and stepped out, I could see the neighbor was with a small group of people near their house and approximately two-hundred feet away from me. Oddly, the neighbor made no gesture to walk toward me or greet me. I tooted my car horn and tried to call out to them, but still, nobody made any move in my direction. Instead, the group just stared at me. It seemed peculiar. Receiving no response and merely distant stares, I got back in my car and left. I tried not to take it personally, but considering I believed we had made amends, something about their lack of neighborly decorum made me feel uneasy. I continued onward with my day.

Upon retrieving my face mask from home, along the way to the store, and just down the street from my house, I made a quick stop at a local township police department. While my own township police department was a twenty-minute drive away, the local township police department was only a two-minute drive down the road. All things considered, I was not feeling very safe or protected by my own township police department; on the contrary. Even more, I was feeling apprehensive about my neighbor. For my own safety, I wanted to provide my contact information to the nearby local police department in case of an emergency.

I was surprised to find the building was open. As I entered, it was empty and eerily quiet. I walked up to a customer window and waited for someone to appear. When an officer finally emerged, he sat behind a desk, crossed his arms, and looked at me but said nothing. I began to explain to him that I lived down the street and was having concerns about my neighbor and my police department. I inquired if he would be able to take my information in case I might require police assistance. The officer said nothing; he just sat in the chair and stared at me. I took my driver's license from my wallet and pushed it through a small opening in the glass window. The officer took my license and looked at it. Still, he said nothing. Feeling forlorn, I requested my license back; however, he would not return it to me. Frustrated, I turned, left, and continued on with my trip to the store.

Five minutes later, I arrived at the big 24-hour big-box store that remained open during Covid. Oddly, there was a row of security guards standing outside along the storefront. I asked a guard what was going on, wondering if the store was open. The guard informed me the store was closed but would not provide further details. The next closest store that would have what I needed was thirty minutes away, so I drove there. Unfortunately, that location was closed as well.

I returned home around 10:30pm. Before pulling through my gate, I stopped at the end of my driveway to take down the 4th of July decorations I had displayed there. It took about ten minutes to take everything down and load into my car. Next, I opened my gate and drove down the driveway to my house. The gate closed behind me.

While parking my car and unloading the decorations, with Ollia still in her sling pouch hung around me, I heard someone call my name. Startled, when I looked up, I saw a bright white light at my driveway gate, presumably a flashlight. Again, I heard a man call me. Then I heard him say he was with my township police and wanted to speak to me. I did not know why the police would be at my gate that time of night; I had done nothing wrong. I hollered to the man that I needed to use the restroom and would be right there.

Cautiously, I got back in my car and slowly drove up my driveway and toward my gate. I barely got twenty-feet when suddenly my gate began to open! I did not open my electric gate, but it was opening! Suddenly, there was a flood of many flashlights scattering and charging toward me fast! Terrified, I put the car in reverse, turned around, and drove across my property to my barn paddock.

No sooner than I stopped my vehicle and headed toward my barn than a swarm of men grabbed me. Yet again, I was attacked and assaulted on my own private property. As the men tackled me and I began to fall, Ollia fell from her pouch! It was dark; I could not see where she went, and I began calling for her, but nobody cared. The men continued assaulting me. By then, I was begging for my life. I pleaded and bartered with the officers, but nothing I could say would help.

Beaten and bloodied, I was put into the back of a police SUV. I kept one foot in the door, which prevented the officer from closing it. While he pondered how to close the door with my foot in the way, he unsuccessfully attempted to move my foot. I wondered if he would simply slam the door closed, despite my foot being there. The stocky police officer was dripping with sweat, breathing heavily, and wiping his forehead with his arm. Despite Covid-19, he was not wearing a mask. The officer never spoke to me; he only spoke about me to others who were present, but I could not see. I was not being arrested, had done nothing wrong, and had caused no disturbances. No information was provided to me. Nobody stated why they were there or what I had possibly done to warrant this attack in the night. Eventually, I set my foot inside the vehicle, allowing the sweaty police officer to close the door. He got into the driver's seat and drove me away from my home. I had no idea what became of my little Ollia after she fell out of my pouch and into the dark of night.

I was transported to a building where inside was a large room consisting mainly of a huge command center desk. There were a lot of people sitting behind monitor screens. I was placed into a small medical examination-type room. There, I was probed and injected with multiple needles. As I grew more drugged and intoxicated, somebody wheeled a rolling cart with a monitor screen into the room. They were telling me to talk to the person, a doctor on the screen. Trying to fight off blacking out entirely from the drugs, I tried my best to politely answer the questions coming from the person on the monitor screen. It felt surreal. Unfortunately, due to the drugs, my speech was too garbled. The cart with the monitor screen was rolled away.

I watched police officers humorously corroborate varying stories about me with unidentified people and each other. Frustrated, I repeatedly asked what was going on, why I was being held captive, and what I did to warrant such detainment. Though I did not engage in any yelling or physical action whatsoever, simply inquiring was deemed combative. That led to me being punished for it; held down, then shackled and restrained to the bed.

Hours passed until I was unshackled. I was placed in a wheelchair, then wheeled down hallways and corridors until I arrived at the same area in a hospital where I had been held captive only weeks before.

Ultimately, nobody provided me with any information as to what warranted such an assault and incarceration. Certainly, I had every right to inquire with my township and police department regarding the identities of the men in green who entered my home on 3/31; I knew I had done nothing wrong.

I had been home alone during the Covid lockdown. During that time, I went shopping, went online, talked on the phone, decorated my home, took care of my animals, and nursed Chad. I had all my receipts from the stores and restaurants I patronized without ever encountering any unusual activity or incident.

While I caused no disturbance, I was assaulted and detained upon returning home from a store one night; people all across America were burning cities, destroying businesses and public property, and rioting without consequence. Nothing mattered; I was provided no answers.

Despite being mentally and physically well, not suicidal, psychotic, or a danger to myself or others, I knew that, according to the law, I would be held for seventy-two hours. Nevertheless, the doctors kept me imprisoned in that hospital for seventeen days: July 13 – July 30.

Recalling when the councilman was at my home, the warning he gave me came to mind – that some may want to discredit me. After I watched a girl in a pharmaceutical drug-induced state repeatedly hit her head against a wall, fall to the floor in a fetal position while she screamed insanities, then be released to go home only hours later, it felt like something significant was afoul for me.

While in the hospital again, despite that it was a time of a global Covid-19 pandemic, there was no enforced social distancing or over-crowding whatsoever. None of the patients in the hospital wore a face mask, including myself. There were no extra precautions or sanitation measures taken. Nobody would have known or guessed that Covid-19 or any pandemic even existed.

The room I was provided had two beds, two nightstands, a sealed window, and a bathroom with a sink and toilet. I shared the room with an obese girl with thin, stringy, knotted blond hair. She was thirty-something. The girl spent twenty-three hours a day lying in bed and did not even rise to use the bathroom. Despite my repeated complaints, none of the nurses did anything to help the girl. They did nothing about the filth she created in the room we shared.

When the girl finally attempted to use the bathroom on one occasion, she left fecal matter spread all over the toilet, floor, and sink. I insisted somebody clean the mess and change the bed linens; it was like living inside a litter box. Housekeeping cleaned the bathroom while a nurse stripped the bed. The nurse left behind clean sheets that she expected the patient to put on the bed. That did not happen. The girl simply continued to lie in the bed without any sheets. Nobody cared. But I did.

Out of sympathy, I tried to help that girl. She was so drugged; it broke my heart. I combed her hair for her and offered encouragement. The girl cried and moaned all day. When she wept and cried out for her mother, I assured the girl I would help her to see her mom. The girl provided me with her mother's phone number. She asked if I could call her mom to help arrange a visit.

I took the number and went to the phone area to call. When the mother answered, I began to explain the dire situation about her daughter to her. She had been unaware of how her daughter was being treated and unaware of any side effects associated with the drugs her daughter was given. As the mother was asking questions, telling me she would visit her daughter, the phone receiver was suddenly ripped from my hand, slammed down. It was a nurse. The nurse had been at the command station and listening to our conversation. She began screaming at me, yelling that I was out of line and not authorized to speak to the girls' mother. Had the nurse helped the girl, I would not have called the mother. The mother did visit the next day; the girl was happy to see her. Even better, she showered for the occasion. I was quite glad I called.

Fortunately, I was also able to call my folks, who had found Ollia. They were at my house caring for her, plus Chad and BG too.

The layout of the hospital area was a rectangular hallway. Patient rooms lined three sides of the perimeter; the nurses' command station and an office were on the fourth side. One hallway also had two small private shower rooms; another had two phones on a wall. In the center was a common area with couches, a TV, and a few round tables with chairs. That's where most of all day, every day, was spent; in the common area.

Every morning began with about two dozen inpatients lining up at the nurses' station for the administering of drugs. One by one, every person was given a cup filled with pharmaceutical pills and another cup filled with water. After that, a tall rolling hot box was wheeled into the hallway. One by one, each person was given a food tray with breakfast. We ate our breakfast in the common area. Following breakfast, we watched TV, colored, did puzzles, stayed in our room, showered, or walked laps around the hallway.

At eleven o'clock each morning, whoever felt like it gathered in the common area for a group therapy session. That consisted of stretching and listening to a nurse or social worker talk about coping mechanisms and personal goals, followed by a one-page worksheet assignment that usually involved drawing or coloring. When that hour was over, the tall rolling hot box was wheeled into the hallway. One by one, each person was given a food tray with lunch. After lunch, everyone was once again left to watch TV, color, do puzzles, walk hallway laps, shower or nap.

The cycle repeated at four o'clock with an afternoon group therapy session in the common area. After one hour of that, the tall rolling hot box arrived with a dinner food tray for each person. Following dinner, the line formed at the nurses' station, and one by one, every person was given a cup filled with pharmaceutical pills and another cup filled with water. Once again, we were left to watch TV, color, do puzzles, read or go to bed.

The next day was an exact repeat of the day before. Occasionally, a nurse would escort a group through the locked doors and out to a small enclosed yard area for twenty minutes of fresh air.

After two weeks in the hospital facility, a social worker told me I would attend a virtual court date hearing. At last, I would get to see a judge! I was hopeful that I would get answers to my questions and gain insight into why I was even there.

Unfortunately, I was not permitted to speak during the court hearing. The only thing I was allowed to do was agree to their outpatient treatment program. I was threatened that if I did not agree to their program, I would be held in the hospital indefinitely. Agreeing to their terms, on the upside, the judge ordered my immediate release that day. On the downside, the hospital did not care what the judge ordered. Instead, they kept me imprisoned there for a full two days more.

When July 30, 2020, came and my discharge was finally being prepared, I was instructed to take a blood test before I left. I refused; I had no reason to provide them with my blood. I was threatened by the nurses and social workers. Also, they prepared a stack of discharge paperwork they wanted me to sign but would not permit me the time to read. I was told if I did not comply, I would not be released. I signed their papers to secure my discharge, never took a blood test, and was set free that day at last.

Though my heart was comforted when I was finally home and reunited with Ollia, Chad, and BG, my head knew there was a lot of research and collection of reports to be done.

Despite being home, the ordeal was not over still. Days after I was released from the hospital, a woman came to my house for a meeting. She was part of a mental health group, Legacy Treatment. She instructed that I was ordered to participate in an outpatient treatment program consisting of mandated pharmaceutical psychiatric drugs plus one hour a week on a Zoom call with a social worker. Even more, every day, Monday through Friday, I was required to attend outpatient classes at a facility from 9am-3pm. I was threatened that if I did not comply, I would be taken from my home and permanently placed in a long-term psychiatric facility.

I could not fathom how such weaponization of psychiatry and mental health was legal. I was not suicidal. I never harmed anyone or threatened to harm anyone. I never caused a scene or disruption anywhere I went, nor had I committed any crime or violation. But out of complete fear of another attack and detainment, I decided it was in my best interests to go along with most of the measures until I could gain answers and secure my emancipation from such vile and unjustified mistreatment.

Beginning August 4, each day, I drove twenty minutes to an outpatient facility. Every day upon entering the building, I was required to leave my car keys with the staff. Then, I went into a room with about fifteen other people to participate in a group therapy class. Mostly we talked about coping mechanisms, drew pictures, and colored. A social worker instructed us not to exchange phone numbers or meet with each other outside of the facility. Regardless, I was curious about those people, their stories, and their personal experiences; I made sure to meet them and obtain phone numbers for follow-up.

Also, I obtained the police report from July 13, the night police opened my gate, stormed my property, assaulted and abducted me. Lo and behold, the police incident report stated:

"Dispatched to location for a report of the neighbor, Dawn Jeronowitz, harassing [Mrs. Neighbor] and her husband [Mr. Neighbor] for the last 4 days. [Mrs. Neighbor] stated that on or about Friday July 10 Ms. Jeronowitz was speaking with her husband [Mr. Neighbor] regarding the fact that she is being watched and "they" are watching the [Neighbor] family as well. Ms. Jeronowitz stated that she feared for the safety of the [Neighbor] family as well as her own from the unknown subjects. Throughout the weekend, Ms. Jeronowitz continued to demand to speak to [Mr. Neighbor], which [Mrs. Neighbor] stated he was not at home and could not speak with her."

Firstly, I never spoke to Mrs. Neighbor. She and I had never engaged in conversation. I would not be able to identify her; we had never met. I had a brief conversation with her husband on July 10 about guns, farming, and landscaping, and I believed it was quite amicable. After speaking with her husband at our property line that day, the only additional attempt I made to speak with Mr. Neighbor was when I briefly pulled into their driveway to inquire about purchasing a big decorative rooster. Despite everything, the police report did not mention any statement from Mr. Neighbor, the person with whom I spoke briefly. The report only presented outlandish accusations made by the neighbor's wife without providing any evidence of harassment at all.

The police report continued:

"This prompted Ms. Jeronowitz to continually drive up and down the street in front of the Neighbor residence beeping the horn for extended periods of time. While on location, police observed Ms. Jeronowitz pull down [the neighbor] driveway while shouting at the neighbor family. Sgt and Officer identified ourselves, which prompted Ms. Jeronowitz to begin shouting obscenities toward us regarding the sum of approximately $50,000. Ms. Jeronowitz then drove toward her home, rapidly turned around and left the residence making a right onto the road."

Fascinating. That July 13 day, when I was headed to the store, I tooted my horn at the neighbor as a friendly hello, then turned the car around to retrieve a face mask from home, but before doing so, I made a brief stop at the neighbor's house to inquire about purchasing the decorative rooster. The police were at the neighbor's house; according to the police incident report, it was police officers who were the small group of people I saw gathered with the neighbor near their house while I was up the driveway in my car. If police officers were at the neighbor's house at that time, it is unclear why none would have simply walked up the driveway to speak with me then. Seemingly, my apprehensive instinct was spot on that day.

The police report continued:

"At this time, Sgt and Officer returned to the station where contact was made with Dawn Jeronowitz's parents which we requested to come to her residence. Sgt spoke to a representative from SCIP [Screening and Crisis Intervention Program] and advised them of the situation. While at the station, police were advised by central communication that Ms. Jeronowitz went to the local township police headquarters and advised them that she was scared and in fear for her life. At this time, Sgt and Officer responded back to Ms. Jeronowitz's residence... and it was discovered that Ms. Jeronowitz was not on location."

I was not on location at my residence at that time because I was going about my own business and shopping at the store. Unbeknownst to me, while I was at the store, the police had been arranging a full-blown sting operation to apprehend me! Once I had arrived back at my property, taken down the July 4 decorations, pulled down the driveway to my house, saw a bright flashlight at my gate, and heard an officer call to me, the police narrative continued:

"*Units responded back to Ms. Jeronowitz's residence to speak with her. Upon arrival, the gate to the driveway was closed, however Police were able to observe Ms. Jeronowitz outside of the home. Sgt and Officer announced our presence and requested Dawn come speak with us at the gate. Ms. Jeronowitz stated she needed to use the restroom but would then drive up to speak with us at the gate. Mr. and Mrs. Jeronowitz stated they think she may run into the woods, and she has done the same in the past.*"

Notably, I do not live in the woods. Mine is a sprawling horse property with paddocks and fields. Also, I have never before run into the woods... at least not since I played in them as a child. The police report continued:

"*Sgt and Officer went around the gate and began walking toward the residence at which time Ms. Jeronowitz began driving toward the gate. Once Ms. Jeronowitz was close enough, our presence was again announced. At this time, Ms. Jeronowitz got back into her vehicle and accelerated rapidly in reverse back down her driveway toward her residence and the rear of the property.*"

Once I got into my car that fateful night and drove toward my front gate to meet with the police officers, I never got out of my car again until after I backed my vehicle in reverse and drove to my barn area. It is unclear why the police narrative states that I got back into my vehicle when I never got out of my vehicle while driving toward my gate in the first place. Even more, the officers did not go around my gate; they opened my gate. Then, they stormed me. If officers announced their presence again to me, I would not have heard that; I was inside my car and driving to meet them at the gate, as I told them I would. Despite all its deception, I welcomed the clarity the police incident report had brought me.

I also obtained the hospital intake records from SCIP. That's where I was able to read the narrative that I watched police contrive when I was first taken into the small medical room after being seized. At that time, due to Covid safety measures, my parents were prohibited from entering the hospital to see me or speak with the medical staff. Instead, the police provided analysis to the medical team. In the hospital report, the police officers were referred to as "Collateral," while I was referred to as "Consumer." It read:

"Consumer is a 50-year-old Caucasian female who was referred to SCIP by Township PD for erratic behavior. Consumer consented to telehealth assessment from the crisis unit at [hospital]. Consumer rambling and incoherent throughout assessment. Consumer denied SI [suicidal ideation]. Information obtained by Collateral. Collateral reports that consumer is Bi-polar with psychotic features and was just discharged on 3/31. Collateral reports that Consumer will tell you what you want to hear; she is very smart; she testified before the FDA against medicating psychiatric patient and has a book published. Collateral reports when she was discharged, she locked everyone out. Collateral reports that the neighbors called PD because she was outside in her driveway screaming for four hours straight when the police got there, she jumped in the car and took off driving erratic; thepolice didn't chase her because they were afraid she would hurt someone. Collateral reports that she isolates herself and she is not taking care of herself; she is not eating there was no food in the house or refrigerator. Collateral reports that consumer also stopped taking care of her horses which she loves. Collateral reports that this time she went to the police and said someone tried to kill her and took off driving erratically, jumped out of the car and hid in the woods because she reported bodies in the house; she is going to hurt herself or someone else if someone doesn't help her."

I took a moment to chuckle; a 120lb unarmed woman with a little dog in a crossbody sling pouch inquiring about splitting the cost of a giant decorative metal rooster must have been a terrorizing threat.

The hospital assessment also noted that I had made no suicide attempt and had no suicidal ideation or history thereof. It stated that I made no attempt at homicide and did not harbor homicidal ideation. It also said that I was disheveled, not destructive, no danger to myself or others, body/motor behaviors were within normal limits, memory unimpaired, speech mumbled, and attitude guarded. It also repeatedly stated that I was "non-compliant with her medications."

Evaluating the statements made by Collateral, it was not clear to me when I would have had time to scream for four hours straight on July 13; my banking statements and receipts from that day included purchases from 7-Eleven, an Italian restaurant, a grocery store, PetValu, Dunkin Donuts, and a gas station. I know I did not scream for four hours; I was out and about that day, shopping and dining with my dog. The same as I did the day before when my banking receipts documented that I was out shopping at Tractor Supply and Barnes & Noble thirty minutes away.

Also, my testimony to the FDA was not "against medicating psychiatric patients," as Collateral claimed. The FDA Psychopharmacologic Drug Advisory Committee Hearing and my testimony were in regard to psychotic and suicidal side effects that were associated with pharmaceutical psychotropic drugs. Thanks to my testimony and the testimonies of all pharmaceutical drug victims who testified, FDA Black Box Warnings on those drugs were expanded that December 2006 day. If only more people heeded them...

More baffling was the claim that the police did not chase me because they feared I would hurt someone. Seemingly if police were fearful a person may hurt someone, then that would constitute even more of a reason for police to go after that person, not retreat. If the police were at the neighbors' house when I stopped in to inquire about the decorative rooster, and they had concerns about me, that would have been the time to approach me if they truly believed I was capable of harming someone, or myself. It was a stretch to imagine police officers would not attempt to prevent harm if they believed I was capable of that and instead simply permit me to continue on my way.

What's more, Collateral acknowledged my pit stop at the local police department two minutes down the road from my home. The narrative claimed I drove erratically, jumped out of the car, and hid in the woods. I remain confident any surveillance video from that night would show that I parked my car in a parking spot near the building, walked into the police building, walked out of the police building, got into my car in the paved parking lot, drove away, and on to the store. I never jumped out of my car or went into any woods. The police department was not in the woods. I did not live in the woods. What was their obsession with the woods? *Where were these woods they spoke of?* I wondered.

Despite the entire July 13 police incident taking place outside my house and nobody else at my home, Collateral reported to the hospital that I had no food in my house, and my refrigerator was empty. In reality, I had plenty of food for myself and my animals and had even been to the grocery and pet store that very day. In addition, I had the bank statements and receipts from my purchases.

When Collateral reported I stopped taking care of my horses, that may have been the most despicable denunciation of all. I had multiple notebooks where I documented Chad's care and everyday activity, including wrap changes, hoof packing, medication administration, every time he stood up, laid down, ate, drank, eliminated, took steps, and walked outside the stall. Chad's vet made weekly, sometimes daily, visits. The hospital report sickened me with insult, on top of injury.

Back at the daily outpatient therapy classes that I was required to attend, or face being locked away permanently, I seized the opportunity to speak with others there. And, listen. The younger generation was especially interesting to hear. They were all highly suspicious of the mental health treatment processes. Each person had alarming stories of their own to tell.

Unsurprised to discover that the youth had never heard about pharmaceutical drug warnings, side effects, or FDA Black Box Warnings, I

254 | DAWN JERONOWITZ

seized the opportunity and provided them with information. I also presented them with a copy of the U.S. Constitution. One young person proceeded to ask me to which political party the U.S. Constitution belongs. Just when I thought things couldn't be more alarming...

One girl in particular really struck my heart. Her name was Sophia. She was twenty years old, medium build, with purple, pink, and blue hair. Sophia was talkative, compassionate, creative, and friendly to everyone. Unfortunately, due to her strong emotions and perceived ADHD, her parents routinely had Sophia admitted to psychiatric hospitals, causing her to miss large parts of her time in school.

One particular day at the outpatient facility, I sat with Sophia during lunch break. She told me she had been pharmaceutically drugged since second grade after being diagnosed with a mental disorder. She was a disorder, not normal; not ok. She required pills to be well. Add more pills, switch pills, increase pill dosage, change pills, more pills; a cycle of drugs was all Sophia knew. Sophia wept as she confessed, she couldn't recall herself without being drugged. She had no memory of that. I informed Sophia about adverse side effects and Black Box Warnings associated with the drugs she had been prescribed since childhood. As I listed a few side effects, Sophia fell to the ground. While on her knees, she cried at my feet and called me "Gold."

One rainy day going to the outpatient therapy classes, I chose not to leave my keys with the staff. Instead, I gave them an old keychain and kept my car keys in my handbag, where they belonged. Good thing I did.

That day, I was asked to take one drug test proving that I was not using cannabis plant products and another proving that I was taking prescribed pharmaceutical psychiatric drugs. The staff threatened me about the drug tests. They warned that if I did not comply, I would be penalized.

At that moment, I had had enough of their threats and abuse. I gathered my notebook and handbag and headed for the door. It was pouring buckets of rain outside. Regardless, I walked out into the hard and heavy rain. I kept on walking and did not dare look back. Nobody followed me into the rain. I walked directly to my car, got in, drove away, and never returned.

No sooner had I got home than my phone rang. It was the Legacy Treatment lady calling to tell me that I had caused big trouble at the outpatient facility; they were not happy with me. I informed the Legacy lady that I was not going to be returning to their outpatient classes. Instead, I had an upcoming event scheduled; I was going to work. And I did just that.

On August 24, 2020, I boarded an airplane to Nashville for a few days of working with my band family and tour crew, like usual. It was the first time during Covid we were permitted to do any work at all. Four days at work; it was purely wonderful! Bliss!

Upon returning home from Nashville, I received more bills for the hospitals, doctors, and medical transport sent from collection agencies. The invoices totaled many thousands of dollars. I responded with a letter asserting that I was not responsible for and would not pay for any goods and services which I did not require, request, purchase, or approve.

When reviewing the hospital invoice, I noticed Medicaid listed as a co-pay. I did not have Medicaid and would not qualify for Medicaid. Curiously, I called Medicaid to inquire about the charge. The woman I spoke with at Medicaid typed in my social security number but found nothing. Confused, she asked for my full name, which I provided. Under my name, the woman discovered over $200,000 charged to Medicaid. I assured the woman I had never filled out an application for Medicaid and would not be eligible for such a program. The woman instructed me to file a fraud complaint with Medicaid. I did.

Although I no longer attended the daily outpatient classes, I was still required to participate in a weekly Zoom meeting with a Legacy Treatment representative. That individual informed me she was looking into another outpatient treatment facility, where I would again attend classes. She said I would be required to participate in the program for at least one year. A year? That was unacceptable to me.

Pressing the Legacy lady, she informed me I would have a hearing with a mental health judge in September. The judge would determine my status. I guessed the judge was my only opportunity to relieve myself of the mistreatment I was forced to endure. I looked forward to the day I would speak to that judge.

While on Facebook, I spotted a fake page created on August 30 using my name, Dawn Jeronowitz. No posts had been made on the page, but the profile was described as "personal assistant." Why did someone create a fake Facebook page using my name? Who would do such a thing? It was obvious to me that whoever did create the fake Facebook page was uninformed about my actual job title.

Also peculiar, I noticed that while I was being held captive inside the hospital for seventeen days, a $100 payment had been made to my mother from my bank account. Nobody had access to my bank account, including my mother. Yet, even though I did not have access to my computer or banking account while I was in the hospital, the transaction was on my banking record. When I inquired with my mother, she claimed she knew nothing about it.

While I reviewed the paperwork I had collected regarding the incidents I suffered, I noticed the report from March 30 was missing. That was the night when the two unidentified men in green first went down my driveway, then left. I recalled when the councilman told me the men in green were from the medical transport company.

When I went to the medical transport company to obtain that record, a small, elderly woman behind the desk took my information and told me to wait. I observed a man with a "Chief" nametag on his uniform whisper something to her. Shortly thereafter, the woman handed me an envelope. She said it had the record I requested. I took the envelope, thanked her, and left.

When I arrived home and opened the envelope, I quickly noticed it was not the March 30 record I had sought. Instead, the report she provided to me was from 3/31. That was the night the two men in green went down my driveway, refused to identify themselves, and ultimately followed me inside my house, then assaulted me; the night I was first removed from my home. What stood out most on the report was the black marker hiding redacted information. Fortunately, I already had a copy of the 3/31 medical transport record, so I compared the two.

As I examined the first copy I had previously obtained in April, I noticed it included the names of two men in the upper right corner of the first page. The names of the two men were also shown on the last page and circled where they signed off on the report: T. Piper and M. Reynolds. However, on the second copy that the elderly woman had just provided me, the names of the two men had been blacked out with a marker on the first page, and their signatures completely removed from the last page.

It was unclear to me why such modifications were made on the second copy of the medical transport report. Moreover, it was confounding why the police department still would not confirm the identities of the two men in green who entered my home on 3/31, despite the police narrative that reported the men told me to verify their identities with police.

When I called the medical transport company to inquire, the elderly woman answered the phone. She explained she could not provide me the report from 3/30 because I did not go with the men that night. Before I could ask any questions, she hung up.

At last, I was provided a mental health court hearing date of September 23. Due to Covid, it was scheduled as a virtual hearing on the computer. The Legacy lady informed me that I would be provided a court-appointed attorney from the treatment program. At that time, I informed her of my intentions to have my case dismissed and my desire to have my own private attorney. That did not please her.

Moreover, the Legacy Treatment lady became irate when she discovered I had video recorded our Zoom meetings. She demanded I delete the videos. I was reprimanded and told I was not permitted to video record any of the ongoings or meetings. Despite this, I did. It was important for me to retain records and documentation of it all. I had even saved the prescriptions bottles and pills they supplied to me, which were abundant.

Days before the hearing, I received a phone call from the court-appointed attorney. I instructed him that I wanted a complete dismissal from the Legacy program and nothing short thereof. I also informed him I would hire a private attorney if need be. The court-appointed attorney told me to stand by; he would make some phone calls.

Shortly thereafter, the attorney called back to inform me that my dismissal request would not be contested by Legacy Treatment. He fully expected the judge to dismiss everything and restore my independence and freedom.

On September 23, that happened! At long last, I presented myself to a judge who immediately dismissed all the outrageous medical demands being forced upon me without a warrant. I was no longer required to participate in any mental health treatment, classes, meetings, tests, or forced drugging. Much to my profound relief, finally, that was all over.

Still, many questions were in need of answers. Justice for all that had been wrongfully done to me was desired. Still, our government offices remained closed due to Covid.

I followed up with the attorney regarding my book, Mr. Harshman. He informed me that due to Covid, the courts in Indiana remained closed; no progress to update.

Though Dog Ear Publishing had been shut down, my book remained available for purchase on book sales sites, including Amazon. It was listed by third-party vendors who were selling my book, priced from $300 - $1300! Despite any efforts, there was nothing I could do about that.

Thankfully, collection agency letters seeking payment for the hospitals, doctors, and medical transport bills stopped arriving. Nothing appeared on my credit report regarding them. No lawsuit seeking payment was brought against me. Nothing. It all ceased.

When checking my book on Amazon, I was startled to discover a book released on November 12, 2020. It had the exact same title as my published book, *Crazy or Not, Here I Come,* and it also had a book cover design with an uncanny resemblance to mine too. The book was written by Walter W. Swinhoe and included the description:

"This book offers a dynamic path to healing by going to the root cause of your present symptoms. If you are stuck in depression, frozen in anxiety, or haunted by past abuse issues, this book will be curative."

Before publishing my book in 2018, I researched my book title; I saw no other books had that title. Perhaps Mr. Swinhoe did not do his research prior to publishing, and the similarity was mere coincidence?

December 7, I got a private message from a friend. She received an Instagram request from a fake account impersonating me: dawn_jeronowitz. Soon after, I received more warnings from friends who were getting similar requests. We reported the fake account but received an Instagram message stating no violation had occurred. The fake account remained active.

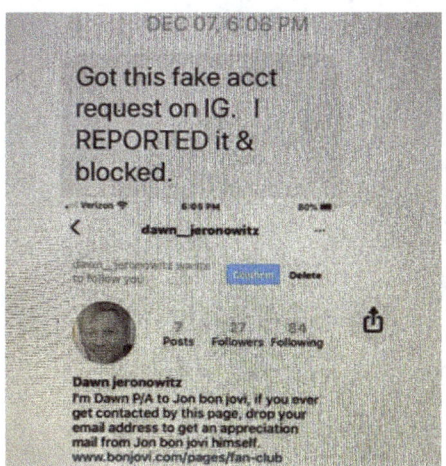

Taking care of Chad in his challenging condition required full attention. The vet made weekly visits. BG was a hero staying in the barn with Chad, comforting him throughout his ordeal. We prepared for a cold winter ahead.

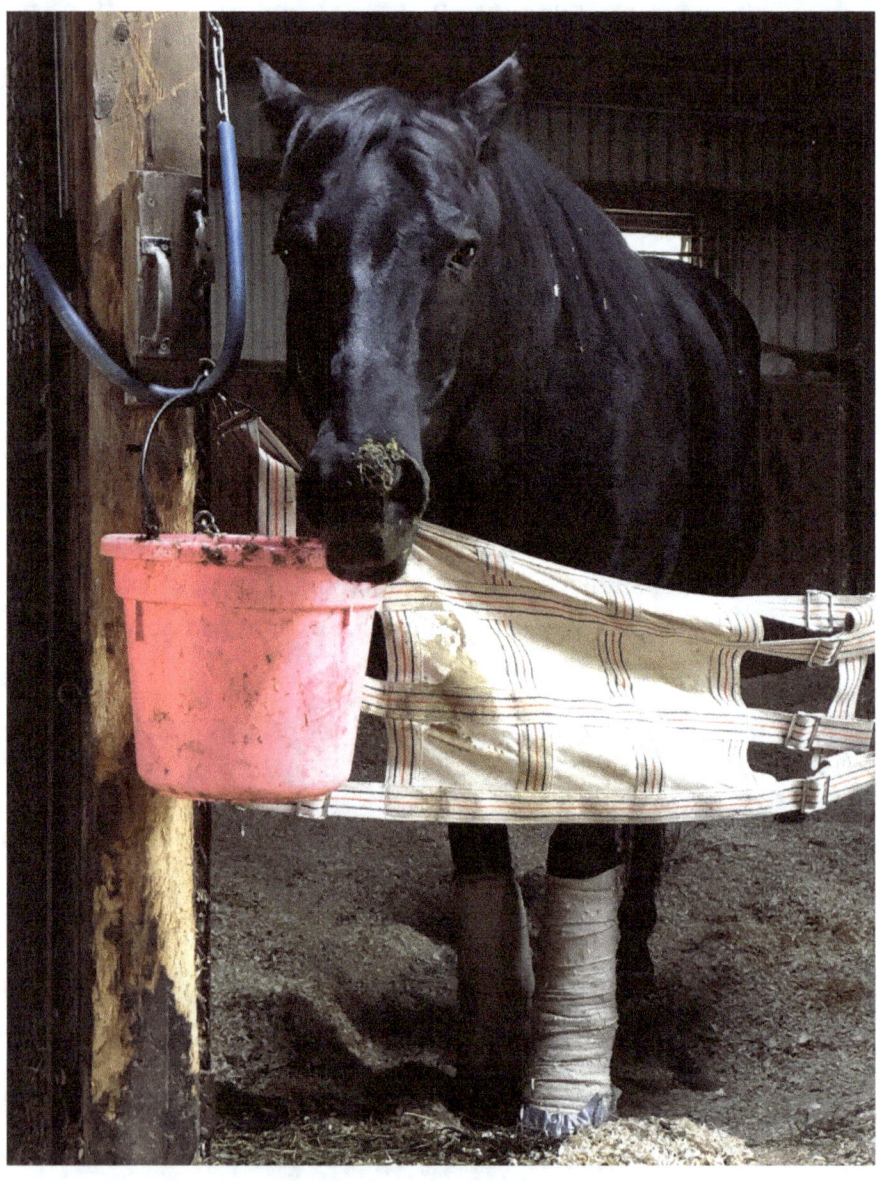

20

New Car

As a less-than-festive 2021 rolled in, Covid-19 lockdowns increased; they became even more restrictive. Covid vaccine campaigns were taking root in countries around the world. President Donald Trump was preparing to leave office, and a new Joe Biden administration was going to be sworn in as President of the United States. Political unrest was on the rise. It had a stench.

January 2021, I was grateful to finally be contacted by Aaron Harshman, the attorney representing authors in the case against Dog Ear Publishing. Mr. Harshman requested authors to each compose a letter to the Indiana Attorney General that described their negative publishing experience and monetary loss. He was going to collect the letters, then impactfully present them to the Office of the Attorney General. Dozens of victimized Dog Ear Publishing authors from our Facebook group participated and submitted letters for the AG review.

Beginning the new year doing outside yardwork, I kept my radio playing at a modest volume, level 2. It was an old mid-century stereo inside the blue 1980 Chevy van parked in my driveway. The van had come with the sale of my property. It had been sitting stationary for a decade by then, a storage space.

One afternoon, after returning from a quick trip to the hardware store, I returned home to discover the wires to my radio had been cut. Somebody had gone onto my property and cut the wires to my radio while I was at the store. My decorative welcome flag was missing too. I repaired the wires, then turned on my radio again. Then, I purchased a new welcome flag and additional cameras.

Despite the new year, due to continued Covid-19 lockdown restrictions, my life as a roadie remained at a standstill. No touring was allowed. Considering Chad remained extremely compromised by his laminitis, I was immensely grateful for the time at home to be with him; he required a lot of daily medical attention. Still, regardless of all the love and care I provided my Chad, the hoof disease had progressed.

After a sudden week of a dire downturn, an appointment was made for Chad to receive X-rays and another expert opinion on his condition. It was most overwhelming and deeply troubling to face the possibility that Chad would not recover. Notwithstanding, my parents stayed with Chad for that intensive appointment while I stayed away from my property and monitored the medical proceeding in the barn from my security camera.

As I could see on the camera the appointment was concluding, I began to drive back in the direction of home. I was on a busy four-lane road with lots of traffic lights, stores and cars. I knew I should have waited to return home for a full update on Chad's exam. However, I called my father from the road.

Ultimately, the medical team had concluded that there were two options: I could send Chad away to a hospital for another surgery with low odds he would recover and return home, or I could relieve his suffering through humane end-of-life means.

Understanding that reality, I was overwhelmed. Very rapidly, my body grew hot, my head light, dizzy. I realized I was going to pass out, yet I was driving my car on a busy road.

Keeping my father on speakerphone, I immediately pulled the car over to the side of the road and onto the shoulder. When I opened the car door and stepped outside in an effort to cool myself with fresh air, I had no muscle in my legs. My legs were weak, wobbly. As I tried to stand, I stumbled uncontrollably onto the highway and across two car lanes. Desperately, I struggled to gain control of my body but could not.

Fighting to remain conscious, several moments passed, and with all my might, I managed to get myself back to the car and inside my vehicle. As I took a sip of water, I thanked God for the miracle that I was not hit by a car. Many pedestrians are killed each year on that busy road. It was by the Grace of God I was not one of them that day.

Suddenly, a car pulled up behind me on the shoulder, then it pulled in front of me and parked. The car door opened, and a man in his late sixties walked toward my passenger side window. He said he had been driving in the opposite direction when he saw me stumble onto the highway and nearly to the median divide. The man turned around to come to see if I was okay and inquired if I needed help.

I informed the man I had just received the most traumatic news and experienced a bout of overwhelming anxiety as a result. I assured him I was on the phone with my father and would not drive until I felt well enough to do so. Of course, I graciously thanked the man for taking the time to turn around and check on me; that was a generously kind, heroic thing for him to do. The man returned to his car, but he did not pull away; not until minutes later when I felt restored enough to do so myself.

Safely, I made it home and into the barn with my Chad. As I wept and hugged him, I comforted Chad with love and provided him with all his favorite treats. He soothed my soul with his beautiful presence in life.

Forthcoming in my lived truth, some things in life remained too much to put into words. Feb 21, 2021, was the day I had to let go of my greatest love, my partner, champion, my boy, my Chad. Of all of the experiences in my life, saying goodbye to him would forever be the most difficult thing I have ever endured. Living without him would remain the greatest challenge of my life. Saying goodbye to him, I could offer neither spoken nor written word to describe the immense grief, heartbreak, loss, and love that consumed me. My beloved, my forever, Can You Imagine, my Chad....

The somber days that followed were a haze. Grief was indeed the price we paid for love.

BG was bereaved. She and Chad had been together for most of Chad's nearly twenty years. Alone, she would not remain inside the barn but instead stayed outside and up the hill, where BG and Chad liked to go.

Chad's birthday, March 1, passed. My birthday followed on the fourth. Then, on March 6, friends began alerting me to another fake Instagram account using my name: the_real_dawnjeronowitz. Many reported the fake account to Instagram; however, it was never removed.

A letter arrived in the mail from my township. It notified me about an upcoming zoning board meeting where the neighbor had an application on the calendar for review. The application was regarding the land use of the neighbors' agricultural farm-assessed property and the storage of their recreational vehicles. Strangely, the application did not include any reference to the subsequent RV rental business that the neighbors had been operating on their property for the past four years, merely the RV storage.

As a homeowner in close proximity to the neighboring property, I was invited by law to offer public comment at the zoning board meeting. Considering that when I looked outside my kitchen window, the once lovely view of a crop field had been turned into a commercial RV parking lot view, combined with other concerns, including the blazing RV fire, I was eager to submit my comments to the zoning board.

On the morning of the zoning board meeting, March 15, 2021, BG and I were on the front lawn. While petting BG, mourning and grieving Chad together in solace, I heard a voice yelling. Although the evergreen trees I had planted along the property line were thick, and I could not see him, the neighbor's voice echoed in a snarky tone as he called out to me, "Are you ready for tonight?" I said nothing and remained focused on petting BG. Again, I heard him call in a sardonic tone, "Are you ready for tonight?" Shaken, I said nothing. Rest assured, I was indeed ready and fully prepared for the meeting. In fact, I had already preemptively emailed pictures to the zoning board to supplement my forthcoming statement at the meeting.

That evening I connected online to the zoning board Zoom meeting. Board members and township representatives posed questions to the neighbor husband about his agricultural property, farm assessment, and RVs. Even better, after seeing the pictures I had sent to them, which included aerial Google images and the RV business website, I was pleased when the zoning board questioned the neighbor about his commercial RV business operations.

Though the neighbor answered a few questions from the zoning board, he had hired a lawyer and engineer to primarily represent the case for his application on his behalf. As anticipated, the neighbors' buddies from across the street attended the meeting too. They spoke in overwhelming support of the RV business and zoning permit.

When my turn came to speak, I presented my pictures and prepared public comments opposing the matter. Surprisingly, a married home-owner couple living behind us spoke up too. They were very disturbed by the visual aspect of the ten RVs parked in our quiet residential neighborhood and the customers going in and out. They were also concerned about the impact on home values that such a commercial business in the neighborhood would affect.

As it turned out, all seven members of the zoning board were satisfied with their established planning and zoning. Not only was the board incensed that a full-service RV rental business was operating on an agricultural farm-tax-assessed property that was not being farmed, but even more, the zoning board had no interest in altering their zoning plans to set a precedent for the neighbor and his RV business. By a unanimous decision, all of his applications were denied. The zoning board said the RVs had to go. I was shocked and relieved.

Even more striking and alarming during the meeting, the neighbor husband began to attack me after the board denied his zoning application. He yelled and proclaimed that I was the reason he was no longer permitted to shoot guns on his property. Then, he held up his telephone to the camera and displayed a decibel count that he had calculated from my radio. "46," the neighbor yelled repeatedly, "46!" Notably, a 46-decibel measure is equivalent to the hum of a refrigerator or speaking conversation. In contrast, the decibel of my work environment at a stadium concert is estimated at 120, and his gunfire 160.

The zoning board was troubled by the neighbors' antics. They interrupted him and firmly asserted to the neighbor that the zoning board meeting was strictly in regard to zoning. Again, they stated that his land-use application remained denied. The board reaffirmed the RVs must be removed from the property. Even more, the neighbor was prohibited from using the third driveway on the property he had installed over the crop field, where the RVs were parked. Finally, the zoning board informed the neighbor he would be assigned a court date for his zoning, land use, and ordinance violations.

Two days later, on March 17, the neighbor went onto Amazon and posted a review of my book, *Crazy or Not, Here I Come*. Accompanied by a lowly one-star review. The neighbor wrote: "Wow. What a lunatic. Denial is not a good look." The review remained posted on Amazon.

In another vicious offense, the neighbor also displayed a sign he made. He took a large piece of plywood and spray-painted it with the words "HORSE KILLER." He then set the sign along our property division line and faced it toward my house. It was unclear to me how the neighbor knew about my Chad.

As I coped with all that had occurred, I focused on the needs of BG. She had never before been alone and without the companionship of another horse. Since we lost Chad, BG had not stayed inside the barn once; not a single muck to clean. She would stand all day on the hill Chad loved and barely wandered about. I knew she needed someone.

After a few attempts with horse rescue organizations, a companion for BG was found from a kind, ailing woman who needed a retirement home for her twenty-five-year-old gelding, Zippy. On April 9, I drove an hour to meet Zippy. Instantly, I knew he would be an ideal match for BG. I immediately sought arrangements for him to be transported to my home.

The following morning, April 10, 2021, I worked on the repair and reinforcement of the old wire fence that divided the properties of myself and the malevolent neighbor. Repeatedly they had gone onto my property, cut my radio and camera wires, and taken my belongings. I hoped that reinforcing the fence would prevent them from further trespassing and destroying my property.

While I was working on the fence project, my phone rang. It was the woman who had Zippy. She called to inform me that she had found a horse trailer service that could transport Zippy that afternoon. Though that was exciting news, I also recognized I had much preparation to do for his rapid arrival that day.

Unfortunately, while I talked with the woman, my camera system alerted me to activity at my property line with the neighbor. When I looked at my camera, I saw the neighbor was removing the fencing I had repaired and was throwing it onto his property.

As I began to walk toward the fence line and suspicious activity, I kept a few things in mind: keep calm, do not fall for their lure, do not yell, do not curse, record everything, and get my father on speakerphone to listen as a witness. I called Debbie, who said she would come over to my house immediately; she was on her way.

After I called my father and put him on speakerphone, I turned on my video and began to record. As I approached the neighbor, I politely asked him to please return my belongings and stay off my property. I pointed out the fence line that divided our property and informed him that he was trespassing and committing theft.

Regardless, the neighbor continued to take down my fencing. He called it trash and piled the pieces onto his property near his RVs. Then, he tossed the 'Horse Killer' sign on top of the pile of my belongings. He made a number of threats that included he had Covid, would fire his guns along the property line, not remove the RVs and cut down my row of thirty-two evergreen trees I had planted a few years prior when the RVs first began to arrive. He claimed my trees were on his property, even though they were on my side of the fence.

I continued to video-record everything.

As the frightening ordeal continued, the wife yelled and harassed me. She called me crazy, said she was terrified of me, that nobody in the neighborhood liked me, the police hated me, and refuted my claims that her husband trespassed on my property. She mockingly asked who would know more, a wardrobe manager or an engineer? When I repeated that I wanted my belongings returned or otherwise I would call the police, the neighbor's wife screamed the police would again take me away. She intended to utilize the weaponization of mental health and psychiatry upon me, as she had done before.

I wanted to call the police for assistance with the frightening ordeal; however, I knew I had to remain focused as I prepared for Zippy's arrival that day. After nearly an hour of the nasty neighbor episode, I had no more time to delay. Calmly, I questioned the neighbor about who would end up in jail first: the husband, the wife, or the kid. Then, I turned and walked toward my barn. As I did so, I heard the wife holler to her husband. He had lunged through the fence toward me, and she begged him to stop. I continued walking away and did not dare look back.

While I prepared the barn, Debbie arrived at my house. Soon thereafter, a truck with a horse trailer pulled into my driveway; Zippy had arrived too. It was a tremendous relief when BG reacted over the moon to have a friend again! And Zippy seemed to like her too.

Whereas the horses usually are free-roaming on my property, I kept Zippy locked inside a stall that first night for safety reasons. As I monitored the barn throughout the first evening, I saw BG remained in position stationed outside the stall where Zippy was contained. I was thrilled; finally, BG would go inside the barn again. Still, I did not permit anyone to enter the stall where Chad had spent his last days; that stall remained closed off, with the imprint of Chad still intact.

The following day, I called my father to inquire if he would accompany me to the police station. Everything considered, I did not feel safe going there alone. I intended to file an incident report and hoped to have my stolen items returned to me. My father met me at my house, and we drove to my township police headquarters.

Meeting two officers outside the station, I explained the trespassing, theft, and harassment complaint and presented the police officers with my property survey. However, the officers said they could neither look at my property survey nor determine property lines. Therefore, they could not say whether or not the neighbor trespassed onto my property.

I presented the police officers with a video from the previous day's incident. Also, security camera images of the neighbor when he took my fencing, pictures of the pile on his property, photos of cut wires, and the Horse Killer sign. The police officers said they could not look at any of it. They said they could not determine to whom the items belonged. I insisted they belonged to me.

Persisting on the matter, with the help of my father's insistence, the police finally agreed to visit the neighbor's house and inquire about my belongings.

While my father and I waited at my house, the police went to speak with the neighbor at theirs. Afterward, the two officers arrived at my house to speak with me. While they were there, the neighbor threw my belongings over the fence and onto my property. An officer pronounced no theft had occurred because the neighbor had returned my items to me.

Before leaving, the officers explained that if I had any disputes, I could bring my concerns to the courthouse and file a complaint there. In a final piece of advice, one officer warned that if he heard I played my music loudly, he would come to break down my gate. My father and I both looked stunned.

The irony was not lost on me. I could not help but recall how the neighbor's wife made unfounded accusations of harassment against me in the previous year. Then, based on my experience, without any evidence provided, police officers organized a sting operation, attacked me at my home, took me into custody, provided false statements in various records, and advocated for my hospital detainment.

Nonetheless, when I sought to file a harassment and trespassing complaint against the neighbor, the police did nothing; they would not even review the cumulative hard evidence I had provided for them that day. I wanted to ask the police officers to reveal the location of the notorious woods. But I bit my tongue and did not.

In the following days, I assembled the evidence I amassed into an organized binder and included the required incident complaint forms for trespassing and harassment committed by the neighbor husband and wife. Since the courthouse was still closed due to Covid, I was instructed to put my binder inside a drop box located outside the court building doors. I did.

In early May, a letter arrived in the mail from the court. I gave a sigh of relief when the letter informed me that a judge had reviewed my complaint and found enough evidence of probable cause to put forth criminal charges against my neighbor.

It came as no surprise that both the husband and wife pleaded not guilty. The case was then scheduled for mediation.

By mid-May, I was alerted to more fake Instagram accounts utilizing my name and likeness and sending messages to music fans. In addition to the the_real_dawnjeronowitz, two more fake accounts became active: dawn_bon9060 and dawnbon_9060. The account holder had blocked me; I was unable to see the existence of the fake accounts from my devices. Fortunately, others who did see them were quick to alert me to the fraud.

The stalker impersonating me had also gone onto my real Instagram account and seized a few of my personal pictures. They incorporated pictures of myself and my Ollia dog onto the fake account, dawn_bon9060. I did not recognize any of the other pictures on the fake accounts. Hoping to prevent further theft of my photos, I adjusted my personal Instagram account to a private setting and deleted numerous dubious followers.

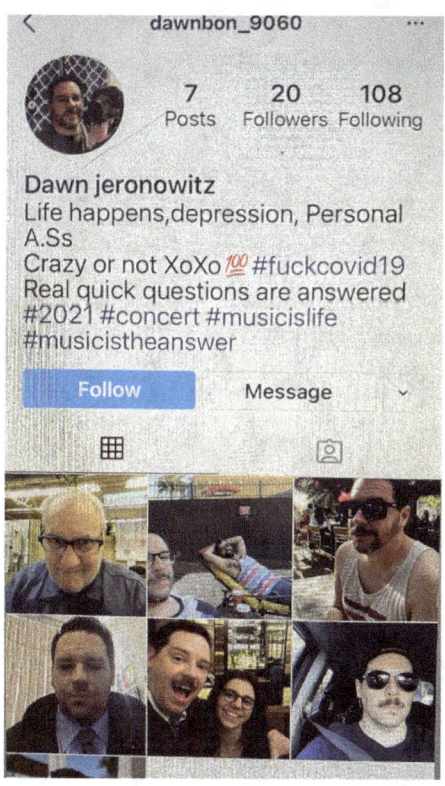

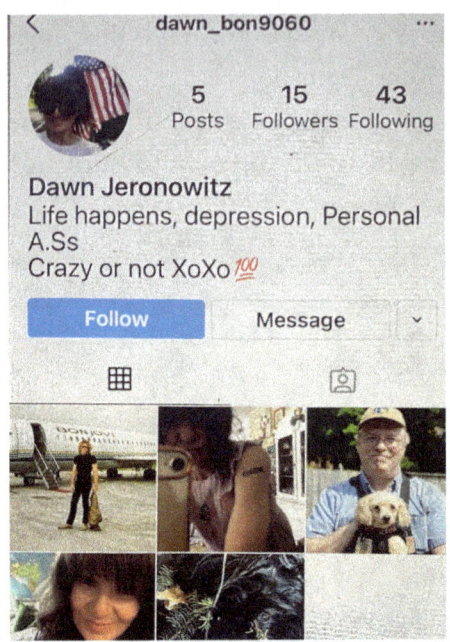

May 10, 2021

Hi Dawn! I know you dont know me but there is this account going under JBJ's posts and contacting fans pretending to be you and being able to link contact between them and JBJ ... now i know how the bizz works and i know it was fishy and no one in your position would be contacting fans willy nelly to put them in contact! I reported and blocked the account but i know im not alone that the account contacted so... just letting you know! 😊 cheers!

Another horror was reported on May 15, 2021 when a forty-year-old woman in Tempe, Arizona, woke up with blood on her hands and no memory of what had happened. A *12 News* article by Erica Stapleton, "Court Records: Tempe mom accused of killing kids has history of domestic violence, mental health concerns," reports the woman, Yui Inoue, had brutally killed her two young children with a meat cleaver. She then went to the police station herself and told officers that she was hearing voices telling her to kill her kids.

An *azcentral* article by Miguel Torres, *Arizona Republic*, "DCS was investigating Tempe mother before she was suspected of killing her 2 children," reports, prior to killing her children, Arizona Department of Child Safety had an open case on Yui Inoue after she was reported for child neglect and took one of her children to an unknown location. When found, the child was returned to the father and Inoue was taken to a psychiatric facility. Undoubtedly, Inoue was medicated in the facility and provided prescriptions for psychotropic drugs upon her release. Based on my experiences, that was a routine procedure. Only two months after her hospital discharge, Yui Inoue murdered her own children.

A mediation hearing with the neighbor via Zoom was scheduled for July 28, 2021, but though it was intended to mediate the situation and bring about a resolution, it did not.

Throughout the meeting, the husband and his wife continued their attacks on me. They were enraged about my security cameras and believed I should not be permitted to have them. When they previously spoke to a family member of theirs on the township police force, he told them I could. Hysterically, the wife told the mediator that it should be illegal for me to face my security camera in the direction of their property. The neighbors proclaimed everything I did to them should be illegal. They even accused me of calling the police on their kids when they played basketball. I was unaware they had a basketball hoop on their property.

Worse, the neighbors took zero accountability for any of their actions, made no apology to me, and instead said that I was crazy and belonged in a mental institution. Finally, after an hour of failed arbitration, the mediator determined no resolution could be achieved, and a trial date would be forthcoming.

Days later, I received a letter. In it, I was advised by the Municipal Court Administrator that the matter with the neighbor was "being scheduled for trial due to the fact that no resolution during mediation was agreed upon."

I still had not received any updates from my attorney, Aaron Harshman, regarding my case against Dog Ear Publishing. I did follow up with the court in Indianapolis myself. They informed me the paperwork for the trial had not yet been submitted. Providentially, I was at least able to acquire my case number on the matter from them.

In mid-September, I received a postal letter from the Office of the Attorney General in Indiana. It was in response to the 2019 complaint I previously filed with them against Dog Ear Publishing and its owner, Ray Robinson. The Indiana Attorney General's letter informed me:

"The Consumer Protection Division has completed its review of your complaint against Dog Ear Publishing. We have determined not to conduct further inquiry or investigation into this matter. We are closing our file."

I was gobsmacked. The letter continued:

"To protect the confidentiality of our review and the deliberative process we worked through in reaching our determination, we cannot provide details of the reason for our determination."

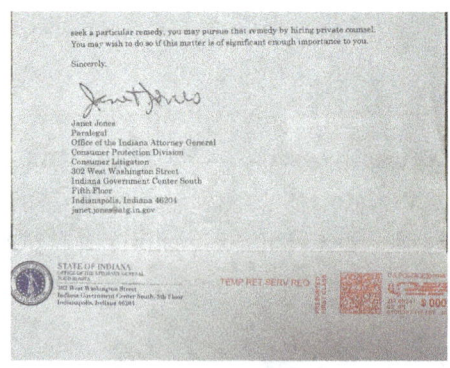

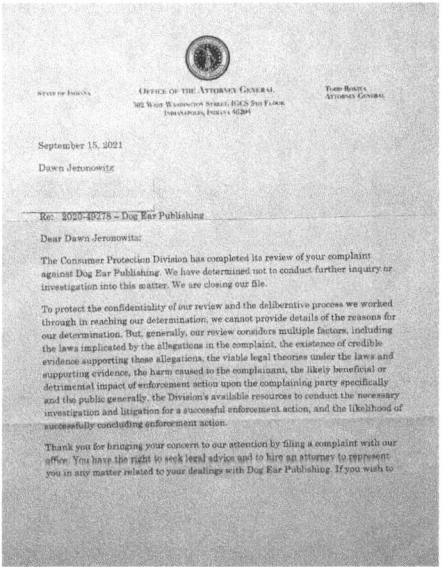

When I followed up with other people in our Dog Ear Authors Revolt Facebook group, many of them had received a similar letter from the Office of the Attorney General in Indiana. Also, from the FBI.

Fed up with relying on others to be responsible, honest, and hardworking, on September 23, I took the initiative; I filed the paperwork to open my own publishing company: Write Road Publishing. I was going to revise and update my book, then publish it myself. Onward!

It was a happy October day in Nashville when I was able to gig again. I flew there for a corporate show at an amphitheater. There were Covid vaccine mandates in order to work; however, despite not getting the jab, I was blessed to be able to do my job. Of course, we had to test negative for Covid prior to entering the building. Ultimately, it was an absolute rockin' good time! So good to be with my road family again.

October 18, 2021, Paris Hilton published an op-ed in *The Washington Post*. In it, she wrote:

"When I was 16 years old, I was awakened one night by two men with handcuffs. They asked if I wanted to go 'the easy way or the hard way' before

carrying me from my home as I screamed for help. I had no idea why or where I was being taken against my will. I soon learned I was being sent to hell."

Paris went on to explain:

"Few people are aware of the abuses and tragedies that occur within the walls of some facilities. I was called vulgar names and forced to take medication without a diagnosis. At one Utah facility, I was locked in solitary confinement in a room where the walls were covered in scratch marks and blood stains."

In addition to the verbal, emotional, and physical abuse she endured, Paris wrote about how her parents 'fell for the misleading marketing of the 'troubled teen industry.' - Hilton, P. (2021, October 18). "Opinion: America's 'troubled teen industry' needs reform so kids can avoid the abuse I endured," *The Washington Post.*

Soon thereafter, on November 12, 2021, Britney Spears was finally freed from her thirteen-year-long conservatorship. After years of what Britney described as manipulations by her mother, control by her father, as well as the state, courts, doctors, prescribers, and teams of people claiming to be serving in her best interest, yet not doing so at all, Britney was freed at last. For her, that was an end to the forced drugging, forced living, forced everything. Britney's life belonged to her once again. I could imagine the stories she would soon tell. I could sincerely empathize with her. I prayed her healing would finally begin; in whatever way she chose for her own self.

By pure coincidence, I toured with Britney Spears back in 1999/ 2000. It was the *Hit Me Baby One More Time* and *Oops, I Did It Again* tours. Every show day, I set up her dressing room and decorated it with things she loved. I recalled running in the rain somewhere in Germany when tasked with buying her an end-of-tour gift. I selected a 1920s vintage white gold and diamond bracelet from an estate sale. On the final show day, while in her dressing room, I presented it to Britney in an old, torn, tattered, aged bracelet box. She squealed with delight.

It was also Britney's tour rehearsals in Florida that I had crashed in 2001 when I was first pharmaceutically drugged and in a psychotic state of mind. That was back when I had Simon and the Winnebago, just before breaking down at the truck stop. I reflected on how far we had come, how much we had endured, and how strong we were. The soul of a survivor was truly indomitable.

By the end of 2021, Covid lockdowns were mildly lifting; however, the Covid drug mandates were being implemented worldwide. Anyone who refused the Covid jab faced life-altering consequences, including loss of employment or access to any public space. Some were even denied medical treatment, including organ transplants. Moreover, simply attending the theatre, going to a museum or gym, or eating inside a restaurant required a paper or QR code showing proof of Covid vaccination.

The definition of the word 'vaccine' was changed when, in truth, the mRNA drug was no vaccine at all; it neither prevented transmission of the Covid virus nor contracting the virus. People who received the drug, and boosters, were still getting Covid. Worse, the drug proved to have side effects, including blood clots, stroke, heart attack, myocarditis, and sudden death.

Unsurprisingly, those the vaccine injured and killed were ignored, taunted, ostracized, and gaslit. From my own experience I knew how that felt. Any mention of adverse vaccine effects was quickly stricken from the media. Those who dared to speak up about the dangers were immediately canceled from society; barred from their social media accounts. Censorship and cancel culture were in full force. The ugliest side of humanity was on full display.

The new year, 2022, rang in. I was thrilled it was planned to head back on tour again by Spring. But as the Covid jab mandates gripped the world, the entertainment industry required all performers and backstage crew to be jabbed with the drug.

Considering my life experiences with pharmaceutical drugs, doctors, FDA, and drug manufacturers, I was not keen on risking further harm. I absolutely was not going to inject an experimental pharmaceutical drug into my body. No needles! No sexy rockstar or traveling the world was going to change that. My memories were too lucid and I valued my life too much. Most unfortunately, the vaccine issue was raised politically. Still, I was not interested in my life ending prematurely. I did not want the burden of worrying about drug side effects, whether physical, emotional, or mental. I chose to live my life all-natural.

Heartbreakingly, as an 'unvaccinated' person, it was determined that I would not be able to go on the upcoming tour dates. Instead, it was decided that I would work from home and do tour preparations. That included a few months of clothing design, wardrobe shopping, rider preparation, and training another backstage person to do my gig on tour. Despite the disappointment, I still welcomed the opportunity to do some of the job I loved and had built a twenty-five-year-long career doing. It was expected that I would be able to return to tour again on the next run. I could only hope while I hurt.

Uvalde, Texas, May 24 – an eighteen-year-old kid, Salvador Ramos, shot his grandmother before going to Robb Elementary School, where he was once a student himself. There, he killed nineteen students and two teachers over the course of an hour before he, too, was killed. *The National Desk* article by Alec Schemmel, "Texas shooter struggled with mental health, family dysfunction, was fascinated by guns," reports that on one occasion, Ramos met up with a friend of his at the park and had cuts all over his face. Ramos told his friend he had cut up his face with knives for fun. *Was any toxicology report or drug analysis done on Salvador Ramos?* I wondered. Did he have a prescriber? Even a car accident could warrant a basic breathalyzer test.

The summer heat burned on. BG and Zippy were settled into a nice routine. Still, Chad's presence was deeply missed. His imprint in his stall still remained undisturbed.

The big, long-awaited court date with the neighbor was approaching. Days before the hearing, I spoke with the prosecutor. He informed me he would not be present at the hearing. Instead, I was told to look for a man wearing a suit. I inquired whether the man in the suit had a name and was provided the first name of his legal associate. Also, I asked if the associate would have the binder of evidence and timeline of events that I provided to him. The prosecutor assured me he would.

August 25, 2022, the in-person trial date with the neighbor finally arrived. It had been over a year of waiting since mediation failed. My father was present as a witness on my behalf.

Before going into the courtroom, I met in a small room with the prosecutor's associate. As we were going over the case, I realized the associate did not have any information about the case. He did not have the binder of evidence I had provided to the prosecutor. It was unclear to me how the associate would prosecute a case without having any evidence or details about the case. Fortunately, I had brought a copy of the binder with all of the evidence, timeline, and details with me. I offered that to the associate, and we briefly reviewed the case.

While I was in the room with the associate and my father, the neighbor husband and his wife arrived. The loud, brash voice of the wife could easily be heard echoing through the hallway. The associate excused himself and went to speak with the neighbor in the hallway. Very quickly, the wife grew even louder; she ranted on with her routine about my craziness and mental state.

A few minutes later, the associate returned to speak with my father and me, still sitting quietly in the small room. He regretted to inform us that the trial would not take place that day after all. The neighbor had determined they wanted a defense attorney.

Still, we all went into the courtroom for proceedings before the judge. The judge was not in the courtroom; instead, he was present on a large monitor screen. My father and I sat in the general seating chairs behind the prosecutor's associate while the husband and his wife sat in the defense chairs to his right. While I wore slacks and a blazer, I noticed the husband wore cargo shorts, a dirty t-shirt, and sandals to the hearing. It was casual day in court.

When the judge spoke to the defense, the neighbors responded that they wanted a defense attorney. Also, they wanted to file counterharassment and trespassing charges against me. The judge instructed they would need to provide evidence of harassment and hire a surveyor to assess the property for trespassing and harassment charges to be considered.

The judge then questioned the husband about his decision to request a defense attorney on the day of the trial. He asked what they had been doing for the past fourteen months and why they had not retained an attorney during that time. The neighbor floundered; he said he believed the case was over after mediation the previous year. He continued making excuses until the judge cut him off. The judge told the neighbors they had two weeks to retain an attorney; he would reschedule pre-trial following that.

I said it before, but wait, there's more.

There's always more...

Nikolas Cruz, the kid who killed seventeen students at Marjory Stoneman Douglas High School in Parkland, Florida, was sentenced to life in prison on November 2. Meanwhile, Henderson Behavioral Health and the doctors who may have over-prescribed psychotropic drugs to a nineteen-year-old Nikolas Cruz remained uninvestigated and unscathed. They walked away with no responsibility or liability, free to drug even more youth. *The Hill* article by Alexandra Kelley, "Florida court finds mental health facility not liable in Parkland massacre," reports: "The judges further ruled that if Henderson did owe a legal duty to the school to disclose patient details, it would undermine the doctor-patient confidentiality relationship and potentially disincentivize mental health professionals from treating students."

Medical professionals recklessly disregarded the expanded FDA Black Box Warnings, homicidal and suicidal side effects associated with the class of drugs they prescribed to Nikolas Cruz; the warnings about which I and others testified to the FDA in 2006 and helped secure. The warnings that were expanded for children, teens, and young adults that December day, people under age 25. At the time of the shooting, a highly medicated Nikolas Cruz was only nineteen. Were the drug warnings and our FDA testimonies in vain?

My country, 'tis of thee, sweet land of drugged misery, of thee I weep. Land where our children die from pharmaceutical drug-induced suicide, the prescription pills doctors prescribe. May sobriety reign.

While many people were helped by the use of psychiatric drugs and hailed their successes, it was erroneous and perilous to ignore people who were critically injured, killed, and tremendously harmed by the pills. What pharmaceutical manufacturers, FDA, and prescribers considered to be side effects, those who endured and survived the drug-induced trauma called it torture. Those who could not withstand the drug-induced torture tragically ended their lives.

> It's weird that a drug can cause such specific behavior, but it does.
> My best friend was a good, well-liked person who was told that he had a "chemical imbalance" after he got depressed when his mother died. He was given SSRIs, and he strangely started talking about shooting everyone at school and collecting guns. He shot himself in the head.
> My other best friend, a musician, suffered hearing loss, got depressed, and doctors gave him SSRIs. He jumped off of a tall building. They were both so smart, talented, and nice, with their whole lives ahead of them.

J. Keebler

There are many many many people who were sensitive, loving people who become absolutely different, crazily angry and violent, almost overnight from these drugs. I have seen it.
It is causal not corrolative.
SSRIs have been shown to work no better than a placebo in the best of cases.

D. Sonntag

████████ you need to check out the complaints from patients on these drugs. I was a perfectly sane person. Was given Zoloft after a floxing. It made me psychotic, then given Seroquel and that pushed me deeper down he psychotic realm. Dr kept increasing the dosages even after telling him I was getting worse. I never had any issues like this. Turns out my genetics (cyp450) can NOT remove these drugs from my body. I was at toxic levels. I took myself off them and it took 3 years to get myself straightened out.

K.H. White

Long story short, I was on 1.5mg Ativan per day for 30 days (45mg total) When the month scrip ran out the doctor didn't renew it over fears it would lead to chemical dependence. I was immediately forced into cold turkey Withdrawal.

What I experienced was HORRIFIC!

Delusion, confusion, memory loss, extreme insomnia (stayed awake for 3 months) terror, panic attacks, unable to eat, psychosis, mania, 3 Seizures, uncontrollable tremors, Akathisia (feels like you're being electrocuted 24/7) isolation, brain fog, nightmares, suicidal thoughts, plans and ideas, skin rashes, hallucinations, depersonalization, tunnel vision, adrenaline rushes, complete sexual dysfunction, tinnitus (loud ringing in ears)

I was completely debilitated and in and out of the hospital for 7 months after only 30 days of Ativan use. I cannot stress this enough.

TAPER PROPERLY!

Survivor

They may work for some but for so many of us they destroy us and it can happen extremely fast. I was given an SSRI for fibromyalgia, 2 weeks later I was depressed, had severe anxiety, psychotic thoughts, dark, scared of everything, spending money like crazy, distant from my new husband, I lost everything bc of these meds... Now almost 8 months off I'm healing but the damage had been done. They prescribe these meds like its one size fits all with no written consent and for off labeled reasons. Had I'd been given all the information I would have definitely taken my

L.R. Harris

Another day, another massacre. November 19, 2022, Anderson Lee Aldrich, only twenty-two years old, shot and killed five people in a nightclub. Colorado, again. *The Gazette* article by Carol Mckinley, "Anderson Lee Aldrich: A history of family travail, personal violence" reports about a broken family, extensive turmoil, and Aldrichs' history of violent threats, including making bombs in the basement. A *Heavy* article, "Anderson Lee Aldrich: 5 Fast facts You Need To Know," reports that, prior to the shooting, Aldrich's mother, Laura Voepel, posted in a Facebook group that her son was dealing with mental health issues. In February of 2022, she posted to the Facebook group, "Hello Sisters. Can anyone please recommend a great trauma/ptsd therapist?" Although I've looked for information about his motivation and whether mind-altering drugs may have been involved, I have seen nothing to indicate it was investigated. Transphobia was to blame. Final.

A *Daily Beast* article by Freddie deBoer, "Stop Denying That Mass Shooters Can Be Mentally Ill," caught my attention when I saw a quote by Democratic Senator Chris Murphy of Connecticut; a Senator who supported the extraordinary efforts to block the release of records in the case of Newtown, Connecticut shooter, Adam Lanza. Regarding the relationship between mental illness and mass shooters, Senator Murphy was quoted as saying, "Spare me the bullshit of mental illness. We're not an outlier on mental illness, we're an outlier on firearms." Perhaps the lives lost in mass killings by means of stabbings, hangings, drownings, meat cleavers, bombs, vehicles plowing through crowds of people, and airplanes flown into mountains are not worthwhile to Senator Murphy?

As I reflected over the decades, it seemed all I tried desperately to help warn against was in full force around the world. We had reached a point of super-saturation, whereas the mass amount of people prescribed psychiatric drugs in the name of mental health had produced a massive amount of people who lived with adverse drug effects: derealization, depersonalization, psychosis, mania, akathisia, religious preoccupation, aggression, agitation, paranoia, insomnia, delusion, hallucination, irrational thinking, impulsive behavior, homicidal & suicidal ideation – all rampant on full public display. It became the culture. Two plus two equated to orange poodles. Ok. To question was to be non-compliant, fascist, racist, white supremacist, xenophobe, transphobe, cis. Men got pregnant.

The new normal.

What was not normal was the ongoing, continuous stream of fake Instagram accounts made by a stalker and created using my name. The accounts were not merely my 'paranoid thoughts about being hacked,' as police and medics alleged about me in their records. The stalker and fake social media accounts were very real. Despite the fake accounts routinely reported to Instagram, nothing was done about it.

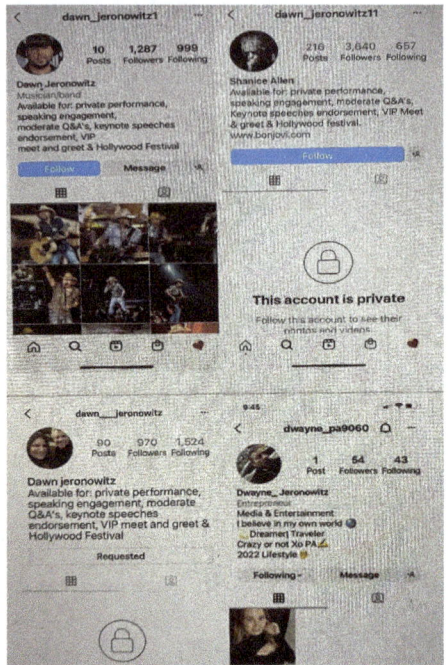

By December 2022, a new trial date for the case still had not been scheduled. The prosecutor said he hoped to settle the case with the neighbors' defense attorney and avoid trial. *When would that be?* I wondered. No countercharges had been brought against me. I did not expect any. Unlike the neighbor, I did nothing wrong.

Barely into my early fifties, and despite all I have endured, I recognize and appreciate that my life has been most amazing and full. When not faced with challenges set in my path, time passed, tours rolled, and I traveled through forty-nine U.S. States, as well as Australia, New Zealand, South Africa, Mexico, Brazil, Argentina, Canada, Peru, Venezuela, Chile, Costa Rica, Puerto Rico, Barbados, Russia, Germany, UK, France, Italy, Spain, Poland, Romania, Netherlands, Belgium, Czech Republic, Greece, Portugal, Sweden, Austria, Switzerland, Bulgaria, Denmark, Finland, Norway, Ireland, Croatia, Latvia, Estonia, Iceland, China, Indonesia, Turkey, Thailand, Japan, Malaysia, South Korea, Jordan, United Arab Emirates, Taiwan, Israel, and Singapore.

While I worked, I was blessed to be welcomed with generous and warm hospitality in each state and country I visited. I wished more people could share my unique and fortunate perspective. It was a beautiful world, rich with texture we had. The diverse and vibrant energy of the people was palpable and contagious. I hoped to share more of those treasured stories one day.

Many mass-prescribed mental health drugs were known to adversely affect the frontal lobe brain functions needed for empathy, impulse control, and forethought. I valued those brain functions greatly and chose not to pollute my body with chemicals that could destroy it. I was fully compliant with myself; that was a priority. Respectful of choices others made for themselves, I was unyielding in my God-given right to remain genuine, natural, and unaltered, like the ancestors who came before me. Not even a Botox or filler; I hoped to age gracefully, with propriety and authenticity. Sans a monthly brunette Naturtint on the roots.

My hope, faith, resilience, strength, determination, and imagination remained unwavering. I reflected on the past but looked ahead to the future: where it goes, no one knows, and nobody knows what the future holds.

My story was just one. There were millions of tragic mental health, pharmaceutical drug, psychiatric treatment, and police mistreatment stories like mine to be told. It occurred on a wide scale; diagnosed disorder. The penalty for non-compliance was severe; the side effects were killing us. It was discussed in social media groups, memes, and posts by victims crying out to be heard, recognized; their lived experience validated. Much fell on deaf ears. Nobody cared. But I did.

I was reminded of my first words when I testified at the 2006 FDA hearing, "I would like to thank myself for the miracle of my being here today." Followed by the closing words of the man who boldly testified after me, "If you think we're going away, you are on drugs."

Nonetheless, 22 Veteran suicides a day... and then some. How many of them were "medicated?"

Can you imagine.

Crazy, or not

Thank You.

Born and raised in New Jersey, Dawn graduated University of North Carolina at Charlotte with a Bachelor of Creative Arts degree in Theatre, then embarked on a decades long backstage career in live event production and the concert touring industry. She traveled all across the United States and around the world, over fifty countries, while specializing in wardrobe, dressing rooms and catering for legendary rockstars. When not touring, she nurtures her passion for animals, food and drug safety, and politics. **dawnjeronowitz.com**

Dawn -- rockin' 'round the world
K. McDowell